WHEN "THE" CHURCH RIDES THE BEAST

THE ANTICHRIST-CENTERED MYSTERY!

(REVELATION CHAPTERS 17, 13 AND 18:1-8)

[REVISED]

FRANKLIN S. FOWLER, JR.

Director, Prophecy Research Initiative

Publisher:
Christian Heritage Foundation
P.O. Box 829
Lucerne Valley, CA 92356-0829 USA
prophecy-research@earthlink.net

These conclusions are always subject to progressive understanding.

Order this book online at www.trafford.com
or email orders@trafford.com

Most Trafford titles are also available at major online book retailers.

Print information available on the last page.

ISBN: 978-1-4907-5960-9 (sc)
ISBN: 978-1-4907-5959-3 (e)

Library of Congress Control Number: 2015909911

First Edition, 2009
Printed and bound in the United States of America.

Library of Congress Control Number: 2009933032
ISBN 0-9789263-1-5

Published by the Christian Heritage Foundation
P.O. Box 829, Lucerne Valley, CA 92356 USA
www.endtimeissues.com

Trafford rev. 08/05/2015

North America & international
toll-free: 1 888 232 4444 (USA & Canada)
fax: 812 355 4082

ACKNOWLEDGEMENTS

This book would not have been possible without the tireless work that my wife, Jeanne, gave to its typing and formatting. The cover design and artwork is a product of her creativity.

My brother-in-law, C. Raymond Cress, devoted valuable time to proofing the manuscript. After my numerous reviews and reworking of the document, his focused scrutiny brought a welcomed polish to the final composition.

CONTENTS

FOREWORD

Presentation of apocalyptic prophecy is frequently done with a journalistic flair. Writers find sensational events which appear to headline a predictive story and then Biblical truth is massaged for the imagination. Those narratives appeal to the fantasy but not the heart. Those purpose-driven messages become based on fear and excitement, not commitment and understanding.

Revelation is a book of war, the universe's last conflict. The final battle scenes between Christ and Satan fill each chapter with drama. Like any well written documentary, the reader – the student – is drawn into each scene. Sides are mentally taken. But different from temporal stories, that identity demands loyalty which becomes irrevocable and eternal. Those prophecies become, then, one of the most solemn studies for mankind!

The sequence of John's missives is written as he was inspired and as heaven wanted them recorded. The order of the commentary flows in a divine pattern. The stories, in turn, come in small packets of information with many "footnotes" of added thought. As the verses progress, there is a beautiful whole that emerges. Thus, I have chosen to follow this phrase-by-phrase study as it is divinely presented.

Chapter 17 is part of an *interlude* or *review* of the beast and its associated church. It actually serves as an excellent foundation or preface to the detailed prophecy of the antichrist beast power in chapter 13. The key timing of 17 begins in 1929 when the papacy and its kingdom state were restored. The timing of chapter 13 is the last three and a half years (42 months) of earth's history, after that restoration period. Together, the final years of Vatican Rome and its emergent religious power are seen as a major terminal world force.

It is my hope that this alarming study will help prepare God's true remnant people for what lies ahead. A merciless campaign against those devoted to God's Sabbath and truth, as it is in Jesus, will be waged. Knowing that story beforehand is a major step in being ready for Satan's final resistance movements.

Author

Notation: There are many who will read this book who might feel offended because its messages "come close" and seem personal. The publisher urges that you set aside prejudice, tradition and personal bias and ask: "What does the Book of Revelation really say?" Chapter 1 of John's Apocalypse states that that book originated with God the Father – the central head of the universe. Giving attention to what He said is our imperative.

Publisher

PREFACE

Following the dramatic imagery of four living creatures, twenty-four redeemed beings and then a weeping Apostle John, comes stunning anthems of joyous praise to the "worthy Lamb that was slain" (Revelation 5:12). The choir proclaiming these praises is made up of "every creature that is in heaven and earth." It portrays the unique celebration moment when the wedding of Groom Jesus is about to be consummated. Yet, despite this amazing picture with the reception of His kingdom (power, riches, honor and glory) presently anticipated, He is described as a "victim" – a bleeding lamb (5:6). Though ready to be the King of kings, the pristine choir still refers to the mighty Savior as a Lamb! The imagery becomes an eternal icon of honor. The *Lamb* will marry His church (19:9). He will lighten the New Jerusalem (21:23) and He will share the Father's throne (22:1, 3). Stunning!

The reader must keep this humble, meek impression of Jesus' character in view as the narrative of the beast unfolds. The Lamb is contrasted with a creature that is called *therion* – a vicious beast. The Lamb died to save, even when hated; the beast lives to kill any who hate it. The Lamb of God accepts its role of humility; the beast wants to be like God through violent acts of tyranny (13:7). The Lamb submitted to death when despised of all men; the beast fights for controlling power over all men to enhance its life (13:7).

The amazing comparison between good and evil, God's people and Satan's, right and wrong, comes sharply into focus right at the end of time. God designed it that way so in earth's final hours there will be only two classes left. The drama will be so intense, every person will take sides. Daniel prophesied of this: "Many shall be purified, and made white, and tried; but the wicked shall do wickedly: and none of the wicked shall understand; but the wise shall understand" (Daniel 12:10). From the divine throne will then come a judicial decree: "He that is unjust, let him be unjust still: and he which is filthy, let him be filthy still: and he that is righteous, let him be righteous still: and he that is holy, let him be holy still" (Revelation 22:11).

The leaders of the armies – Christ and Satan – will employ vastly different tactics to draw followers. God's witnesses will be known by their characters (cleansed by the Lamb's blood – Revelation 7:14, 12:11). Their testimony message (from and about Jesus – Revelation 12:11, 17) will be filled with the convicting power of the Spirit of God (seen from the oil of the two olive trees – Revelation 11:3-4).

Satan's key witness is known as being vicious, defying God and having power over the earth. It is associated with a woman/church so evil she is called a harlot. This sea beast comes out of water depicted as filthy with slime, washing up on its beaches (Isaiah 57:20-21). To make its picture more graphic, God told John that that filthy beast had a partner in evil – an earth beast just as violent but known as a "prophet." God says a "false prophet." That means it has a religious aura.

The duo works together with such deception (Revelation 13:14) that the world is enamored even when engaged in evil. For the saints, the remnant that resists, the beast's followers eventually plan their death (13:15).

Scholars dance all around the meaning of these beasts. The majority, however, conclude that the key sea beast on which the harlot rides is a religious power in Rome. Though noting "an eschatological prophetic theme," their applications infrequently focus on the Roman Catholic Church, the only possible explanation.

That denial mocks the purpose for which God gave the prophecy; it is to be understood, used as a warning and a missive to give to a deceived world. Refreshing exceptions exist. Frank E. Gaebelein, editor of the Expositor's Bible Commentary, is one. He notes:

"Irenaeus (d. 202) gives the first extensive discussion of the Antichrist. He is to be an unrighteous king from the tribe of Dan, the little horn of Daniel 7:8, who will reign over the earth during the last three and one-half years of Daniel's seventieth 'week' (Dan 9:27). Irenaeus identifies the Antichrist with the first beast of Revelation 13 and the 'man of sin' ('lawlessness,' NIV) of 2 Thessalonians 2:3-4, who will exalt himself ... (*Contra Haereses* 5.25.1-5; 5.28.2; 5.30.2; ANF, 1:553, 556-59).

"Luther, Calvin and other Reformers adopting this general view identified the beast with the papacy of the Roman Catholic Church."[1]

In an era when public criticism of powerful religious icons, such as the pope, is viewed with cultural distain, the author appeals to the moral and eternal concerns the God of the universe presents in these chapters. The storyline was not given to entertain or to cover up the identity of the "performers." In clear, metaphorical language we can see unified, suppressive control over all people by the Roman Catholic Church and apostate Protestantism. This represents the final scenes on earth's theater stage.

We are not observers in the audience to enjoy a sitcom. We are thrust on stage into each scene. The key opposing actors relish harm and death to all of God's followers. Jesus has gently promised, as a Lamb, that if you overcome, "I will ..." Then follows the richest promises anywhere in Scripture.

From the stories of malicious people, countries, kingdoms and leaders come the invitation: "Fear none of those things which thou shalt suffer: behold, the devil shall cast *some* of you into prison, that ye may be tried; and ye shall have tribulation ten days: be thou faithful unto death, and I will give thee a crown of life" (Revelation 2:10).

---

[1] Gaebelein, Frank E.; *The Expositor's Bible Commentary,* vol. 12 (Zondervan Publishing House, Grand Rapids, MI), 1984, pp. 521-522.

CHAPTER 1

WHEN BABYLON COMES TO ITS END

The Bible is full of predicted "ends"! Some bring the deepest sadness; others, great happiness. The very first one came as a warning when the world was perfect, without sin or any sadness. Adam and Eve were told that eating of the Tree of Knowledge would lead to death (Genesis 2:17), an "end" they had never experienced. Adam sinned, and the record says he "lived … and he died" (Genesis 5:5). That first couple was given a promise that they could be restored to their original favor. There would be a Savior, and He would bring an end to sin and death. When Jesus arrived He announced, "I am come that they might have life, and that they might have it more abundantly" (John 10:10b). When He comes again He will bring that gift.

The very last prophecy of the Bible is: "Surely I come quickly. Amen" (Revelation 22:20). That will be the end of all adverse experiences from sin. He is the only hope of eternal life, which will be endless! Another "end" is forecast beyond the time of that *parousia*: "And death and hell were cast into the lake of fire. This is the second death [a final end].... And I saw a new heaven and a new earth [a beautiful beginning]: for the first heaven and the first earth were passed away [the end]" (Revelation 20:14, 21:1a,b).

That terminus is the *end of the line* for sin and sinners. It is the point in time when the universe experiences closure of all wrong and rebellion.

Biblical *cessations* are usually the wrap-up of something allied to Satan. This takes on two forms: (1) God brings an end to a sinful event, experience or rebellion; (2) God terminates some freedom as punishment for a sinful act. As powerful as the devil is, God is always in control. He has the *last word*. At the "finish line" Satan loses.

Satan's Agents are Shattered

One of his dramatic failures comes during the seventh Vial, or Plague. This is where our story begins, right where there is a major end!

"And the <u>great city</u> was divided into <u>three</u> parts, and the cities of the nations fell and great Babylon came in remembrance before God, to give unto her the cup of the wine of the fierceness of his wrath" (Revelation 16:19a).

"Babylon" is Satan's ally in the last conflagration. The antichrist, referred to by many symbols, is its earthly leader.

<u>"and great Babylon came in remembrance before God, to give unto her the cup of the wine of the fierceness of his wrath." (vs 19b)</u>

God has great patience, but the time comes when He will act. The cue is when it says, "God remembered." Divine justice is often intimately linked with the expression of divine remembrance.[1] The

1   Aune, David E.; *World Biblical Commentary; Revelation 17–22*, vol. 52c (World Books Publisher; Dallas, Texas – 1997), p. 902.

total destruction of Babylon is described in that Plague. Its end is complete.

Babylon was introduced to students of John's apocalypse in the second "flying in the midst of heaven" angel (Revelation 14:8). There it is identified as (1) "that great city" and (2) as "fallen." "Fallen" (*epesen*) is written in "prophecy perfect" language. That means it is presented as though it already happened but is actually still in the future as an event.

John's prophecy is a second application to that "city." "And, behold, here cometh a chariot of men, *with* a couple of horsemen. And he answered and said, Babylon is fallen, is fallen; and all the graven images of her gods he hath broken unto the ground" (Isaiah 21:9) – that was the first prophecy.

Literal Babylon fell to the Persian king, Cyrus, in 539 B.C. Belshazzar's apostasy against God and that city's military fall became a prophetic metaphor for the moral fall of apostate Christianity at the end of time. As God's people then came out of literal Babylon and journeyed to Canaan, so the cry goes up at the end to "come out of Babylon," "be not partakers of her sins." Prepare for the journey to the heavenly Canaan (cf. Jeremiah 51:9).

Babylon's fall, in this apocalyptic urgent warning to the world, informs us that its doom is imminent. It gives everyone a final chance to heed that ominous cry: "Flee the precincts of that influence. Judgment against Babylon is coming." Just as the Babylonian king was judged because of his defiance of God, so will the latter-day Babylon be punished for the same reason. This judgment predicted in the third angel's message of Revelation 14 is the same as when the "cup of the wine of God's wrath had come" (16:19c). That will be the beginning of its end.

"And the great city was divided into *three* parts, and the cities of the nations fell" (vs 19a)

The "splitting" of Babylon into three parts, in that seventh Vial, heralds that judgmental end. But why three parts?

That great city represents not only Rome, but in the next chapter we will see that it is associated with all of apostate Christianity.[2]

There, the harlot church is actually named "Babylon the great."

As Satan takes unprecedented measures to deceive the world at the end, one of his insidious advances conveys solidarity with three powers (some call it a "false trinity"). "Babylon" characterizes the apostate *unity* of those powers.

John was given stunning imagery of those three allied forces.

"And I saw three unclean spirits like frogs come out of the mouth of the dragon, and out of the mouth of the beast, and out of the mouth of the false prophet" (Revelation 16:13).

These three figures are all mentioned in Revelation 13, though the beast from the land of 13:11-17 is here designated the *false prophet*. John will be told that Babylon is the "habitation of demons and prison of every unclean spirit" (Revelation 18:2). "Unclean" suggests that they have a deceptive nature.[3]

The papacy (sea beast), apostate Protestantism and spiritualism are all at variance with God's will. At the end they deceive the world.

---

2   Mounce, Robert H.; *The Book of Revelation* (Wm. B. Eerdmans Publishing Co., Grand Rapids, Michigan – 1977), p. 303.

3   Beale, G. K.; *The New International Greek Testament Commentary; The Book of Revelation* (William B. Eerdmans Publishing Company, Grand Rapids, Michigan – 1999), p. 831.

One of the Exodus plagues was frogs (Exodus 8:1-15) – one of the Egyptian gods. God instructed Israel that frogs were unclean (Leviticus 11:9-12, 41-47). Symbolically, they capture their prey with their tongues. Their croaking is meaningless; they are slimy, thus hard to catch.

The spirits "like frogs" are hard to pin down – being camouflaged by deceit and falsehood.

Expositor White noted that these frogs are spirits and spiritualism.

"Satan has long been preparing for his final effort to deceive the world. The foundation of his work was laid by the assurance given to Eve in Eden: 'Ye shall not surely die.' 'In the day ye eat thereof, then your eyes shall be opened, and ye shall be as gods, knowing good and evil.' Genesis 3:4, 5. Little by little he has prepared the way for his masterpiece of deception in the development of spiritualism. He has not yet reached the full accomplishment of his designs; but it will be reached in the last remnant of time. Says the prophet: 'I saw three unclean spirits like frogs; … they are the spirits of devils, working miracles, which go forth unto the kings of the earth and of the whole world, to gather them to the battle of that great day of God Almighty.' Revelation 16:13, 14. Except those who are kept by the power of God, through faith in His word, the whole world will be swept into the ranks of this delusion. The people are fast being lulled to a fatal security, to be awakened only by the outpouring of the wrath of God."[4]

These demonic agencies will work signs – many through spiritualism – which ties directly to the wonder working of the false prophet and Satan (Revelation 13:13-14).

Three powers – Satan, beast, false prophet – make up Babylon. Yet from Revelation 13 the sea beast is the *visible*, functioning "head" of those three because, there, the earth beast or false prophet causes all on earth to worship that beast (13:12). And the dragon gives it power (Revelation 13:4) over "all kindreds, and tongues, and nations" (Revelation 13:7). In chapter 17, because the harlot is called "Babylon," it speaks for and personifies Satan, the beast and the false prophet.

Stunning! No wonder God reaches a point where He "remembers" those apostate, blasphemous powers and destroys them.

When it says that the cities of the nations fell, a difficult state of the world begins as Babylon weakens. Revelation 18:8-18 describes some of their amazing reactions.

How do we know those powers are deceptive and blasphemous?

"For they are the spirits of devils, working miracles, which go forth unto the kings of the earth and of the whole world, to gather them to the battle of that great day of God Almighty" (Revelation 16:14).

Those agencies for evil go out to the world by their words and representatives, called "spirits of devils." Out of Christ's mouth (Revelation 1:16, 19:15) went a sharp sword, representing truth (Ephesians 6:17, Hebrews 4:12). Out of the mouths of the false trinity comes a deceptive influence over the world.[5] In the New Testament false religious leaders lead people astray (Mark 13:22, II Thessalonians 2:9-10, II Peter 2:1-2). The influence and power of this work reaches to the "kings of the earth." "The 'kings of

---

4   White, Ellen G.; *The Great Controversy*, pp. 561-562.

5   Osborne, Grant R.; *Revelation* (Baker Book House; Grand Rapids, MI), p. 591.

the whole world' are often identified with the ten kings in Revelation 17:12-14 and 16-17."[6] World leaders will rally to Rome, the leader of Babylon.

Then those "spirits" rally the world to battle God's people. This is depicted in numerous prophecies.

*"And when they shall have finished their testimony, the beast that ascendeth out of the bottomless pit shall make **war** against them, and shall overcome them, and kill them.... And the dragon was wroth with the woman, and went to make **war** with the remnant of her seed, which keep the commandments of God, and have the testimony of Jesus Christ.... These shall make **war** with the Lamb, and the Lamb shall overcome them: for he is Lord of lords, and King of kings: and they that are with him are called, and chosen, and faithful"* (Revelation 11:7, 12:17, 17:14; cf. Joel 3:2, Zechariah 14:2).

Fall of Babylon

God directs the last act over Babylon and its agencies when that great city is divided into three parts. The cities of the nations go down with her. That great Babylon crossed a line and God began the fierceness of his wrath. *"For the LORD shall rise up as in mount Perazim, he shall be wroth as in the valley of Gibeon, that he may do his work, his strange work; and bring to pass his act, his strange act"* (Isaiah 28:21).

It will be time for God to respond. If God were not to punish evil and rebellion, the great divine theme of a moral universe would have to be discarded. God's wrath is described in numerous ways in inspiration (Jeremiah 25:15, 26-29, 33; Isaiah 34:2-4; Joel 3:9, 11-13). It comes at the time of the seventh Vial, which is associated with the sixth Seal (Revelation 6:12-17) and His second coming. So – Babylon comes to its end. The work of the dragon, the beast and the false prophet ceases, and the Vial vision ends.

It is in this setting that chapters 17–19 begin. They represent an "interlude" in the flow of apocalyptic truth being given to John. Those chapters fill in amazing details of messages already given, like this fall of Babylon. The "details" are "must haves" to grasp the meaning of key visions.

We're in for a surprise. It seems as though the work of the Vial angels is now done. But it isn't. John is going to get a personal visit from one of them. Let's listen in!

---

[6]   Aune, *op. cit.,* pp. 894-895.

CHAPTER 2

REPORTING FROM HEAVEN ONCE AGAIN

"And there came one of the seven angels which had the seven vials, and talked with me, saying unto me, Come hither; I will show unto thee the judgment of the great whore that sitteth upon many waters:" (Revelation 17:1).

Visiting Vial Angel

The angels assigned to pour out those terrible Vial woes just completed their busy assignment (Revelation 16). Devastation to earth's inhabitants has been momentous. Most important, the triumvirate of Babylon has been decimated (16:19). Those triune apostate powers so long bent on muffling the voice of God included Satan. His crowning acts of spirit manifestations and appearing as an angel of light have now been thwarted. He's impotent and powerless. That's why the seventh Vial heralds a decisive change in redemptive history. It comes when a voice out of the temple in heaven is declaring, "It is done" (16:17; cf. 11:19)!

Angels are assigned curious tasks when working with human beings. The most mysterious tasks were assigned (right at the end) to a select few. Those majestic beings appointed to work with Christ must have expressed awe and honor at their sacred mission. One of the Vial angels is now given a unique instructive task.

"And there came one of the seven angels which had the seven vials, and talked with me, saying unto me" (vs 1)

John must have been excited, though he doesn't admit it. He has seen stunning heavenly activity. There were the 144,000 on a sea of glass. They sang in one of heaven's great choirs. Just recently a living creature gave the seven angels their destructive Vials; a general voice from the temple (likely God the Father speaking) ordered those angels to begin their fearful mission; and then he saw those terrible woes come upon the earth. What could this Vial angel now be coming to John to talk about?

Before we listen in, a visit to God's prophecy center will be extremely helpful. He chose to give John these sacred prophecies in a variety of ways. That array permits us to better grasp their intent and significance.

Revelation is divided into different message packets:

1. Visions/auditions of earthly events
2. Visions/auditions of events in heaven
3. Commentary inserts – comments to add information, often "out of the clear blue" – "Oh, by the way" thoughts
4. Interludes – vision/audition messages that review what was just given but fill in important details
5. Orientation statements as to time and/or place

This vial angel is about to begin an *interlude* of special details that go way back into chapter 12! Those intervening chapters were filled with astonishing prophetic facts. But God wants us to know even more information. This special bulletin continues on through chapter 19, verse 10. It is clearly extremely important, or such a special mission would not be occurring!

Attention on Harlotry

"Come hither; I will show unto thee the judgment of the great whore" (vs 1)

In the second angel's message (Revelation 14:8), Babylon is fallen. In the third, there is a warning of receiving God's wrath if anyone identifies with the mark of the beast – the insignia of Babylon's kingdom. In the seventh Vial the fall of Babylon is said to have happened because of the cup of the wine of anger of God's wrath (16:17). The Vial angel is going to fill us in on what led to unleashing His wrath. It is an amplification of "why" the seventh Vial or Bowl occurred. You will be stunned to know that Babylon is a harlot. Another Vial angel will later come to John and tell him about another "lady," the bride of the Lamb (21:9)! This book is filled with amazing paradoxes. God's bride was first introduced in 12:1 as a pure woman with a crown of victory. The most amazing is how Satan tries incessantly to mimic things God does.

This Vial angel is now speaking: "Come hither; I will show unto thee the judgment of the great whore that sitteth upon many waters" (17:1).

Those are the same words He will use in 21:9 about the "bride"! We are to know about those two "women": a harlot (with many husbands) and a bride (with one – Jesus). They are also called two cities: Babylon and the New Jerusalem. Lest we become mired in information overload, the angel is going to explain everything to make it all clear.

What are John, you and I, going to be shown? The *"judgment* of the great whore" (17:1).

We won't be told until verse 5 that this harlot is Babylon. But we will know much about her beforehand. "Harlot" is *pornes* (Gr.) and matches the attributes of Babylon in 14:8, where she's guilty of fornication (*porneias*). It suddenly tells us that she is active in *spiritual adultery*. She is involved with illicit religious practices. In prophecy, prostitution, adultery or fornication is the same as *idolatry* or religious *apostasy!* (Isaiah 23:15-17; Jeremiah 2:20-31, 12:27; Hosea 2:5).

It is most amazing that we already were told centuries ago that Nineveh (Nahum 3:1, 4), Tyre (Isaiah 23:14-17) and Babylon (Jeremiah 23:17) were adulterous cities.

Even before we get the harlot's facts, we know she is the epitome of spiritual idolatry. Because of God's wrath we know she is an abomination to Him. She represents a false religion.[1]

She Can't Get Away with Evil

The angel said that that false religion will face future judgment. Repeatedly (vss 2, 5, 15-16; 18:9; 19:2), words are used for her proselytizing religious corruption. Her existence is a travesty to the worship of the true God. We are now going to witness what occurred leading up to Babylon's demise (developing in the sixth Vial and *final judgments* in the seventh).

Babylon's judgment echoes Jeremiah 51:12-13, where the fall of literal Babylon, the city associated with "many waters," is in view. The destruction of spiritual Babylon comes as a final answer to the saints' cry under the fifth Seal, "How long, oh Lord, how

---

[1] Thomas, Robert L.; *Revelation 8–22 – An Exegetical Commentary* (Moody Press, Chicago – 1992), p. 283.

long" (6:10). Thus, that great city became "an eschatological symbol of satanic deception and power,"[2] which God finally destroys.

Wielding Her Power

<u>"that sitteth upon many waters:" (vs 1)</u>

This next clue tells us of her power.

The *"many waters"* are explained in 17:15. They represent "peoples and multitudes and nations and tongues." That list collectively symbolizes **the whole world**. Since the harlot is evil, it depicts the wicked earth. Since Babylon was situated on the Euphrates River, in prophecy we can deduce that that body of water epitomizes wicked people supporting the city (Isaiah 57:20-21). This is helpful in other contrasting apocalyptic studies [Revelation 16:12, Daniel 8–12 – Hiddekel and Ulai Rivers ("east" of the Euphrates River) are righteous people].

"Sitting" on the waters portrays rulership or enthronement.[3] This is substantiated in the next chapter when Babylon replies: "I sit *as* a queen" (18:7). It also represents judicial authority over (Daniel 7:9 – "Ancient of days did sit"). All examples portray "control over." She is controlling the world!

We will be presented with new instances of her "sitting" (vss 3, 9, 15). Each will inaugurate a fresh line of information to this woman's seductive, controlling power.

It's All About Religious Power

Before we visit the next verse, it is important to observe what is being introduced. A woman in prophecy represents a church (Ephesians 5:24-27, Jeremiah 6:2, II Corinthians 11:2). A pure woman was already presented to John's readers in 12:1-2. She symbolized God's true church with a crown of twelve stars, representing its first leaders (the apostles). The harlot is a fearful presentation, noting that at the end God's church will apostatize. We can lean on one amazing promise – there will be a remnant left.

"And the dragon was wroth with the woman, and went to make war with the remnant of her seed, which keep the commandments of God, and have the testimony of Jesus Christ" (Revelation 12:17).

Side by side these two women – these two churches – will compete for followers. One headed by Christ, the other by Satan. Satan will have one advantage – deception. That is why Jesus repeatedly addresses: "Take heed that no man deceive you" (Matthew 24:4). Knowing truth, having a precise understanding of prophecy, is vital to avoid the devil's traps.

The contrast between the pure woman and the impure woman is striking. We can now anticipate prophetic details about God's church in rebellion at the end. The timing of this event, the players and the outcome are all unfolded. But what is that apostasy over? There must be something that Satan wants earth's Christians to revolt against. The Bible does tell us. It relates to the beast and its mark. Those details will emerge as we navigate deeper into God's anticipatory mysteries.

2   Gaebelein, Frank E.; *The Expositor's Bible Commentary,* vol. 12 (Zondervan Publishing House, Grand Rapids, MI), 1984, p. 554.

3   Aune, David E.; *World Biblical Commentary, Revelation 17–22,* vol. 52c (World Books; Publisher, Dallas, Texas – 1997), p. 930.

"The Pure Woman (Revelation 12)	"The Impure Woman (Revelation 17)
Clothed with heavenly bodies (v. 1)	Arrayed in purple and jewels (v. 4)
Mother of Israel's remnant (vs. 17)	Mother of harlots (v. 5)
Threatened by the waters (v. 15)	Sits on the waters (v. 1)
Attacked by the red dragon (vs. 13)	Allied with the scarlet beast (v. 3)
Exiled because of attacks (v. 6, 14)	Sits enthroned as a queen (v. 1, 4)
Alone in the wilderness (v. 6, 14)	Feasts with kings in wilderness (v. 2, 4)
Fed by God Himself (v. 6, 14)	Feeds on the saints' blood (v. 6)
Receives God's deliverance (v. 14)	Receives God's judgment (v. 1)"[4]

When she becomes the Lamb's bride (19:7):

- She is called the New Jerusalem (21:2)
- Her clothing:
  - Arrayed in fine linen – clean and white (19:8)
- Her Jewels:
  - Light was the glory of God (21:11, 23) – like jasper stone
  - Is a city of pure gold – like glass (21:18)
  - Foundations are made up of twelve precious stones
  - Has twelve gates of pearl (21:21)

---

[4]   Osborne, Grant R.; *Revelation* (Baker Book House; Grand Rapids, MI), p. 608.

CHAPTER 3

THE HARLOT'S EVIL INFLUENCES THE WORLD

World Leaders Enamored with the Harlot

"With whom the kings of the earth have committed fornication," (Revelation 17:2a).

In dramatic language a picture is painted of religious prostitution. It portrays secular leaders being emotionally captivated with the harlot. The language is intimate. There must be a "drawing card" towards this symbolic harlot! This same accusation occurs two more times in this interlude (18:3, 9).

This harlot – Babylon (an ecclesiastical power) – as we will further observe, is carried by a beast (kingdom). In that coupling (church and state), she seductively "controls" the world through her devoted followers, the world leaders! The religious influence of the prostitute (sounds absurd, doesn't it?) is exactly how the Bible paints it. Something the harlot "stands for" bonds world leaders to a false "religious" or "moral" issue that God despises. The worship of God, within His moral parameters, is debased.

This imagery reveals a global sacrifice of spiritual principles. We catch a glimpse of how devoted earth's kings are from chapter 13, where the world "worships the beast" (13:8), which carries the harlot here in chapter 17. Thus, that church/ state, harlot/beast, receives idolatrous loyalty from leaders and people globally.

God is betrothed to us (Hosea 2:19). The betrothal contract is called a covenant. It was originally classified as the ten commandments (Deuteronomy 4:13). Just before the wedding, its principles will be part of us (Hebrews 8:10). Thus, fornication must have something to do with breaking that covenant or the law.

Isaiah 23:17 notes Tyre as being another city symbol for apostasy of God's people – "she fornicated with all the kingdoms of the earth." The word "fornicate" or to be a "prostitute" is frequently used figuratively to illustrate Israel's faithless behavior against Yahweh. This designation is, again, based on a defiance of God's ideal – a covenant coalition (between Yahweh and Israel) with marriage contracts (Lev 17:7; 20:5-6; Num 14:33; 15:39; Deut 31:16; Judg 2:17; 8:27; 1 Chr 5:25; 2 Chr 21:11; Ps 73:27), a metaphor found with particular frequency in the prophets Hosea (1:2; 2:4 [MT:6]; 4:15; 9:1), Jeremiah (2:20; 3:2, 9, 13; 5:7, 11; 13:27) and Ezekiel (6:9; 16; 23; 43:7, 9).[1]

The harlot rejects God's great restoration covenant agreement, the Decalogue. This was prophetically foretold by Daniel:

> "have indignation against the holy covenant" (Daniel 11:30).

> "such as do wickedly against the covenant" (Daniel 11:32).

---

[1]   Erlandsson, *TDOT* 4:202-4.

There, the leading actor is first called a "vile person" (11:21); then the "king of the north" (11:36-45). That antichrist

Influenced First (17:2a):	Influenced Second (17:2b):
Kings of earth	Inhabitants of earth
• Commit fornication	• Drunk with wine of fornication
• Tie with religious prostitute	• Accepts service of prostitute
This creates an alliance	They join the alliance

drama parallels the one depicted here by John for the "beast," "harlot" and "Babylon." Those entities, adversely influencing the world, are described as "whose names have not been written in the book of life" (Revelation 17:8). They are eternally lost. The harlot/Babylon/ Rome story/prophecy relates to eternal death.

God is describing, through His servants, terrible the risk of divorcing from the betrothal bond He has with His people.

The world's populace accepts the harlot's beliefs.

"and the inhabitants of the earth have been made drunk with the wine of her fornication" (Revelation 17:2b).

A cup of fruit beverage ("wine," grape juice) is an intriguing metaphor that God uses in prophecy. The pure grape juice (I Corinthians 11:35) symbolizes the blood of a sin-pardoning Savior; the fermented juice symbolizes the mind-numbing drink/ beliefs of the harlot. The thoughts are so deranged that falsehood is received as truth. The world drinks enough from her cup that it gets drunk. It is unable to decipher right from wrong.

This fearful report came as a warning in the second angel's message. Babylon fell **because** "she made all nations drink of the wine of the wrath of her fornication" (14:8).

"What is that wine? – Her false doctrines. She has given to the world a false sabbath instead of the Sabbath of the

fourth commandment, and has repeated the falsehood that Satan first told to Eve in Eden,–the natural immortality of the soul. She has spread many kindred errors far and wide, 'teaching for doctrines the commandments of men.'"[2] The Sabbath is at the center of the Decalogue and is the sign of that covenant (Exodus 31:13).

Note the fascinating sequence in this verse: The word for fornication is *porneuo*, which means the "practice of prostitution or sexual immorality."[3]

This harlot, centered in Rome, as we will see, endorses appalling behavior, beliefs and power within the Roman Church. The "marriage" (illicit) to the inhabitants of the earth is repugnant and hints at victimization of the people because of darkness.[4]

In the Old Testament Babylon is condemned for making "the whole earth drunk" – and they "*have* gone mad" (Jeremiah 51:7; cf. Isaiah 51:17).

The scene now changes. It seems as though John was in a literal real-time conversation with the angel. In the brief encounter, he was invited to "Come hither, I will shew thee ..." John was to observe something far more dramatic and explicit. The event-driven circumstances that led to the harlot's demise will now unfold!

---

2   White, Ellen G.; *The Review and Herald,* December 6, 1892.

3   Brown, Colin, editor, *New International Dictionary of New Testament Theology,* vol. 1 (Zondervan, Grand Rapids, MI), 1986, p. 497.

4   Aune, David E.; *World Biblical Commentary, Revelation 17–22,* vol. 52c (World Books; Publisher, Dallas, Texas – 1997), p. 932.

This graphic account builds on several "known facts": (1) The harlot rules or has power over the world, (2) her doctrines or beliefs have been accepted by the world's leaders and (3) the populace of earth is totally enamored with her wine; it is entrancing and controlling!

Can you imagine how this powerful, world-controlling Roman Church might come to its "end"? That's what now follows in a stunning blow-by-blow account. That is why the angel came to John. We are to know what apostasy brought God's eternal rejection.

CHAPTER 4

INTO THE DESERT AND WHAT DID HE SEE?

"So he carried me away in the spirit into the wilderness: and I saw a woman sit upon a scarlet coloured beast, full of names of blasphemy, having seven heads and ten horns" (Revelation 17:3).

This *chapter* begins with a personal visit from one of the Vial angels. He describes why he came. His mission was to disclose the circumstances surrounding God's destructive wrath against the harlot (Revelation 16:19). A new information phase has now commenced.

The Vision Story Begins

"So he carried me away in the spirit" (vs 3)

One's imagination can quickly add to this narrative when John suddenly notices he is being taken away. How did it feel? What was his immediate reaction? He shares few details except that he was "carried away." This suggests that he was lifted up and out of the region he was in – perhaps sensing the absence of gravity – then a mystical journey to a *specific* destination – a wilderness.

Notice that it was the Vial angel that carried John. He was holding him in some manner, yet, he was "in the spirit." One experience of Ezekiel is described as being taken by "a lock of mine head" (Ezekiel 8:3). The apocalyptic writer will once again be "carried" by a Vial angel ("to a great high mountain" – Revelation 21:10) to see "the bride," the "New Jerusalem." Fascinating language, isn't it. It actually

describes a supernatural experience between a created earth being and a heavenly being – associated with the Holy Spirit. Ezekiel had many other encounters which he graphically recorded (Ezekiel 2:2, 3:12, 8:3, 11:1, 37:1, 43:5). There, he identified the supernatural being as the Spirit that "entered into me" (Ezekiel 2:2). John is entering "another dimension."[1] Details are not, however, described.

As with others, this imbues John with special prophetic insight.

"into the wilderness:" (vs 3)

The word for "desert" (*eremon*) represents an isolated place where something *exclusive* can occur. It becomes a metaphor for many illustrations. Examples of how it is used include:

1. Refuge (Ezekiel 34:25, Mark 6:31, Revelation 12:14)
2. A place to be alone (I Kings 19:4-7)
3. Its flatness, an easy place to make a "spiritual highway" (Isaiah 40:3)
4. A place to pray (Mark 1:35)
5. A place to be punished (Psalm 95:7-10)
6. A symbol for destruction (desolation) (Isaiah 1:7)
7. A place to be tempted (Matthew 4:1)

Prophetically, it is best seen as a place to hide or a place of protection (Jeremiah

1   Beale, G. K.; *The New International Greek Testament Commentary; The Book of Revelation* (William B. Eerdmans Publishing Company, Grand Rapids, Michigan – 1999), p. 850.

31:1-2, Revelation 12:14). Here, it is a place to hide to deceive (Isaiah 13:21, Revelation 18:2). Since the harlot is evil, we anticipate she misleads, or falsifies truth. Her real nature or actions are being masqueraded. Expositor Brighten rhetorically asked, "Does this harlot also station herself in the desert so that she can pretend that she is the true church and thus by her immoral deceptiveness wean people away from the church of Christ?"[2]

Amazing! Just from this "wilderness" *attribute* alone, we assume God is going to convey special insight into Satan's end-time deception. The whole vision of Revelation 17 unfolds this very allusion.

First Glimpse of the Harlot

"and I saw a woman sit upon a scarlet coloured beast," (vs 3)

As John arrives in the wilderness he sees a woman on a beast. Since he had already been told that the visionary material would be about the harlot, he undoubtedly knew that this was the person. He said, "I saw a woman" (17:3) sit (seated) on a beast. In verse 1 she was seated on many waters.

As we previously noted, "woman" represents a church (Isaiah 54:5-6, Jeremiah 3:14, II Corinthians 11:2, Ephesians 5:31-33). A beast symbolizes a king or kingdom (Daniel 7:17, 25) – a secular/civil power. A harlot would allude to an unfaithful church practicing spiritual adultery (Jeremiah 3:20; Ezekiel 16:28, 32). The position of "sitting on" suggests

enthronement,[3] control or total influence[4] over the beast.

- Woman (apostate church)
- Ruling over the beast (secular power – civil power)
- These suggest judicial control.

Immediately, we must think of an end-time church that has a close association with a civil power or government. There is no equal to that of the Holy See, which is made up of the Catholic Church and Vatican City. As of 2013, there were 179 countries with full diplomatic ties with ambassadors to the Holy See.[5] That is not to Vatican City but to the unit of both! The Holy See also is a Permanent Observer to the United Nations.

The significance of this is astounding. The Roman Church even redefines the ultimate meaning of the Holy See as the *Pope (Bishop of Rome).* He, therefore, is an *institution, having a legal personality* and is the *central government* of the Roman Catholic Church. Here is the official position of how these "entities" intermingle: "On 11 February 1929 the Holy See and Italy resolved the '*Questione Romana*' following the cessation of the Papal States by signing the Lateran Treaty. By means of this Treaty, *Vatican City State* came into existence (see Appendix I). Article 12 of the Treaty notes that diplomatic relations with the Holy See are governed by the rules of International Law. Years later the Vienna Convention on Diplomatic Relations (1961), convened

---

2   Brighton, Louis A.; *Revelation* (Concordia Publishing House, Saint Louis, MO – 1999), p. 439.

3   Aune, David E.; *World Biblical Commentary; Revelation 17–22*, vol. 52c (World Books; Publisher, Dallas, Texas – 1997), p. 934.

4   Thomas, Robert L.; *Revelation 8–22 – An Exegetical Commentary* (Moody Press, Chicago – 1992), p. 285.

5   http://www.ewtn.com/vnews/getstory.asp?number=124481

for the purpose of codifying diplomatic law, went even further by formally recognizing the practice accepted by any receiving [a] State regarding the precedence of the representative of the Holy See within the Diplomatic Corps (Art. 16, §3).

"Vatican City is the physical or _territorial_ base of the Holy See, almost a pedestal upon which is posed a much larger and unique independent and sovereign authority/rule: that of the Holy See. The State of Vatican City itself also possesses a personality under international law and, because of such, enters into international agreements. However, it is the Holy See which internationally represents Vatican City State. In fact, when the Holy See enters into agreements for Vatican City State, it uses the formula: 'acting on behalf and in the interest of the State of Vatican City.' In October 1957, in order to avoid uncertainty in its relations with the United Nations, it was affirmed that relations are established between the United Nations and the Holy See. And it is the Holy See which is represented by the Delegations accredited by the Secretariat of State to international organizations.

"In the Listing of Country Names, published annually by the United Nations, a note is added to the Holy See's entry, stating that – in United Nations documents – the term 'Holy See' is to be used except in texts concerning the International Telecommunications Union and the Universal Postal Union, where the term 'Vatican City State' is to be used. States, then, do not entertain diplomatic relations with Vatican City State, but with the Holy See [which includes the Roman Catholic Church].

"Basically, the term '_Holy See_' refers to the supreme authority of the Church, that is, the Pope as Bishop of Rome and head of the college of Bishops. It is the central government of the Roman Catholic Church. As such, the Holy See is an institution which, under international law and in practice, has a legal personality that allows it to enter into treaties as the juridical equal of a State and to send and receive diplomatic representatives. As noted above, it is the 'Holy See' that is present at United Nations Headquarters in New York and at UN centers abroad, as well as at other international organizations such as the European Community, the Organization of American States, the African Unity, etc. At the time of this revised publication, the Holy See maintains full diplomatic relations with one-hundred and eighty (180) countries out of the one-hundred ninety-two (192) member countries of the UN."[6]

This means that at the United Nations those 180 nations with diplomatic ties have a legal bond to the pope and the Roman Catholic Church. Vatican City is the only _place_ where they are headquartered. Prophetically – one can view the woman as typifying the central power of Babylon [she sits upon or controls the beast (Vatican City) (vs 3), waters (people of the world) (vs 1, 15) and Rome (depicting location) (vs 9)].

Thus, the imagery of a beast with multiple heads would also represent the full "kingdom" with its leaders. This is similar to the imagery of the sea beast of Revelation 13:1. They are the same.

Scarlet is the Color

Isaiah warns Judah of its waywardness in chapter 1. Then in merciful language he shares, "though your sins be as scarlet, they shall be as white as snow" (Isaiah 1:18). That color represents the guilt of the

---

6   http://www.holyseemission.org/short_history.html (emphasis added).

sinner as there typified "with blood on his hands" (Isaiah 1:15). In beautiful typology every sin crucifies Jesus; He bears the guilt of blood/death on His hands. Consequently, our stain can be washed away. Our record then will be "as white as snow" – clean hands and a pure heart.

For the whole beast to be scarlet is highly symbolic that it has "blood guiltiness" and is full of sin. Scarlet is also one of the colors of the woman's garment (vs 4). Historically, the color of royalty was often scarlet. It represented luxury (II Samuel 1:24) and authority, and was one of the colors of the pomegranates on the hem of the priest's robe (Exodus 28:33).

In the nineteenth century Albert Barnes noted: "It is remarkable that nothing would better represent the favourite colour at Rome than this, or the actual appearance of the pope, the cardinals, and the priests in their robes, on some great festival occasion. Those who are familiar with the descriptions given of Papal Rome by travellers, and those who have passed much time in Rome, will see at once the propriety of this description, on the supposition that it was intended to refer to the Papacy. I caused this inquiry to be made of an intelligent gentleman who had passed much time in Rome – without his knowing my design – what would strike a stranger on visiting Rome, or what would be likely particularly to arrest his attention as remarkable there; and he unhesitatingly replied, 'the scarlet colour.' This is the colour of the dress of the cardinals – their hats, and cloaks, and stockings being always of this colour. It is the colour of the carriages of the cardinals, the entire body of the carriage being scarlet, and the trappings of the horses the same. On occasion of public festivals and processions, scarlet is suspended from the windows of the houses along which

processions pass. The inner colour of the cloak of the pope is scarlet; his carriage is scarlet; the carpet on which he treads is scarlet. A large part of the dress of the body-guard of the pope is scarlet; and no one can take up a picture of Rome without seeing that this colour is predominant. I looked through a volume of engravings representing the principal officers and public persons of Rome. There were few in which the scarlet colour was not found as constituting some part of their apparel; in not a few the scarlet colour prevailed almost entirely."[7]

The beast is depicted as sinful, even murderous. The harlot is an evil ruler – all FROM THE COLOR OF *kokkinos* and what is next attested to.

"Blasphemy" is His Name

"full of names of blasphemy," (vs 3)

As "scarlet" represents sin on the beast, so the name of "blasphemy" epitomizes utter rebellion and dishonor of God. The word alone seems not to be enough to convey how horrible God sees this beast. John is inspired to tell us the beast was "full of names of blasphemy." It is degradation at its height and reveals how low the Roman Church has sunk. It has become a supreme enemy of God.

Intriguingly, "The blasphemies are not so much directly spoken against God by the beast as they are implied by his self-deification."[8] "The beast sets himself up as the 'god of this world.'"[9] He conveys illicit behavior that mocks God's ideals.

[7] http://www.studylight.org/com/bnn/view.cgi?book=re&chapter=017

[8] Mounce, Robert H.; *The Book of Revelation* (Wm. B. Eerdmans Publishing Co., Grand Rapids, Michigan, 1977), p. 310.

[9] Osborne, Grant R.; *Revelation* (Baker Book House; Grand Rapids, MI), p. 611.

Physical Characteristics of the Beast

"having seven heads and ten horns." (vs 3)

This creature has seven heads and ten horns, thought to be an allusion to a similar beast seen in Daniel 7. There, an eleventh horn "speaks great words against the Most High" (7:25). Here it is specifically identified with the "great red dragon" and sea beast, which had blasphemous names upon their heads (Revelation 12:3, 13:1).

A direct identity with the sea beast is invited. Why? It is the immediate preceding beast with seven heads and ten horns called therion – vicious in Revelation.

Chapters 17 and 18 are interludes which review visionary material and messages recently presented. Thus:

1. The sea beast receives its power from the dragon (13:2).
2. It, too, has names of blasphemy.
3. It is associated with death (Revelation 13:15) through the facilitation of the earth beast, just as the scarlet colored beast here in 17 is represented by its harlot rider drunk with the saints' blood (17:6)!
4. The fourth beast of Daniel 7 appears to represent the same power. There, Daniel talks about when its dominion will come to its end (7:26).

We have a woman (church) and a beast (state) representing Satan's wishes. The world is fascinated by its leadership, and gives it "worshipful" allegiance.

The world's most profound deception is unfolding. God is putting us right into its very center through John's prophetic journalism! We are warned by being informed: "have nothing to do with these powers."

ALLUREMENTS OF THE HARLOT

"And the woman was arrayed in purple and scarlet colour, and decked with gold and precious stones and pearls, having a golden cup in her hand full of abominations and filthiness of her fornication:" (Revelation 17:4).

Recall what the Vial angel said was the purpose of these insights – to show us "the judgment of the great whore" (17:1). Babylon, the descriptive three-part city, was made ineffective by the *cup of God's wrath* described as the "wine of the fierceness of his wrath" (Revelation 16:19). Allied with these prophecies is the "man of sin" or "that Wicked" whom "the Lord shall consume with the spirit of his mouth, and shall destroy with the brightness of his coming" (II Thessalonians 2:8) and the third angel's description of God's wrath (Revelation 14:10).

The end of all apostasy, Babylon and wickedness, is typified by the final history of this woman. Her last story serves as an event-driven warning to all who would be careless and rebellious. The whole world –

Muslims, Buddhists, atheists and, tragically, most Christians – will give her allegiance. "All that dwell upon the earth shall worship him [the beast/antichrist/head of the Holy See]" (Revelation 13:8).

The world *dominance* of the United States will be doomed as this Roman-based Vatican City/Catholic Church emerges as the headquarters of religious, civil and international power.

"Thus, as the moon receives its light from the sun ... so the royal power [state] derives from the Pontifical authority the splendor of its dignity.... The state of the world ... will be restored by our diligence and care ... for the pontifical authority and the royal power ... fully suffice for this purpose. – Pope Innocent III (1198-1216).[1]

"And the woman was arrayed in purple and scarlet colour" (vs 4)

Purple, another color of royalty (Judges 8:26, Daniel 5:7, Esther 8:15, Lamentations, 4:5), and scarlet, the color of wealth (Nahum 2:3, II Samuel 1:24, Proverbs 31:21, Jeremiah 4:21) were expensive dyes. Thus the woman/church is typified as powerful and rich. The cardinals of the Roman Church dress in scarlet, as often do the popes. Scarlet shoes and stockings are their norm. Though wealth is portrayed, the color of scarlet reminds us again of the color of the beast (*kokkinonl*), which is the imagery for sin and murder (blood). Purple is seen with the bishops and archbishops, belying their leadership roles over distinct areas or institutions.

Stunning! Purple and scarlet were the two colors used to describe the mockery robe put on Christ to taunt Him (Matthew 27:28 – scarlet; Mark 15:17, 20; John 19:2, 5 – purple). The costly and spectacular garb of this prostitute should also be contrasted with the "fine linen, bright and clean," worn by the "Bride of the Lamb" (Revelation 19:8).[2] The next chapter

---

1   Documents et Civilisation, de la Prehistoire a nos jours, classiques Hachette, Innocentii III Romani Pontificis Regestum sive Epistolarium, Epistula CCCCI, > P.L., 214, col. 337, p. 37.

2   Mounce, Robert H.; *The Book of Revelation* (Wm. B. Eerdmans Publishing Co., Grand Rapids,

talks more about Babylon, which is here depicted as the harlot. There it says, "The great city, clothed with linen and purple and scarlet" (Revelation 18:16) – another parody trying to mimic Christ with His city bride.

Its riches and regal state are "covered" by its constant appeals to the world that its wealth needs to be distributed to the poor. All the while its prelates wear gold and icons [idols] that are made of tons of gold and precious gems. The Roman Church often talks about a "Vatican budget deficit," yet their travels, dress, art and edifices are opulent.[3]

That is a facade to control and raise even more funds.

"The Catholic church is the biggest financial power, wealth accumulator and property owner in existence. She is a greater possessor of material riches than any other single institution, corporation, bank, giant trust, government or state of the whole globe. The pope, as the visible ruler of this immense amassment of wealth, is consequently the richest individual of the twentieth century. No one can realistically assess how much he is worth in terms of billions of dollars."[4]

"... the most formidable financial empire the world has ever seen."[5]

The expensive clothing reflects the attractiveness by which the whore tries to seduce others (Jeremiah 4:30). "Harlot Israel 'dresses in scarlet' and 'decorates [herself] with ornaments of gold.'"[6] That

is a metaphor for this end-time Roman apostate power!

"and decked with gold and precious stones and pearls" (vs 4)

The word "decked" means that she was excessively dressed with these precious adornments. She is enhancing her appearance to allure her paramours. Prophecy reveals that she will be successful (Revelation 13:3).

"The papacy will appear in its power. All must now arouse and search the Scriptures, for God will make known to His faithful ones what shall be in the last time. The word of the Lord is to come to His people in power."[7]

"having a golden cup in her hand" (vs 4)

The Roman Catholic Church represents herself as a woman holding a cup in her right hand! This is actually portrayed in many Vatican coins. As we saw previously, that Roman Vatican City "houses" the Holy See. The cup is shown with the sun emanating from it. That is the subject of the next phrase. The "heart" of that woman is on the opposite side of that coin – the pope!

Pope Paul VI – 1963

Michigan, 1977), p. 310.
3 *The Catholic World Report* Oct. 2008, p. 6.
4 *Vatican Billions,* Avro Manhattan – 1980.
5 Tony Bushby, *The Papal Billions,* Joshua Books, February 2008.
6 Beale, G. K.; *The New International Greek Testament Commentary; The Book of Revelation* (William B. Eerdmans Publishing Company, Grand Rapids, Michigan – 1999), p. 854.

7 White, Ellen G.; *Manuscript Releases,* vol. 21, p. 437.

Pope John the XXIII – 1959

Pope Pius XII – 1958

The right hand suggests that the meaning of the cup and its contents is not only of major significance but protected by the Roman Catholic Church. It is what she offers the world. She is symbolized as the world's paramount source of "goodness" by the word fides located beneath the woman. This equals virtue. The Bible says that she is a harlot!

She would have you think that that chalice holds goodness, like the Sun of Righteousness (Malachi 4:2). Her deception is embellished by a cross she holds in her **left** hand. It is of **secondary** importance to what she can get others to "drink" from her right-hand cup.

This is what she really thinks of the Cross! It is on the left – the side of rejection. Another example? The pope's chair (right) has an upside-down cross on its back. In his article,[1] Professor J. S. Malan says this about that inverted cross: "This cross is not broken, but turned upside down. It indicates the rejection of

---

[1] Malan, J. S.; *The Kingdom of Satan* (2001).

Jesus Christ and contempt for the gospel of salvation."

Is it a virtuous drink she is holding? No! The cup is:

"full of abominations and filthiness of her fornication" (vs 4)

The word here for abomination is *bdelugmaton*, meaning something detestable to God. This draws on themes in the Old Testament (Ezekiel 8:6, 9, 13, 15, 17 and Daniel 9:27, 11:31, 12:11). Jesus referred His end-time students to Daniel, where it talked of those abominations associated with desolation (Matthew 24:15). This was described as the wine of her fornication (17:2).

This cup is given to others to drink. The "wine" is filth that God equates to immoral behavior. Jeremiah uses a golden cup to picture the horrible influences Babylon has around her (Jeremiah 51:7).

Filth is also used in the New Testament to refer to unclean spirits (Matthew 10:1, 12:43), idolatry (II Corinthians 6:17) and religious prostitution (Ephesians 5:5).

The Roman Catholic Church, in this end-time setting, is promoting, sharing, some "belief" that God hates. As we saw in verse 2, it is against God's covenant law. From Daniel we understand it is related to the fourth commandment. The "transgression" that leads to desolation

POPE VISITS HOLY SITE OF SERMON ON THE MOUNT
CNN LIVE

comes from a Hebrew word, *bepesha,* which describes the sin against God's **authority**, **law** and **covenant**. That represents the amazing spectrum of all that the Sabbath stands for.

The "sun," which the Vatican portrays in its cup, symbolizes the ancient sun worship she adopted from Mithraism. This alludes to that sun god and suggests a false day of worship. The Sabbath commandment is dishonored. Sunday, the first day, is promoted from the sun god of Mithra. Historically, this is validated:

"Every Sabbath on account of the burial (of Jesus) is to be regarded in execration (denunciation) of the Jews ... In fact it is not proper to observe, because of Jewish customs, the consumption of food and the ceremonies of the Jews."[2]

"On the **venerable day of the Sun** let the magistrates and people residing in cities rest, and let all workshops be closed. In the country however persons engaged in agriculture may freely and lawfully continue their pursuits because it often happens that another day is not suitable for grain-sowing or vine planting; lest by neglecting the proper moment for such operations the bounty of heaven should be lost."[3]

"'Let the course of all law suits and all business cease on Sunday, which our fathers have rightly called the Lord's day, and let no one try to collect either a public or a private debt; and let there be no hearing of disputes by any judges either those required to serve by law or those voluntarily chosen by disputants. And he is to be held not only infamous but sacrilegious who has turned away from the service and observance of holy religion on that day.'"[4]

Since the Greek word used for abominations refers especially to a pagan religious practice,[5] it would be consistent with these allusions to the ancient worship of the sun. Could a false day of worship represent the "mark" of the harlot? Jeremiah 51:8 suggests that there is an association between her wine that makes the nation mad (vs 7) and her fall. The identity of what is in her cup is now vital for us to grasp. That "wine" is her mark. It is what she shares with the world. It is an adulterous gesture, mocking our betrothal to Jesus. The drama gets intense in the next verse!

4   http://community-2.webtv.net/Tales_of_the Western_World/
5   Aune, David E.; *World Biblical Commentary, Revelation 17–22,* vol. 52c (World Books; Publisher, Dallas, Texas – 1997), p. 935.

2   Sylvester I, Bishop of Rome, 314 A.D.
3   Constantine, *Dies Solis* on March 7, 321 A.D. (emphasis added).

CHAPTER 6

NAMED AFTER HER CHARACTER

"And upon her forehead *was* a name written, MYSTERY, BABYLON THE GREAT, THE MOTHER OF HARLOTS AND ABOMINATIONS OF THE EARTH" (Revelation 17:5).

Thus been privy to a progression of amazing information regarding the harlot.

Harlot sitting on waters	Kings/leaders of earth have illicit relations with her through her despicable wine	Harlot sitting on beast – a kingdom	Harlot, dressed as wealthy and royal, has cup filled with abominations

This data relates to a ***period when*** the harlot comes to her ***end*** (18:8)!

From this brief revelation we can deduce many things:

1. The harlot has controlling power over the people of the world – from the word "sitteth" (vs 1).
2. The leaders of the world have made themselves subject to her doctrines or beliefs – wine (vs 2).
3. She has controlling power over a kingdom/nation – beast – from the word "sit" (vs 3).
4. Wine in the cup refers to something specific that God calls an "abomination" – some falsehood (vs 4).
5. Since the cup is *full* – there appears to be something very distinct that the Roman Church is dispensing to the world – enough for the whole world (vs 4). She is focused on that one thing at this end time!

We have alluded to the Book of Daniel, which echoes the abominable doctrine of a false sabbath. Contextually, that sin originates after the joining of a civil and an ecclesiastical power (beast/harlot).

The abomination also echoes the rebellion against God's covenant (Daniel 11:31-32). That aligns with His Decalogue (Deuteronomy 4:13), representing God's sanctifying sign (Exodus 31:13). God's law is challenged in a way that He sees as abominable!

This imagery now changes. Her forehead names are clear labels of her true character. They are what God sees in her. They will give us, therefore, insight as to God's perception of what the harlot is like – which justifies His final judgment (16:19).

"Upon her forehead was a name written" (vs 5)

In John's time prostitutes had a custom of putting their name on their foreheads, announcing that they were harlots.[1] The forehead also represents what is in the mind or the very heart of the individual (assumed also in the followers of the beast – 13:16, 14:9, 17:5, 20:4.

Therefore – the names we are about to observe are given by God to help us fully understand the nature of the Roman Catholic Church. This, in turn, will help us to compare these traits with God's people who are sealed in their foreheads (7:3, 9:4). Later, John notes the Father's name (14:1) and the Lamb's name (22:4) are on the foreheads of the 144,000 (His servants).

It was to the overcomers of the Philadelphia Church that Jesus said He would "write upon him" (Revelation 3:12). The names on the harlot are a dramatic contrast! Let's now look at these intriguing labels!

"MYSTERY" (vs 5)

There is a question whether this is part of the name or refers to "mysterious names" on her forehead. There is riveting evidence, however, that the name "mystery" is a harbinger of darkness and deception of ecclesiastical Rome. It is a noun (*mysterion*) and represents a deception that must "be revealed."[2] It implies that a new revelation regarding this harlot is about to be unfolded.

Intriguingly, the Roman Church claims a *dogma of mysteries* which serves as threatening indictments against the doubter of their hidden power.

"The existence of **theological mysteries** is a doctrine of **Catholic faith** defined by the Vatican Council,

which declares: 'If any one say that in Divine Revelation there are contained no mysteries properly so called (*vera et proprie dicta mysteria*), but that through reason rightly developed (*per rationem rite excultam*) all the dogmas of faith can be understood and demonstrated from natural principles: let him be **anathema**' (*Sess. III, De fide et ratione, can. I*)."[3] Anathema = damned, excommunicated, abominable, hated, lost forever.

This Catholic position introduces two elements:

1. Doctrinal mysteries transcend spiritual discernment. Church leaders can only clarify truth. The next logical conclusion is that one must submit to the church's teachings.
2. Denying their authority brings damnation on the person.

This rises to the level of religious arrogance, exhibits moral tyranny over an individual and lacks any admission of understanding from God's Spirit. The more broadly a position is labeled "mysterious," the more vulnerable it is to depraved interpretation! This chapter is an unveiling of the horrors of the Babylon harlot – depravity is at the center of that church.

The name "mystery" occurs in the Greek Old Testament with an eschatological theme (Daniel 2:18-19, 27-30, 47 LXX). Here, it is again emphasized in an end-time association when the whole vision relates to the destruction of Babylon immediately preceding Christ's second coming (cf. 17:10-18). "Mystery" has previously been used by John within end-time connections (1:20, 10:7).[4]

1 Swete, H. B.; *Apocalypse of St. John* (Kregel – reprint of 1906), 1977, p. 217.
2 Thomas, Robert L.; *Revelation 8-22 – An Exegetical Commentary* (Moody Press, Chicago – 1992), p. 289.
3 http://en.wikisource.org/wiki/Catholic_Encyclopedia (1913)/Mystery (emphasis added).
4 Beale, G. K.; *The New International Greek*

The "mystery harlot" also represents Rome personified through *Dea Roma*, "the goddess Rome" that was established at the time Jerusalem fell under Emperor Vespasian. That goddess is shown sitting on the seven hills of Rome in a coin struck at that time.

Coin minted in A.D. 71[5]

Some historians conclude that her position and the symbol to her right is one of prostitution. Most interesting, John's book was written shortly after this coin was struck. In verses 6-7 (our next study) the angel adds new intrigue. He promised John that he would explain the "mysteries" of this harlot and beast!

"BABYLON THE GREAT" (vs 5)

"Apparently Tertullian, late in the second century, is the first ['']church father['] to use 'Babylon' as a name for Rome. The seven hills noted in 17:9 and the great city (17:18) is proof that 'Babylon' means Rome."[6] The association was even noted by Peter when he alluded to Rome as Babylon (I Peter 5:13) in approximately 64 A.D.[7] Others of antiquity made similar

associations [2 Bar. 11.1; 67.7; 79.1; Sib. Or. 5.143, 159; 2 Esdr. (4 Ezra) 3:2].[8]

"Babylon" was to be understood symbolically, as were the names "Balaam" (2:14), "Jezebel" (2:20) and the city prefigured as "Sodom and Egypt" (11:8). Their collective characteristics typify rebellion against God and truth.

Babylon is a theme in Scripture, beginning in Genesis 10:9-10 and continuing through the last book. It is noted as a false religion in Genesis 11:1-9. The tower and its city represent an ancient church/state (Micah 5:6)[9] that became symbolic of resisting and defying God.[10] Thus, at the end, it ties directly to Rome as the great center of religious apostasy. Again, the evidence is stunning that the end-time prophecy of the harlot represents the Roman Catholic Church – a symbol for prostitution of truth and worship.

Her power and arrogance have not ceased to grow.

"Every cleric must obey the Pope, even if he commands what is evil; for no one may judge the Pope."[11]

"The First See [Rome/papacy] is judged by no one. It is the right of the Roman Pontiff himself alone to judge … those who hold the highest civil office in a state….

"There is neither appeal nor recourse against a decision or decree of the Roman Pontiff."[12]

Edition (Thomas Nelson Publishing, 1975), "Time and Place of Writing," p. 1160.

[8] Osborne, Grant R.; *Revelation* (Baker Book House; Grand Rapids, MI), p. 612.

[9] Hunt, Dave; *A Woman Rides the Beast* (Harvest House Publishers, Eugene, OR), p. 53.

[10] Gaebelein, Frank E.; *The Expositor's Bible Commentary,* vol. 12 (Zondervan Publishing House, Grand Rapids, MI), 1984, p. 556.

[11] Pope Innocent III (1198-1216).

[12] Coriden, James A.; Green, Thomas J.; Heintschel, Donald E.; eds., *The Code of Canon Law* (Paulist Press, 1985), Canons 1404, 1405, and 333, sec. 3, pp. 951, 271.

Testament Commentary; The Book of Revelation (William B. Eerdmans Publishing Company, Grand Rapids, Michigan – 1999), p. 858.

[5] http://www.icollector.com/Roman-Empire-Vespasian-69-79-Sestertius-71-28-39g_i9258028

[6] Thomas, *op. cit.,* p. 289.

[7] Authorized King James Version, The Open Bible

Nebuchadnezzar, while walking in the palace, said: "Is not this great Babylon, that I have built, for the house of the kingdom by the might of my power, and for the honor of my majesty?" (Daniel 4:30).

Thus, Babylon was used by God as a symbol for anti-God apostasy, arrogance and power, centered in Rome. Again:

"Thus, as the moon receives its light from the sun ... so the royal power [state] derives from the Pontifical authority the splendor of its dignity.... The state of the world ... will be restored by our diligence and care ... for the pontifical authority and the royal power ... fully suffice for this purpose."[13]

The Protestant Reformation was based on the growing recognition that the Roman Catholic Church was the antichrist – the "man of sin." That great preacher Charles H. Spurgen even noted:

"It is the bound duty of every Christian to pray against Antichrist, and as to what Antichrist is no sane man ought to raise a question. If it be not the Popery in the Church of Rome there is nothing in the world that can be called by that name.

"It wounds Christ, robs Christ of His glory, puts sacramental efficacy in the place of His atonement, and lifts a piece of bread in the place of the Savour....

"If we pray against it, because it is against Him, we shall love the persons though we hate their errors; we shall love their souls though we loathe and detest their dogmas."[14]

"Since the female figures of these chapters (12, 17, 19 and 21) represent purely religious realities, Babylon must also be essentially religious."[15] She is further designated as a mother.

"THE MOTHER OF HARLOTS AND ABOMINATIONS OF THE EARTH." (vs 5)

When this seductive whore with all her false attractions is exposed, Christ's bride will be revealed in all her innocence, purity and beauty (Revelation 21:9-10). The woman of Revelation 12 gave birth to the church. This harlot of Revelation 17 tries to exterminate that church.

This woman has the two sinful ingredients that filled her golden cup in verse 4: (1) idolatry and (2) sexual promiscuity. In Hosea 2:2-5 (cf. Isaiah 50:1), Israel is personified as a mother who has played the whore and has bastard children.[16] This typifies God's view of apostate Christianity at the end of time. If the Roman Catholic Church is here the great whore, those who bond to her ecumenically are her illegitimate daughters.

Babylon, the mother of harlots, makes her the progenitor of everything anti-Christian. The Roman-based church, in turn, is the epitome of what God does not tolerate. She *is* an abomination by being the mother of abominations.

There are numerous beliefs and practices that the Catholic Church holds that mock God's Holy Word. These range from honoring tradition equal to or above the Bible, the infallibility of the pope, the co-redemptrix role of Mary to the "sacrifice" of the eucharist. All of its rebellion can be summarized in the dogma found in a myriad of papal and Vatican decrees on salvation:

---

13 Pope Innocent III (1198-1216).
14 Spurgen, Charles H.; cited in Michael de Semlyen, *All Roads Lead to Rome?* (Dorchester House Publications, England, 1991). P. 183.

15 Beale, *op. cit.,* p. 859.
16 Aune, David E.; *World Biblical Commentary, Revelation 17–22,* vol. 52c (World Books; Publisher, Dallas, Texas – 1997), p. 937.

"There is one holy Catholic and apostolic church, outside of which there is no salvation.... It is altogether necessary for salvation for every creature to be subject to the Roman Pontiff."[17]

"If anyone says that the sacraments of the New Law [of the Roman Catholic church] are not necessary for salvation but ... that without them ... men obtain from God through faith alone the grace of justification ... let him be anathema. – Council of Trent, 7, General, 4."[18]

The Catechism of the Catholic Church teaches that:

"... all salvation comes from Christ.... Through the [Catholic] Church ..."

"... the [Catholic] Church ... is necessary for salvation ..."

"... Christ ... affirmed ... the necessity of the Church which men enter through Baptism as through a door."

When Pope Benedict XVI was Cardinal Joseph Ratzinger, he was head of the Congregation for the Doctrine and the Faith. He wrote, "Dominus Iesus" as a special document presented to the Catholic Bishops of America. In it was this section:

"VI. The Church and the Other Religions in Relation to Salvation

"20. Above all else, it must be *firmly believed* that '**the Church**, a pilgrim now on earth, is necessary for salvation: the one Christ is the mediator and the way of salvation; he is present to us in his body which is the Church. He himself explicitly asserted the necessity of faith and baptism (cf. Mk 16:16; Jn 3:5), and thereby affirmed at the same time the necessity of *the Church* which men enter through baptism *as through a door*."

"The Church is the 'universal sacrament of salvation', since, united always in a mysterious way to the Saviour Jesus Christ, her Head, and subordinated to him, she has, in God's plan, an indispensable relationship with the salvation of every human being."[19]

These defy the wonderful truth, such as:

"For God so loved the world, that he gave his only begotten Son, that whosoever believeth in him should not perish, but have everlasting life" (John 3:16).

"I am the door: by me if any man enter in, he shall be saved, and shall go in and out, and find pasture" (John 10:9).

"For by grace are ye saved through faith; and that not of yourselves: it is the gift of God:" (Ephesians 2:8).

"He that believeth on the Son of God hath the witness in himself: he that believeth not God hath made him a liar; because he believeth not the record that God gave of his Son. And this is the record, that God hath given to us eternal life, and this life is in his Son. He that hath the Son hath life; and he that hath not the Son of God hath not life. These things have I written unto you that believe on the name of the Son of God; that ye may know that ye have eternal life, and that ye may believe on the name of the Son of God" (I John 5:10-13).

The Roman Catholic Church is the harlot of Revelation 17, filled with heresy and blasphemy against the God of the universe! She spreads her falsehood to the kings of the world. She is *the* apostate Babylon of prophecy. This echoes the abomination" of Daniel the prophet

---

[17] From the papal bull of Pope Boniface VIII, *Unam Sanctam*, A.D. 1302.

[18] Schroeder, H. J., O.P., trans; *The Canons and Decrees of the Council of Trent* (Tan Books, 1978), p. 52.

[19] *Dominus Iesus*, August 6, 2000.

(chapters 8–12) that are part of earth's final prophecies (Matthew 24:15).

Intriguingly, many scholars point to Rome as the end-time focus of this harlot/Babylon prophecy. Yet, their description quickly reverts to ancient Rome and her excesses, persecutions, idolatry and Christian apostasy. They all seem to be afraid of a contemporary application.

CHAPTER 7

GIDDY WITH MURDER

"And I saw the woman drunken with the blood of the saints, and with the blood of the martyrs of Jesus: and when I saw her, I wondered with great admiration. And the angel said unto me, Wherefore didst thou marvel? I will tell thee the mystery of the woman, and of the beast that carrieth her, which hath the seven heads and ten horns" (Revelation 17:6-7).

John Reacts

In verse 2, 4 and 5 the woman is associated with "evil beverage" imagery that develops into the meaning of this verse (see box below).

"And I saw the woman drunken with the blood" (vs 6)

This is stunning language and is understood as a metaphor from the "OT (Isa. 34:5, 7 LXX; 49:26; Jer. 46:10; Ezek. 39:18-19) and from ancient writers (Josephus, J.W. 5.8.2 §344; Suetonius, Tiberius 59). It pictures the great joy with which depraved armies would slaughter entire families as well as opposing armies."[1]

This woman, a church, indulges in this heinous drunken orgy though representing "Godliness" to the world. That heinous influence is seen by the world accepting her counsel and teaching, beginning with its leaders (kings). Can you imagine what God is really saying about the Roman church? The end-time horrors of persecution are concentrated within the parochial walls of Catholicism. No wonder God wants to assure His people that this despicable religious order will come to an end.

Scholars often refer this imagery to the massacre of Nero when Rome burned (A.D. 64) or an allusion to the Dark Ages, when the Roman Church was involved with the slaughter of millions. But this is prophecy of the end of earth's history! It ties directly to other eschatological prophecies regarding this time:

Wine (vs 2)	Of her (Babylon's) fornication (deceptive beliefs)	World made drunk with this drink (14:8, 17:6) (giddy with identity to the harlot)
Cup (vss 4-5)	Full of abominations and the evil of her fornication	Called "mother" of earthly abominations
Blood (vs 6)	Woman drunken	Giddy from saints' deaths (13:7) because they resisted abominable beliefs

---

[1] Osborne, Grant R.; *Revelation* (Baker Book House; Grand Rapids, MI), p. 613.

- Dragon hated God's true church (woman) and made war against her offspring (Revelation 12:17).
- Holy City (God's true people) is persecuted 42 months (Revelation 11:2).
- Beast makes war with the saints 42 months (Revelation 13:5, 7)
- God's holy people persecuted time times and an half – then the end (Daniel 12:7)

That can only mean the Roman Church – *the* Roman Catholic Church – will be involved with horrifying butchery and carnage in the very near future.

"Many will plead that there is no prospect that popery will ever be revived. If it shall regain its lost ascendancy, it will be by Protestantism's giving it the right hand of fellowship. If it shall be legislated into power by the concessions of time-serving men, the fires of persecution will be rekindled against those who will not sacrifice conscience and the truth for the errors of the papacy. Once let the minds of the Christian world be turned away from God; let his law be dishonored and his holy day trampled upon, and they will be ready to take any step where Satan may lead the way."[2]

"Let there be a revival of the faith and power of the early church, and the spirit of persecution will be revived, and the fires of persecution will be rekindled."[3]

"with the blood of the saints, and with the blood of the martyrs of Jesus:" (vs 6)

This text doesn't intend to describe two separate groups of individuals. The saints are those who have patience, keep God's commandments and have the faith of Jesus (Revelation 14:12). It is from that loyal group that those killed become martyrs. But we are told: "He that leadeth into captivity shall go into captivity: he that killeth with the sword must be killed with the sword. Here is the patience and the faith of the saints" (Revelation 13:10). The earth beast (the United States) "causes that as many as would not worship the image of the beast should be killed" (Revelation 13:15).

John saw that drunken woman. The angel explained that it was from drinking blood from God's people. No wonder John then said:

"and when I saw her, I wondered with great admiration." (vs 6)

John's response is similar to Daniel's at his hearing of the imminent demise of the Babylonian king: "he marveled greatly" (Daniel 4:19), "Then Daniel … was astonished for one hour." A drunken woman on a beast in the desert will only become more astonishing with the facts being fully explained! She's a murderess – and it is first degree homicide!

The seer had expected to see how the harlot – Babylon – came to her end. So far she seems to have been triumphant, tyrannical and murderous against God's people. The prophetic setting was designed as a preamble to the explanation that follows.

- A beautiful woman
- Seductively dressed
- On a strange beast
- Is suddenly observed to be drunk
  - With blood
  - From God's people

---

[2] White, Ellen G.; *The Review and Herald,* January 1, 1889.

[3] White, Ellen G.; *The Great Controversy,* p. 48.

His curiosity and puzzlement, as ours would be, is at its peak. He is ready for what follows.

Before we go on, there are important observations that must be made: The saints are the people of God who conquer Satan by "the blood of the Lamb and by the word of their testimony. They did not love their lives even to the point of death" (Revelation 12:11).

- This is a golden thread that draws together these many themes in this book.
- God's people remain faithful in spite of end-time persecution.
- AND ... "There is no hint anywhere that during this terrible persecution the saints are hiding in forests, caves, and remote places lest they be killed. Rather, they engage in fearless witness throughout this period."[4]
- God's people are not to be isolationists! There is a mission of completing the work of bringing the gospel to the world. Then the end comes – not before.

"And the angel said unto me," (vs 7)

The vial angel has been "talking" with and "showing him" this visionary experience all along. It appears that John's emotional reaction to the last scene brought an abrupt response from this angel. John admits, before the prophetic communiqué resumes, that he was personally admonished.

"Wherefore didst thou marvel?" (vs 7)

"Why are you filled with wonder and perplexity?"[5] This also appears to be rhetorical. "Don't be so dismayed. At the end Satan will work through his agents/ agencies and reveal the true nature of his heart. You must understand how evil he is and the character of those loyal to his leadership." This imagery (John's reaction) and heaven's response are for us to fully decipher, completely discern and explicate. We will have a similar reaction as this seer! "How can this really happen?"

In God's sovereign foreknowledge He has already revealed the temporary triumph of Satan's malicious power in Revelation 13. He now wants to strengthen our faith by demystifying that future. Terrible ordeals are to be encountered. God will triumph in the end along with a great body of loyal subjects (Revelation 13:10).

Intriguingly, the woman has dress colors close to that of Aaron and his priest sons. They represented redemptive themes and the very character of God. The only key color absent from this harlot is blue, which symbolizes the purity and nature of God's law. Thus, this portrayal undoubtedly added to John's emotions. The harlot defies God's law.

All this describes the emotional transition between the vision of the harlot and the interpretation of her symbolism. What now follows is a focus on the beast. The imagery of that creature will now unfold deeper issues regarding the harlot church.

"I will tell thee the mystery of the woman, and of the beast that carrieth her, which hath the seven heads and ten horns." (vs 7)

The mystery or secret that surrounds the woman is now also tagged to the beast. This suggests that they both share one mystery. The fate of one is inextricably tied to the other. Information regarding the evil of one will be explicitly associated with the other.

---

4   Osborne *op. cit.,* p. 614.
5   *Ibid.*

It is significant to note that the woman sat on the beast (vs 3) in an administrative leadership portrayal. Here, she is carried by the beast. This suggests that without that kingdom/state (the Vatican), the Roman Catholic Church would be ineffective. This is stunning and extremely important prophetically. This symbiotic relationship is the Holy See. It is the Holy See that has a "Permanent Observer" relationship with the United Nations (since 1945). It is the Holy See that exchanges ambassadors with other nations.

Thus, the Roman Catholic Church, by being "carried by the Vatican state," has by default diplomatic ties to 180 (2015) countries around the world.[6]

Like no other church/state (woman/beast) is this, which began legally in 1929.

Thus, as the mystery is now unfolded, end-time cues related to that Rome-centered power will come into view! What is about to be shared is vital information for God's people to prepare and relate to the stunning heartaches and victories that will be their companions for many months.

---

[6] http://www.ewtn.com/vnews/getstory.asp?number=124481

CHAPTER 8

FULFILLMENT OF A 2000-YEAR OLD PAPAL PROPHECY!

"The beast that thou sawest was, and is not; and shall ascend out of the bottomless pit, and go into perdition: and they that dwell on the earth shall wonder, whose names were not written in the book of life from the foundation of the world, when they behold the beast that was, and *is* not, and yet is. And here is the mind which hath wisdom. The seven heads are seven mountains, on which the woman sitteth" (Revelation 17:8-9).

"The beast that thou sawest" (vs 8)

The angel is so accommodating. He makes sure John is reminded that the information he is now going to get refers to the beast he just saw (vss 1-6). It is possible that there was a time break between verses 7 and 8. John is apparently given time to write what he saw. A similar gesture will occur in verses 12, 15, 16 and 18. Why? Every tidbit of new material must be carefully joined with the other for a total picture of this beast kingdom. In turn, it becomes introductory to the imagery of the sea beast in Revelation 13 and, finally, to information in 11:7-8.

Revelation 17 and 18 review and fill in details of visionary messages previously given. Every particular enlightens those apocalyptic stories and prepares us for what's ahead.

"was, and is not; and shall ascend out of the bottomless pit, and go into perdition:" (vs 8)

The beast was worshiped in a previous vision (13:4-6b, 8, 15). Now it parodies another picture mimicking God. Christ is the One who "was, and who is, and who is to come" (Revelation 1:4, 8; 4:8; 11:17; 16:5). It refers to His resurrection. "I am he that liveth, and was dead" (Revelation 1:18). The beast as the "god of this world" (II Corinthians 4:4) is trying to be like God in just the same way. Intriguingly, he lived, then was wounded by a "sword" (13:14) and did live ("which deadly wound was healed" – 13:12). Satan was once an angel of light. Then he was cast to the earth (12:9). He will once again be seen as an angel of light (II Corinthians 11:14). Is he this beast? The color is different from the dragon in 12:3. Also, the *context* in chapter 17 draws on an *earthly* beast/religious caricature that is worshiped, which is acting like Satan. God's people are persecuted, and other kingdoms are supportive of this beast in this end-time story.

There are many allusions of Satan and his minions mimicking Christ and the end-time events. It is his final hour, and he knows "that he hath but a short time" (Revelation 12:12) to work. He deceives. He makes the world think that his nature, teachings and representatives stand for right – but like the harlot, he beguiles, then ensnares. His great forte is through earthly mediums!

Here, an earthly kingdom – the papacy/the Vatican – is in view. It had been a world power with kings giving it obeisance. It had presided over the world's most hideous carnage and evil – *"It was"* the one "who lived" [past tense].[1]

Then, on February 10, 1798, its *ecclesiastical power* was broken when Napoleon's French General Berthier took Pope Pius VI prisoner. Its *civil arm* was later crushed on September 20, 1870 when the final papal land/states – Rome – fell to Italian troops and Pope Pius IX became a vassal to his own church without power and without a kingdom. *Then*, it was *"not"* "who [had] lived."[2] The loss of kingdom (beast) power fulfilled John's prophecy of the beast with precision in 1870.

This final event is reviewed in this brief but fascinating account:

"Rome was declared Capital of Italy in March 1861, when the first Italian Parliament met in the kingdom's old capital *Turin* in Piedmont. However, the Italian Government could not take possession of its capital because *Napoleon III* kept a French garrison in Rome protecting *Pope Pius IX*. The opportunity to eliminate the last vestige of the Papal States came when the *Franco-Pussian War* began in July 1870. Emperor *Napoleon III* had to recall his garrison from Rome for France's own defense and could no longer protect the pope. Following the collapse of the French Empire at the *battle of Sedan,* widespread public demonstrations demanded that the Italian Government take Rome. King *Victor Emmanuel II* sent Count Ponza di San Martino to Pius IX with a personal letter offering a face-saving proposal that would have allowed the peaceful entry of the Italian Army into Rome, under the guise of offering protection to the pope.

"The Pope's reception of San Martino [early September 1870] was unfriendly.

Pius IX allowed violent outbursts to escape him. Throwing the King's letter upon the table he exclaimed: 'Fine loyalty! You are all a set of vipers, of whited sepulchers, and wanting in faith.' He was perhaps alluding to other letters received from the King. After growing calmer, he exclaimed: 'I am no prophet, nor son of a prophet, but I tell you, you will never enter Rome!'"

"On September 20, the Italian Army, commanded by General *Raffaele Cadorna*, entered Rome and annexed the remnants of the papal kingdom to Italy.

"This event, described in Italian history books as a liberation, was taken very bitterly by the Pope. The Italian government had offered to allow the Pope to retain control of the *City* on the west bank of the *Tiber*, but Pius rejected the overture. Early the following year, the capital of Italy was moved from Florence to the royal palace of the Kings of Italy. Pius IX withdrew into the Vatican in protest, where he lived as a self-*proclaimed 'prisoner.'"* [3]

The United States had diplomatic ties with the papacy between 1797 and 1870. These relations lapsed when the Papal States were lost.[4]

"After the overthrow of the *Papal States, Italy's Law of Guarantees* accorded the *Pope* certain honors and privileges similar to those enjoyed by the *King of Italy*, including the right to send and receive *ambassadors* who would have full *diplomatic immunity*, just as if he still had *temporal power* as ruler of a state.

"Pope Pius IX and his successors refused to recognize the right of the Italian

---

[1]   Aune, David E.; *World Biblical Commentary; Revelation 17–22*, vol. 52c (World Books Publisher; Dallas, Texas – 1997), p. 940.

[2]   *Ibid.*

[3]   1. Raffaele De Cesare, *The Last Days of Papal Rome* [Archibald Constable & Co, London (1909) Chap. XXXIV], p. 444.
      2. De Cesare, *Op. cit.,* p. 440.]
      [References as noted in http://en. wikipdia. org/ wiki/Vatican_during_the_ Savoyard_Era_ 1870%E2%80%931929:] (emphasis added).

[4]   http://www.state.gov/r/pa/ei/bgn/3819.htm

king to reign over what had formerly been the Papal States, or to be mollified by the Law of Guarantees.

"That 'law' offered an annual financial payment to the pope, but he perceived it as reducing the pope to a 'chaplain of the King of Italy.'

"Pope Pius IX, asserted that the *Holy See* would maintain absolute independence from the Italian state, finally rejecting the *Law of Papal Guarantees of 1871.*

"The Pope maintained that since the beginning of the Italian kingdom in 1861, and especially since the confiscation of the Papal States in 1870, an international settlement issue remained open. This is referred to in history as the 'Roman Question.' Many nations recognized that this issue needed resolution. Italy did not [address it] until Victor Emmanuel III became its king (1900) and Benito Mussolini became its Prime Minister (1922)."[5]

In the meantime, the pope's refusal to accept the Law of Guarantees was fulfilling prophecy. Though he could have been head of a *state* (woman/beast), he remained an *ecclesiastical head* only. There was *no beast* being ridden by a woman. Then, Mussolini became a fascist dictator of Italy. His foremost priority was the subjugation of the *minds* of the Italian people and the use of *propaganda* to do so – whether at home or abroad. And here his training as a journalist was invaluable. Press, radio, education, films – all were carefully supervised to create the illusion that fascism was *the* doctrine of the twentieth century, replacing Italy's budding democracy.

Victor Emmanuel III Italy

In 1927, Mussolini was *baptized* by a Roman Catholic *priest* in order to take away certain Catholic opposition, which was still very critical of a regime that had taken the "papal property" and virtually *blackmailed* the Vatican. However, Mussolini was never known to be a practicing Catholic, and was privately very hostile to the Church. Mussolini and King Victor Emmanuel III, however, wanted to "settle" the "Roman Question."

"out of the bottomless pit, and go into perdition: and behold the beast that was and yet is [present]" (vs 8)

This imagery points to a final appearance of this apostate power at the end of history.[6] The beast ascending from *the* abyss was already described in:

1. The destruction of the two witnesses (11:7) – then
2. From the sea to join the dragon in his war against God's people (13:1, 7)

In keeping with the angelic theme on how the harlot and beast come to their end, those two stories *follow* the prelude described here in verse 8. It is part of a counterfeit resurrection.[7] The abyss is the abode of demons (Luke 8:31, Revelation 9:1-2, 11). This beast not only supports a sinful "woman" but found its citadel where Satan has his stronghold.

Its rising and being destroyed has a similar ring to the little horn in Daniel (7:11,

5   Pollard, John F. (2005). *Money and the Rise of the Modern Papacy: Financing the Vatican, 1850-1950* (Cambridge University Press), p. 10.

6   Beale, G. K.; *The New International Greek Testament Commentary; The Book of Revelation* (William B. Eerdmans Publishing Company, Grand Rapids, Michigan – 1999), p. 865.

7   Osborne, Grant R.; *Revelation* (Baker Book House; Grand Rapids, MI), p. 616.

17-18, 23, 26; 8:25). It goes into perdition – "the beast was taken" … "cast alive into a lake of fire burning with brimstone" (Revelation 19:20).

The beast (antichrist kingdom) was, is not and now ascends or rises again. This parallels the sword-wounded beast being healed (13:12, 14).[8] The date of 1929 fits exactly with this "resurrection." The end of its rule – kingdom power – will once again be anticipated. One might now conclude that the rest of the prophecy will reveal the steps the papacy will traverse from the ascension to world power, then to perdition. That is actually unfolded in the "rest of the story" in subsequent verses – and then comes chapter 13!

The rise of the beast out of the bottomless pit is also a metaphor for its "eschatological coming." It arrives and the world wonders in awe and worships it, revealing a distinct religious loyalty (Revelation 13:3-4, 8). One exception is noted: those written in the "book of life of the Lamb" (Revelation 13:8).[9] They stand in firm opposition.

Repeatedly, Jesus said of this time that the parousia was imminent: "I am coming" (3:11; 16:15; 22:7, 12, 20). Satan does all possible to make himself or the key "beast" appear as though it was the Messiah answer. The world is unaware that it will be shortly destined to hell.

The beast will in the end be shown to be false and destroyed. Christ will be seen as "alive forever" (1:18, 2:8). Since 17:8 notes that it goes to destruction as it does in verse 11, those verses become the "covers" of a descriptive prophecy "booklet." Verses 8-11 can be seen as a unique unit of information about the harlot and the beast.

Here is how it came out of that abyss (only to return there later – forever):

On February 11, 1929 a concordat with the **Vatican** was signed, the **Lateran Treaty**, by which the Italian state was at last recognized by the **Roman Catholic Church**, and the independence of **Vatican City** was recognized by the Italian state. The 1929 treaty also included a legal provision whereby the Italian government would protect the honor and dignity of the Pope by prosecuting offenders. This is when prophecy once again was fulfilled.

Now the beast ascended out of the "bottomless pit." This beast is further described at the end of the verse: "Behold the beast that was, and is not, and **yet is**" ("will come" – or "will be present"). It suggests a time when the papacy will have its kingdom back. That is exactly what was accomplished by the Lateran Treaty.

The political power and diplomatic standing of the Catholic Church, that had been lost, was re-established. The pope once again became an independent sovereign ruler, as he was throughout the Middle Ages – though his temporal realm, still established today, is the smallest independent state in the world and probably in all history.

Benito Mussolini reads his credentials prior to signing the Lateran Treaty on behalf of King Victor Emmanuel III. Cardinal Gasparri (seated), signed on behalf of Pope Pius XI.

8   Gaebelein, Frank E.; *The Expositor's Bible Commentary,* vol. 12 (Zondervan Publishing House, Grand Rapids, MI), 1984, p. 557.

9   Beale, *op. cit.,* p. 864.

Mussolini signs the Lateran
Pact of 1929, which brought into
being the Vatican City State.

Cardinal Gasparri and Benito Mussolini (seated)
after exchanging treaty ratifications in the Hall
of Congregations, the Vatican, June 7th, 1929.

Cardinal Gasparri signs the Lateran
Concordat as Mussolini looks on.

Pope Pius XI

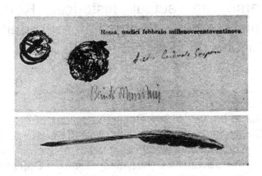

The seals and signatures
of Benito Mussolini and
Cardinal Gasparri

That agreement signed by Benito Mussolini and Cardinal Gasparri, on behalf of King Victor Emmanuel III and Pope Pius XI, restored the full diplomatic and political power of the Holy See of Rome. Can you imagine this prophecy being fulfilled so recently?! We are truly right at the end. Today, all the world indeed "wonders" at the revived power of the Roman Catholic Church, the epitome of Church and State combined and a major player in global politics. The kingdom beast was restored and *now is*. Pope Pius XI himself commented on the concordat, and his restored power, in the first ten paragraphs of a new encyclical he wrote on December 23, 1929.

Quinquagesimo Ante (On His Sacerdotal Jubilee) Pope Pius XI. "[Part] 12. Arrived, then, at the end of the year and looking at the world around Us, We are greatly rejoiced to see that many nations have already, by public conventions, entered upon relations of friendship with the Holy See, or else are on the verge of making or renewing Concordats."

The wound was healed. The Church/State, the harlot/beast, the Roman Catholic apostate church and the Vatican, had legally and prophetically been brought together!

"and they that dwell on the earth shall wonder," (vs 8)

Stunning! The wound was healed. That will be a specific ***reference point*** when Revelation 13 is studied! This helps to develop the link between the stories of Revelation 17 and 13! The beast (scarlet in color), mocking God, will later be seen with key characteristics of the prophetic leopard kingdom in Daniel 7 and morphed again in mocking God (13:1). That is when it wields its final destructive authority against God's people.

"Earth dwellers" have begun to wonder after this beast (17:8). This reaches its zenith at the very end when "all the world wondered after the beast" (13:3). Before that can be studied in full, God has more compelling issues to tell us about what will make it all happen.

See 13:8 for discussion on the Book of Life.

"And here *is* the mind which hath wisdom." (vs 9)

The angel prepares to move deeper into the interpretation of the beast by this statement. A similar announcement will be made again regarding the number 666. "Here is wisdom. Let him that hath understanding …" (13:18). ***When*** these expressions are used:

1. It requires special inspiration from the Holy Spirit to solve the apocalyptic riddle.[10]
2. It relates to the time when Jesus' second coming occurs.
3. This wisdom is also needed to avoid deception regarding the beast.[11]

God used similar language with Daniel, which tied to apocalyptic prophecies (Daniel 1:4, 17; 9:22; 11:33; 12:10). Why is special skill needed here? John is going to be given special clues as to the meaning of the seven heads of this beast. God does not want errors in its interpretation. But shy of the Holy Spirit, all views will fall short of its rich meaning.

"The seven heads are seven mountains," (vs 9)

Anciently, the "seven mountains" often referred to Rome because it was built on seven hills.[12]

Amazing! The "Seven Hills" association became an actual historical Roman festival, the Septimontium, during Domitian's reign (81-96 A.D.).[13]

---

10 Osborne, *op. cit.,* p. 617.
11 Aune, *op. cit.,* p. 941; Beale, *Op. cit.,* p. 867.
12 Cicero, *Att.* 6.5; Pliny, *Nat. Hist.* 3.66-67; … The city began with an amalgamation of groups living on the seven hills (Aventine, Daelian, Capitoline, Equiline, Palatine, Quirinal, Viminal), and during Domitian's reign a festival (the *Septimontium*) celebrated it.
13 Jones, Brian W. (1992). *The Emperor Domitian.* London: Routledge. ISBN 0-415-10195-6.

Those seven hills overlooked the Vatican Hill across the Tiber River where the center of this prophecy would unfold. Thus, God used contemporary clues to make it unequivocal that those seven heads of that blasphemous beast represent Rome.

Vatican Hill was outside the city limits during this first century. It was the location of Rome's major cemetery, where the dead were buried. How intriguing that on that cemetery St. Peter's Basilica was built, and bones, found in one grave, were "declared" as that of the Apostle Peter! Mysterious? No! Deceptive.

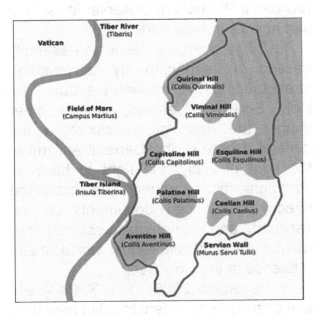

The Temple of Jupiter, on the Capitoline Hill in Rome, had a bronze statue to that god. Emperor Domitian gave him special obeisance. During Roman Emperor Valentinian III's reign, the Bishop of Rome, Leo I, felt the need of power and obtained it from the emperor in a special decree on June 6, 445, through a civil recognition of papal primacy *based on the merits of Peter.* This was the beginning of the Roman Church's claim to apostolic succession from Peter and the first time the bishop of Rome was called *Papas* (pope).

Leo I took the bronze statue of Jupiter from its temple (now belonging to the Church of Rome) and had its hands and right forearm recast with the cultic sign of peace and Peter's key. Then he placed it on a marble throne and called it St. Peter.[14] Another mystery? No! Deception.

Statue – "St. Peter"
(really the god Jupiter)

No wonder the angel declared that one must have wisdom regarding the kingdom associated with Rome. Deception is tied to that city and church. To protect the expanding base of the papacy, Pope Leo IV (848-852 A.D.) enlarged Rome's walls to encompass Vatican Hill – then there were eight official hills in Rome!

Seven heads and an eighth recall the beast we are reviewing. Verse 11, in an "eighth" symbol, draws on a power that follows the seventh. Stay tuned (with wisdom).[15]

"on which the woman sitteth." (vs 9)

The imagery of "sitting" again suggests that she is enthroned. One of

14   http://www.biblicist.org/bible/history.shtml
15   http://www.aloha.net/~mikesch/wheel.htm

the apocryphal books states that when the Lord comes in glory at the *eschaton,* the woman will be ruling on seven hills (1 Enoch 24.1-25.3). In prophecy this always has judicial implications. The lordship is based on laws related to the "sitting" leader.

The apostolic Roman Catholic Church controls, in this end-time imagery, a kingdom known now as Vatican City. An evil king is prophesied by Daniel, who exalts his sovereignty over God and persecutes God's people (Daniel 11:33, 12:10) for a period of time. That parallels the timing prophecies of Revelation 11:2 and 13:5. All are tied to people/powers that mock God in a fascinating bond between secular (Gentiles) and ecclesiastical (woman) power. *The woman and the beast* are symbols of church/state power in supreme apostasy (blasphemy) at the end.

The woman sits or rules over water (people of the world – 17:1, 15). Now she is on a kingdom associated with Rome. Seven denotes "completeness."[16] In this setting, there is a complete number of heads to the Vatican kingdom in its church/state bond. Though many scholars have attempted to put this as seven periods of history (based on heads being kingdoms – Daniel 7:23), *we must relate to verse 1 and the original purpose of this vision.* It is to show how the harlot (the apostate church) *came to its end* at the seventh plague. This implies that the focus is events leading up to the second coming of Jesus. The intent is to review events/ powers/ peoples associated with the demise of that harlot called Babylon.

Since there is a double meaning to the heads, mountains (hills of Rome) and kings (noted in the next verse) – and the harlot is over or controls them – the identity of the woman is irrevocably made. There is no church in charge of a bonified kingdom other than the Roman Catholic Church with its papal heads. The **unit** of the church, kingdom and its head is, once again, called the Holy See.

If this "unit" is a prophetic power, a world influence, then there must be some fulfillment or evidence that the Holy See is a recognized "woman/beast" with unprecedented prestige. Let's look once more at the relationship between the Holy See and the United Nations.

Although the Holy See is not a member state of the United Nations, since 1964 it has had a Permanent Observer Mission to that agency in New York.

In 2004 the U.N. General Assembly passed a resolution by acclamation strengthening the mission's status. The Holy See now enjoys, among other things, the right to participate in the general debate of the General Assembly, the right of reply, the right to have its communications issued and circulated directly as official documents of the assembly, and the right to co-sponsor draft resolutions and decisions which make reference to the Holy See.

In December 2006, the U.S. Congress authorized the president to grant members of the observer mission the same diplomatic immunity and privileges that the United States, as host country, grants to U.N. ambassadors and their staffs.

Archbishop Celestino Migliore is apostolic nuncio and permanent observer (2009) of the Holy See to the United Nations. He is the fourth Permanent Observer.

In addition, the Holy See participates in many conferences sponsored by the United Nations and takes an active role in the work of U.N. agencies.[17]

16   Beale, *op. cit.,* p. 869.

17   April 10, 2008 by usccbdigitalmedia.

The convergence of end-time apostate prophecy is in this dual imagery. World leaders, cultures and religious powers pay deference and reverence to the papacy. This homage is an unprecedented phenomenon, a prodigious cultural anomaly. Yet – it is an explicit fulfillment of prophecy presented in various ways in Daniel and Revelation. This chapter is unequivocally positioned to assure no equivocation as to *who* it is and *when* it is!

Daniel noted that a king of fierce countenance will arise, understanding "dark sentences" (specializing in deception) (8:23). This occurs when "transgressors are come in full" – when rebellion against God's authority, law and covenant reaches its peak. "And his power shall be mighty, but not by his own power" (8:24) – though his "craft" will prosper and he shall magnify himself (8:25). Can you imagine a church wielding that much power, as at the U.N.? Can you imagine a church with such clout as to have ambassadors? It is an aberration unparalleled in human history.

"The federal government of the United States does not name ambassadors to represent us with any other faith tradition. Moreover, as long as the position has existed, it has gone to a Roman Catholic, which raises additional questions about a possible religious test for public office and church–state issues."[18]

Yet, the United States understands and accepts the "mission of the Holy See." "The term '*Holy See*' refers to the supreme authority of the Church, that is, the Pope as Bishop of Rome and head of the college of Bishops. It is the central government of the Roman Catholic Church. As such, the Holy See is an institution which, under international law and in practice, has a legal personality that allows it to enter into treaties as the juridical equal of a State and to send and receive diplomatic representatives."[19]

The next incredible message from the angel is about the "heads" (leaders) of the "beast" (papal Rome) following 1929. Stunning! Let's listen in.

---

[18] http://www.washingtonmonthly.com/archives/individual/2008_12/015892.php

[19] http://www.holyseemission.org/short_history.html (emphasis added).

CHAPTER 9

"HEADINGS" OF THE BEAST

"And there are seven kings: five are fallen, and one is, *and* the other is not yet come; and when he cometh, he must continue a short space" (Revelation 17:10).

The prophetic canvas of Revelation has ever-changing graphics to typify the progression of prophetic events. The "waters" revealed what the harlot had power over (peoples of the world – vs 1). The seven "hills" (Rome) identified the central location of the woman and the beast (the Roman Catholic Church and the Vatican – vs 9). Therefore, we must conclude that at some point in time (just before her fall – 16:19, 17:1), the papacy will have world power. This Biblical portrayal was noted by expositor White long ago:

"The papacy will appear in its power. All must now arouse and search the Scriptures, for God will make known to His faithful ones *what shall be in the last time*. The word of the Lord is to come to His people in power."[1] It is recognition that those who penetrate the deeper Biblical truths will understand these end-time messages.

"The Roman Church is far-reaching in her plans and modes of operation. She is employing every device to extend her influence and increase her power in preparation for a *fierce and determined conflict* to regain control of the world."[2] Her global leadership will be gained through a horrific power struggle.

As the woman/church is over the Vatican beast, that kingdom power is additionally described as having seven unique kingly heads. Most important – they are sequenced!

"And there are seven kings:" (vs 10)

Notice that the woman sits on the heads (vs 9) (has ultimate authority over) – but the beast carries her (vs 7). The Roman Church is seen here as over the leaders of the beast. That "headship" is formally defined by the papacy as:

"The Pope exercises supreme legislative, executive, *and* judicial power over the Holy See and the State of the Vatican City."[3] This means, though he is head of state over the Vatican, he is also over the giant system of the Church and State. Thus, the head of the beast is also over all.

The heads are not numbered (like, for instance, the Seals and Trumpets), but they are in *sequence* by their description. They distinctly represent a series of papal heads. There are seven popes (the "eighth" issue is dealt with as a separate issue in the next verse). Note again that this woman–beast/church–state genre did not emerge until 1929.[4] Thus, that list contextually begins with Pope Pius XI.

The phrase "seven kings" (*hepta basileis*) symbolizes *a complete number of leaders* trying to usurp God's position as leader of an emerging spiritual kingdom

[1]   White, Ellen G.; *The Great Controversy*, p. 565 (1887).

[2]   White, Ellen G.; *Manuscript Releases*, vol. 21, p. 437 (1906).

[3]   http://www.state.gov/r/pa/ei/bgn/3819.htm

[4]   http://www.cia.gov/library/publications/the-world-factbook/print/vt.html

that will know no end. Their thoughts, plans and designs take the place of God's. This is delineated by their leadership over a beast full of names of blasphemy (17:3) – and with the woman having such a name embedded in her forehead! All this illustrates the subtle ways Satan tries to displace God's authority.

The sequence begins from the time the woman and the beast are together – when the woman (Roman Catholic Church) becomes dependent on the beast (Vatican State) for its global influence and power!

"Five are fallen," (vs 10)

The word "fallen" (*epesan*) is a euphemism for death.[5]

These are the five popes who have succeeded each other from 1929 on:

Pope Pius XI – Number One: [6]

He presided over the Lateran Treaty in 1929. He reigned as Pope from February 6, 1922, and as *sovereign of Vatican City* from 1929 until his death on *February 10, 1939*.

Pope Pius XII – Number Two: [7]

He reigned from March 2, 1939 to October 9, 1958. He invoked *ex cathedra papal infallibility* on November 1, 1950 when he defined the dogma of the assumption:

"By the authority of our Lord Jesus Christ, of the Blessed Apostles Peter and Paul, and by our own authority, we pronounce, declare, and define it to be a divinely revealed dogma: that the *Immaculate Mother of God*, the ever Virgin Mary, having completed the course of her earthly life, was assumed body and soul into heavenly glory."

This reveals one of the blasphemous issues that the "woman" is identified with.

Pope John XXIII – Number Three: [8]

He reigned from October 28, 1958 to June 3, 1963. He called the *Second Vatican Council* (1962-1965) – but did not live to see it to completion because of his untimely death.

Pope Paul VI – Number Four: [9]

He reigned from June 20, 1963 to August 6, 1978. He completed the Second Vatican Council work and fostered improved ecumenical relations with Orthodox, Anglicans and Protestants, which resulted in a number of historic meetings and agreements. He met many U.S. presidents and was in power when the first and only Catholic President, John F. Kennedy, was assassinated.

---

5   Osborne, *op. cit.*, p. 617.
6   http://en.wikipedia.org/wiki/Image:Ratti1922.jpg
7   http://en.wikipedia.org/wiki/Image:Pacelli12.jpg

8   http://www.catholic-forum.com/saints/pope0261.htm
9   http://www.omsoul.com/catalog/pope-paul-vi-m081.html

Pope John Paul I – Number Five:[10]

He reigned from August 26, 1978 to September 28, 1978 (33 days). Much controversy surrounds his death. He was known as the "smiling pope," and many world leaders were comfortable talking with him. He was a scholar/theologian and grasped issues quickly.

These five popes died. By this prophecy, they would fulfill "five have fallen." Our challenge comes with the next phrase:

"and one is," (vs 10)

The next head was Pope John Paul II. **Three popes** were in power during the year of 1978.

Pope John Paul II – Number Six: [11]

He reigned from October 1978 to April 2, 2005. Though he has now passed away, stunning issues occurred during his reign to validate this prophecy! He was a unique person, and his reign was the second longest in papal history. He traveled more than any other pontiff – and was seen in person by more than any other human being! Heads of state visited him virtually every week during his tenure. This is when the world began to wonder after the papacy. This *begins* to develop a foundation for a complete fulfillment of the prophecy of Revelation 13:3 – "and all the world wondered after the beast," which occurs at the very end of time.[12] His funeral was the single largest gathering of heads of state in history, surpassing the funerals of **Winston Churchill** (1965) and **Marshal Tito** (1980). Four **kings**, five **queens**, at least 70 **presidents** and **prime ministers**, and more than 14 leaders of other religions attended alongside the Catholic faithful. It is also likely to have been the largest single gathering of Christianity in history, with numbers estimated in excess of four million mourners gathering in Rome.

"Pope John Paul II was buried in a Vatican crypt. Millions around the world watched the funeral."[13]

Funeral of Pope John Paul II

There are other incredible milestones related to the "one that is." The United States would be seen as a "moral partner," beginning a relationship noted in Revelation 13 [the sea beast (Papacy–Vatican State) and the earth beast (United States)]. That alliance is of special importance. It is a prophetic mandate to fulfill the Revelation 13 alliance!

---

10 http://en.wikipedia.org/wiki/Pope_Paul_I
11 http://en.wikipedia.org/wiki/John_Paul_II

12 White, Ellen G.; *Manuscript Releases,* vol. 19, p. 282.
13 CNN.com. Retrieved on 2008-10-19.

45

The United States and the Holy See announced the establishment of diplomatic relations on January 10, 1984. On March 7, 1984, the Senate confirmed William A. Wilson as the *first* U.S. ambassador to the Holy See. Ambassador Wilson had been President Reagan's personal envoy to the Pope since 1981. The Holy See named Archbishop Pio Laghi as the first Apostolic Nuncio (equivalent to ambassador) of the Holy See to the U.S.

"The U.S.–Holy See relationship is best characterized as an *active global partnership* for human dignity. Establishment of diplomatic relations has bolstered the *frequent contact and consultation* between the United States and the Holy See on many important international issues of mutual interest. The *commitment to human dignity* at the core of both the U.S. and the Holy See approach to the world gives rise to a common agenda for action to promote *religious freedom, justice, religious and ethnic tolerance, liberty, respect for women and children* and for the rule of law."[14]

"Reagan's key Administration players were all devout Roman Catholics – CIA chief William *Casey*, Allen, Clark, Haig, Walters and William Wilson.... They regarded the U.S.–Vatican relationship as a *holy alliance*."[15]

Countries that Pope John Paul II visited[16]

Indeed, there has been a growing bond between the Vatican and the United States. There is an amazing crescendoing *political* unity between these countries, just like Revelation 13 predicted, since Pope John Paul II had come into power in 1978.

The time of the end, when all will occur within one generation, appears to have begun in the fall of 1978 when the "one [that] is" became pope. The timing concept that "this generation shall not pass away, till all be fulfilled" (Luke 21:32) suggests this to be within a generation of 40 years. This is affirmed by another contextual tie:

"And when these things begin to come to pass, then look up, and lift up your heads; for your redemption draweth nigh" (Luke 21:28).

Notice the emphasis on "begin." This refers to the wars, calamities, pestilence and celestial signs. They statistically began to be significant in the 1978 window from the end-time clues given by Jesus (see graph on next page).

It is as though God is saying: That is when the end of time begins. That is when the details of the end of the harlot start. When "one is," is when this prophecy becomes of utmost importance.

The expressions "five are fallen" and "one is" illustrate what the angel said in verse 1. This is the story of how the harlot comes to its end. As five came to their end, this "one [that] is" will also – as is implied for the seventh as well. But the endgame for the harlot begins with the "one [that] is." If the beast goes into perdition – so will its heads! These are striking lessons from John's prophetic symbols. The final history of the Roman Catholic Church began in 1929. It is on a forward trajectory that will see its demise – very soon – within one generation from 1978!

---

14   http://www.state.gov/r/pa/ei/bgn/3819.htm (emphasis added).

15   http://www.mosquitonet.com/~prewett/holyalliance 1of2.html (emphasis added).

16   http://en.wikipedia.org/wiki/John_Paul_II

Natural disasters reported – 1900–2011

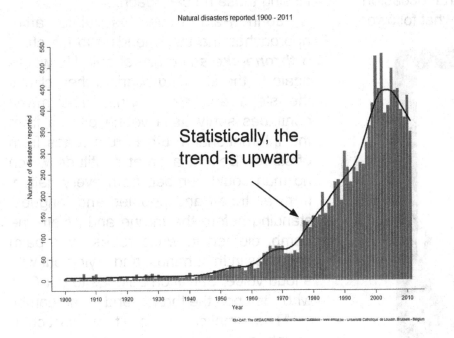

Natural disasters reported 1900 - 2011

Statistically, the trend is upward

EM-DAT: The OFDA/CRED International Disaster Database - www.emdat.be - Université Catholique de Louvain, Brussels - Belgium

Statistically – 1978 confirms an upward trend in significant intensity disasters.
http://www.emdat.be/Database/Trends/Trends_IMGs/Natural/eveyr2.pdf

But there is more to discover. John said in 13:3 that one of the beast's heads was "as it were wounded to death." Wounded (*sphazo*) is in the perfect tense. It had been wounded in the past. When? It doesn't say – but John did note: "I saw one of his [beast's] heads as it were wounded to death." "Saw" (*eidon*) is second aorist and suggests that it was in the past also. This means that the great issues of this prophecy occur with a head that we can

Pope John Paul II – shot May 13, 1981

look back and see had been wounded! There is stunning additional information on this: the "deadly wound was healed" (13:3). In spite of that wound, he "did live."

If Pope John Paul II is the pope when the final phases of these end-time prophetic events begin, did he have a deadly wound and still live? On May 13, 1981, he was shot three times by a Turkish assailant, Mehmet Ali Agea.[17]

The pope underwent a five-hour operation and lived. This is a second application of this prophecy. First, the papal kingdom (beast) was healed in 1929. Now a specific head is wounded and healed. No one could see this second meaning until after the 1981 incident – nor could the tie with Pope John Paul II be fully seen until the diplomatic ties were formally set in 1984.

Again, if Pope John Paul II was the one that "is," another incredible mark of distinction must be present. The adulation of this "head" must be seen in wonder (*thaumazo* – passive). What the pope does enthralls the world (13:3) – AND – he is worshiped (*proskuneo* – active). It's a voluntary response towards this **man**! (13:4).

In August 1993 a dazzling eyewitness account of patrons' reactions to this pope was made. It was World Youth Day in Denver. Pilgrims had fasted and walked 15 miles to Cherry Creek Park for an all-night vigil in veneration of "Our Lady of the New Advent." This painting was made by a

---

17   http://news.bbc.co.uk/onthisday/hi/dates/stories/ may/13/newsid_2512000/2512533.stm

Jesuit, William McNichols, specifically to be presented to the pope at that occasion. To all Christians the report of what followed

Our Lady of the New Advent
http://puffin.creighton.edu/
jesuit/andre/advent_3.html

should bring horror. Daniel's ancient prophecy said of this time that "he shall magnify himself … he shall stand up against the Prince of princes" (Daniel 8:25). Here's the report:

"Suddenly, the whirring of the white-topped helicopter is heard above the music. 'It's the Pope! Papa … The Crowd becomes ecstatic … people press forward. Some are clutching rosaries … crying … [others] cheer … the orchestra begins the *Abba Ojcze Fanfare,* the Pope's entrance music.

"The crowd noise now is deafening as the small figure of Pope John Paul II walks out … [onto] the stage … smiles and waves to the crowd.... The adoration of this man by these people is amazing to behold.... *In his presence people lose ordinary defenses.* They are vulnerable under this high-caliber 'spirituality.' He

smiles with approving eyes, hugging and kissing those he can reach....

"John Paul II in his white attire approaches the steps leading to his chair, a *throne-like structure* of oak. He waves again to the standing pilgrims then climbs the steps and sits down.... The music continues softly as a young person from the International Youth Forum reads from offstage: 'Behold a great multitude which no man could number, from every nation, from all tribes and peoples and tongues, standing before the throne and before the Lamb, clothed in white robes, with palm branches in their hands, and crying out with a loud voice, Salvation belongs to our God who sits upon the throne, and to the Lamb!'

"The implication of that particular Scripture in this setting … induces a sense of alarm and dread from Protestants. The Scripture is from Revelation 7:9-10 and presents a view of Christ on his throne in heaven. 'The great multitude which no man could number' is the true church, the Bride.... However, at Cherry Creek Park the pope sits on a throne among youths of many nations and tongues. They cry out to him as this Scripture is read.

"Is this pope insinuating that he is Christ on his throne and the youths below him are his sheep …?... The arrogance is overpowering despite John Paul's seeming humility. However, those unaware of Scripture and the translated meaning of the Polish hymn neither see nor sense arrogance. They see and sense love.

Pope John Paul II

"Pope John Paul II definitely has an enormous spirit of seductiveness …

respond[ing] to *Abba/Father* while sit[ting] in white vestments on a throne....

"Youths dressed in native costumes and representing each of the continents come forward carrying their national flags. They proceed up the center steps and place their flags at the podium, literally at John Paul's feet."[18]

This man *is* the sixth head!

"and the other is not yet come; and when he cometh, he must continue a short space." (vs 10)

Pope Benedict XVI – Number Seven:[19]

When the "one is" is seen and applied, the next pope or papal head "is not yet come." On April 2, 2005, Pope John Paul II died. On April 19, 2005, Joseph A. Ratzinger became the seventh pope of the seven-headed beast, Pope Benedict XVI.

The Bible says that he will reign only a "short space." This is from the word *oligos*, which means here a small period of time (cf. Revelation 12:12). This is a relative word, suggesting that something will occur that identifies his reign as a "short space." As prophecy "limited," Pope Benedict XVI reigned, and his papacy ended March 13, 2013.

Benedict XVI

Are there any other clues that help us to know that he and his predecessor are *the* end-time popes? Prophecy clearly states that a pivotal issue at the end will revolve around the seventh-day Sabbath.[20]

Expositor White also notes: "The Sabbath question will be the issue in the great conflict in which all the world will act a part. [Rev. 13:4-8, quoted.]

"'If any man have ears to hear, let him hear.' This warning is given to every son and daughter of Adam; and it is repeated over and over again.

"'He that leadeth into captivity shall go into captivity: he that killeth with the sword must be killed with the sword. Here is the patience and the faith of the saints' [Rev. 13:10]. This entire chapter is a revelation of what *will surely take place*. [Rev. 13:11, 15-17, quoted.]"[21]

She is seeing the entire chapter of Revelation 13 as future to 1887.

Has there been any special identity to the Sabbath–Sunday issue with these last two popes?

On May 31, 1998, Pope John Paul II outlined the plans for the Jubilee 2000 year celebrations.

In those plans he wrote an apostolic letter 50 pages long on the Sunday worship issue entitled *Dies Domini.* Quoting:

"66. In this matter, my predecessor Pope Leo XIII in his Encyclical Rerum Novarum spoke of Sunday rest as a worker's right *which the State must guarantee*."

"67. Therefore, also in the particular circumstance of our own time, *Christians will naturally strive to ensure that civil legislation respects their duty to keep Sunday holy.*"

Bishop Piero Marin noted regarding Sunday concerns of this pope:

"... asking Sunday [to be] holy, is placed above all in the framework of the

---

18 Hayes, *NRI, Trumpet,* October 1993.

19 http://en.wikipedia.org/wiki/ File:BentoXVI-30-10052007.jpg

20 Fowler Jr., Franklin S.; *Sacred Time for the End of Time,* Christian Heritage Foundation (2007).

21 White, Ellen G.; *Manuscript Releases,* vol. 19, p. 182 (1887).

preparation for the Great Jubilee.... Though the pope's letter is directed at Catholics, his concerns reach beyond the Vatican and *into other religions*."[22]

The pope not only promoted Sunday worship, he called for civil power to make sure it was honored as a sacred obligation. This end-time pope was calling for Sunday legislation.

Not long after Pope Benedict XVI was in office he noted in a homily:

"Without Sunday we cannot live....

"We cannot live without joining together on Sunday to celebrate the Eucharist. We would lack the strength to face our daily problems and not to succumb....

"The Sunday precept is not, therefore, an externally imposed duty, a burden on our shoulders. On the contrary, taking part in the Celebration, being nourished by the Eucharistic Bread and experiencing the communion of their brothers and sisters in Christ is a need for Christians, it is a joy; Christians can thus replenish the energy they need to continue on the journey we must make every week."[23]

That was an appeal to Catholics, specifically. Then in 2007 his appeal became more pointed:

- "73. To lose a sense of Sunday as the Lord's Day, a day to be sanctified, is symptomatic of the loss of an authentic sense of Christian freedom, the freedom of the children of God.(206) Here some observations made by my venerable predecessor John Paul II in his Apostolic Letter *Dies Domini* (207) continue to have great value. Speaking of the various dimensions of the Christian celebration of

Sunday, he said that it is *Dies Domini* with regard to the work of creation, *Dies Christi* as the day of the new creation and the Risen Lord's gift of the Holy Spirit, *Dies Ecclesiae* as the day on which the Christian community gathers for the celebration, and *Dies hominis* as the day of joy, rest and fraternal chairity.... "Sunday thus appears as *the primordial holy day*, when *all believers*, wherever they are found, can become heralds and guardians of the true meaning of time....

- "74. Finally, it is particularly urgent nowadays to remember that the day of the Lord is also a day of rest from work. It is greatly to be hoped that this fact will also be recognized by *civil society*, so that individuals can be permitted to refrain from work without being penalized. Christians, not without reference to the meaning of the Sabbath in the Jewish tradition, have seen in the Lord's Day a day of rest from their daily exertions."[24]

Here is a veiled appeal for civil laws that assure worshipers that a Sunday rest day would not bring retaliation in any work setting. Note also a subtle appeal to Sabbath/Saturday keepers. "You need a day of rest."

On September 2007 he made a theological statement regarding the change from Saturday to Sunday.

"Sine dominico non possumus"! Without the Lord and without the day that belongs to him, life does not flourish....

"For the early Church, the first day increasingly assimilated the traditional meaning of the seventh day, the Sabbath. We participate in God's rest, which embraces all of humanity. Thus we sense on

22 Vatican Information Service, July 7, 1998.
23 Homily of Pope Benedict XVI, Sunday, May 29, 2005.
24 Pope Benedict XVI, Apostolic Exhortation: *Sacramentum Caritatis*, February 22, 2007.

this day [Sunday] something of the freedom and equality of all God's creatures."[25]

In a myriad of events and statements, this prophecy of the harlot and the beast is distinctly end-time, and its focus is on the last two popes and the power that immediately follows! We have entered that perilous time, all within the final "one generation" block of prophecy.

Since we have come to the end of the seventh head, the continued progression of prophecy must be of critical eschatological importance! The end of earth's "last generation" is in sight. Global changes are to be seen relative to Rome's power. A geopolitical era that has geo-religious overtones is expected.

---

25   Homily of Pope Benedict XVI, Sunday 9, 2007.

CHAPTER 10

"SATAN" AND THE LAST EARTHLY KINGDOM

"And the beast that was, and is not, even he is the eighth, and is of the seven, and goeth into perdition" (Revelation 17:11).

Have you noticed that though the purpose of this angel's message is to define how the harlot came to her end (a divine judicial act – a "judgment" – 17:1; cf. 16:19), we are asked to rivet so much attention on the beast? Remember – that beast carries the woman! Without that kingdom she would be helpless and there would be restricted ability to relate to the world (ambassadors, seat at the United Nations, concordats with nations, consultants to nations). But – with a world-renowned country (the smallest at that) with charismatic male leaders dressed as women, with mystical liturgical intrigue and opulence, it demands everyone's attention!

John was just given a ringside view of the past, present and future of those powerful leaders (previous verse) **when** the church and state would once again be mutually dependent on each other. Initially, the beast was described as the creature with seven heads and ten horns (vss 3, 7). Next, the focus was on its seven heads or leaders.

Since the story of the heads is sequential, since their total number is seven and since the harlot is at all times on that beast (from verse 3), it is a story of *after the beast ascended out of hell* (11:7, 17:8)!

Was – is not – shall ascend (vs 8)

There is fascinating information regarding this in two verses of Revelation 13, referring to the sea beast (the same beast – different focus):

13:12   "to worship the first **beast,** whose **deadly wound was healed."** (ascended, restored)

13:14   "they should make an image to the **beast,** which had the **wound by a sword, and did live."** (ascended, restored)

[Note: There was a **head** that was wounded and lived (13:3). Our focus here is the beast that lived.]

Connecting each of these we have this stunning **beast** picture:

17:11: Was — is not — is [out of bottomless pit – 17:8]

13:12: Lived — deadly wound — healed

13:14: Lived — wounded by sword — did live

The beast ascended (8a) (alive 13:14), is come (17:10) (survived 13:3, 12) and now "is the eighth" (11a).

The reference to the beast of the past (i.e., vs 8) does not detail the "ascent" or "is come" but directs us to the **immediate present.** The first beast period is during the seven heads (papal teachers). This beast is now "the eighth" and reveals a second "beast period." Linking all these verses helps us. This eighth now moves through new prophetic time related to the very end.

It is in this context that we move into the next beast phase of this amazing story.

Now an existential briefing regarding that *beast* unfolds:

"And the beast that was, and is not," (vs 11)

This immediately refers back to that similar language in verse 8. Then information is added regarding this red colored beast.

1. It did rise; it came to life and was resurrected – out of the grave of evil – the bottomless pit. It *had been there* where demons live.
2. It was a kingdom centered in Rome that brought recognition and power to the Roman Catholic Church (just as the Lateran Treaty started in 1929) (see Appendix I).
3. The seventh "head" (leader) of the beast (Vatican) was Pope Benedict XVI. He ruled for a short period. Now – the "eighth."
4. That *eighth* is not identified as a head but as the *whole beast*. It follows that beast period of seven heads and is obviously a transitioned "kingdom" power.

"even he is the eighth," (vs 11)

In some mysterious way, the *beast* is related to the seven heads by this numerical sequence but he is identified only as *the* beast rather than another head.[1]

1 Thomas, Robert L.; *Revelation 8–22 – An Exegetical Commentary* (Moody Press, Chicago – 1992), p. 299 (emphasis added).

When all the Papal States were removed from the Roman Catholic Church in 1870 and added to the territory of Italy, the beast had a wound, which was healed in 1929. Thus, prophecy is precise!

How then do we decipher this eighth? The number shows that *another "leader"* supersedes Pope Benedict XVI (the seventh). But now *it is not another "head" alone.* Benedict completes the papal seven that God distinctly foretold. Thus, a different "leader," one that comes to power under very new imagery, is prophesied. It apparently still carries the harlot (assumed because of 16:19).

The key is a *redirected focus* – the "beast … is the eighth." When it assumes power, this means that another kingdom expression, a redirected kingdom prophecy, has emerged. In Revelation 13 details of that beast are embellished in its third and final prophetic period.

"and is of the seven, and goeth into perdition." (vs 11)

The Greek expression here is distinct (*ek ton hepta estin*) – "out of the seven is." The "out of" or *ek* has been extensively studied. It expresses many characteristics:

1. Part of the seven
2. Out of the likeness of the seven
3. According to the seven
4. Separate but with a close connection to the seven

Scholars adopt mainly the theme that this eighth powerful kingdom *shares characteristics with all the heads.* The beast kingdom changes. It serves as its own *moral and* political force. Since it goes to perdition (from where it arose), it displeases God. It is demonically driven.

Two prophetic phases will be described:

Beast ascends out of the
bottomless pit (vs 8)

A kingdom
with seven
identifiable
leaders
(Rev. 17:10)

Then a global
evil kingdom
at the end
(Rev. 17:11-13; 13)

Prediction it will
go into perdition
(papal kingdom)
(vs 8-9)

Goes into perdition
(global kingdom)
(vs 11)

Perdition means destruction or ruin. Metaphorically, it alludes to the doom of God's enemies. Judas Iscariot was called the "son of perdition" (the one doomed – John 17:12). The eschatological "man of sin" is called the "son of perdition" (II Thessalonians 2:3).

When the beast goes to perdition (Revelation 20:10), it goes to destruction – total ruin – the fate of evildoers. This must not be confused with the "bottomless pit" or "abyss," where Satan and his host are "contained."

This eighth represents a transition to another phase of the **beast prophecy** (17:12-14). Revelation 13 carries on its final story when the beast comes out of the sea! Between the ascension/coming and perdition (eternal end) three papal beast prophecies are sequentially given!

1. **1929–2013:** Seven sequential popes, ending with Pope Benedict XVI (17:10 – "heads")
2. **2013–?:** Ten world powers (New World Order) give growing support to the beast (harlot/beast) (17:12 – "ten horns"). They will war against Christ (17:14a).
3. **42-month period:** Era of the dragon-supported sea beast (which

becomes a world power – 13:7b) and the earth beast (Revelation 13). This coalition blasphemes God (13:5-6) and wars (persecution and martyrdom) against the saints (13:7, 15; 17:14).[2]

Phase 2 above has now been entered, where soon the "ten horns" will have "one mind" with the beast (Revelation 17:13). This is the specific focus of the next chapter. But – there is something dramatic that must be observed.

- The beast receives geopolitical power from its horns (ten world divisions – vs 13). Later, in chapter 13, the dragon gives the beast his power, his seat and his authority (13:2).

Collectively, it is apparent that a secular/demonic mission is seizing the Holy See. It will wield global authority (13:3-4, 7b). Satanic elements will drive its work.

1. Speaking against God (13:5)
2. And, with another "beast partner," it will kill those who do not have the "image to the beast" (13:15).

The raw power of Satan is expected to appear. Though under a guise of "supreme good," God's people will suffer.

The Eighth "Number"

"Eight," Biblically, represents "beginning again." On the "eighth day" a new week begins. On the "eighth day" Christ arose and the Christian dispensation began. But "calling the beast an "eighth" is another

---

[2] White, Ellen G.; *Manuscript Releases,* vol. 19, p. 282.

way of referring to his future attempted mimicry of Christ's resurrection on the eighth day."[3] This prophecy now reveals the full presence of the dragon in the beast with renewed power![4]

"He is an eighth in the sense that he is distinct from the other seven. He is Antichrist, not simply another Roman emperor. He is an expression of evil itself. He belongs to the cosmic struggle between God and Satan that lies behind the scenes of human history. He will appear on the stage of history as a man. He is 'of the seven' (*ek ton hepta*) – not 'one of the seven' – in that he plays the same sort of role as his earthly predecessors. He belongs to another sphere of reality. His period of hegemony is … ***[just] preceding the return of the Messiah.***"[5]

There is more to this deceptive eighth. It has eschatological significance! Sunday, in early Christian tradition, was occasionally called the "eighth day."[6] This beast, covered with the names of blasphemy (17:3), comes at the very end to promote "an eighth" and ***dispense*** with the seventh. Some stunningly see this as an indicator that Sunday worship will be promoted. Gaebelein, Schemenann and Shepherd embellish this thinking:

"This pattern of seven-to-eight-equals-one was familiar to the early church. It is a concept those raised in the great liturgical traditions can grasp. The eighth day was the day of the resurrection of Christ, Sunday. It was also the beginning of a new week. The seventh day, the Jewish Sabbath, is held over, to be replaced by the first of a new series, namely Sunday.

Austin Farrer has noted how even the whole theme of the Apocalypse is integrally related to this idea. 'Sunday is the day of Resurrection.' The week with which the Apocalypse deals extends from the Resurrection of Christ to the General Resurrection, when death has been destroyed.' He further states the relation between the seventh and eighth:

"'God rests from his completed work, but in so resting he initiates a new act which is the eighth-and-first day. We may compare the Gospel once more. On the sixth day Christ conquered, and achieved his rest from the labours of his flesh. But the sabbath-day which follows is in itself nothing, it has no content: it is simply the restful sepulcher out of which, with the eighth and first day, the resurrection springs. (*A Rebirth of Images; the Making of St. John's Apocalypse* [London: Darce, 1949], pp. 70-71).'

"Each of the series of sevens in the book, except for the seven churches, follows a pattern of the seventh in the series becoming the first of a new series; thus seven to eight equals one. The eighth was the day of the Messiah, the day of the new age and the sign of the victory over the forces of evil (Alexander Schememann, *Introduction to Liturgical Theological* [London: Faith, 1966], pp. 60-64). Shepherd also calls attention to this phenomenon in Revelation (Massey H. Shepherd, Jr., *The Paschal Liturgy and the Apocalypse* [Richmond: John Knox, 1960], pp. 20-21, 80)."[7] Interesting, isn't it?

---

3   Thomas, *op. cit.*

4   Beale, G. K.; *The New International Greek Testament Commentary; The Book of Revelation* (William B. Eerdmans Publishing Company, Grand Rapids, Michigan – 1999), p. 875.

5   Mounce, Robert H.; *The Book of Revelation* (Wm. B. Eerdmans Publishing Co., Grand Rapids, Michigan, 1977), p. 318.

6   Aune, David E.; *World Biblical Commentary; Revelation 17–22*, vol. 52c (World Books; Publisher, Dallas, Texas – 1997), p. 950.

7   Gaebelein, Frank E.; *The Expositor's Bible Commentary,* vol. 12 (Zondervan Publishing House, Grand Rapids, MI) (1984).

These scholars, unaware of the Sabbath issues at the end, are sensitive to the fascinating sentiments related to Sunday, first day, Messianic resurrection missives – "the eighth."

The beast now takes on a new meaning:

- Seven-headed kingdom
  (papal power)
  End of Time
  (Revelation 13:3, 17:3, 8)

- "Eighth" – Vatican – Rome
  Represented by beast, per se
  A kingdom transition
  (consolidating power)
  (Revelation 13:14-15, 17:11)

Emerging Satanic Influences

This may be an area new to many. Here is a challenging question:
Do you think Satan knows the Bible and end-time prophecy?

- He not only knows Scripture, but he has used demonically inspired followers to write his parallel prophecies, obviously to his end-time advantage.

There are numerous satanic predictions directly related to our time! They have important parallels to Bible prophecy. Here are a few:
St. Malachy O'Morgair in the twelfth century (1102 A.D.) allegedly gave:

- Sequential predictions of papal heads, which have been uncannily close.
- His "last pope" – Benedict XVI – was to be followed by a leader called *Petrus Romanus* (Peter the

Roman). Then – the understanding of "Babylon's mysteries" would occur (the harlot of Revelation 17:1-6)!

- He is number "eight" (Revelation 17:11).
- Malachy said that he would guide the final period of the "Church."
- But at the end – it would be destroyed. Interesting!

Of deepest interest is his imagery of this last leader as the **antichrist,** which matches the "man of sin" (II Thessalonians 2:3). Prophecy notes:

- He will be involved with ten world powers in an illicit relationship (17:12) and will war against Christ (17:14).
- He blasphemes God (13:6).
- He persecutes saints (13:7).
- He is under the control of Satan (13:2).
- He is directly associated with murdering God's people (17:6).

Evidence weighs heavily that this last "leader" will be a charismatic individual of "distinguishing character." The world will wonder after him (13:3). Then he will become a "king of fierce countenance" (Daniel 8:23).

- *"And the king shall do according to his will; and he shall exalt himself, and magnify himself above every god, and shall speak marvellous things against the God of gods, and shall prosper"* (Daniel 11:36).

Following Malachy, **Saint Francis of Assisi** (1182–1226) noted that at the time of the end "a man, not canonically elected, will be raised to the Pontificate, who, by his cunning, will endeavor to draw many into error and death ... [he will not be] a true Pastor, but a destroyer."[8]

A Marian apparition from LaSalette, France (1846), approved by Popes Pius IX and Leo XIII, regarding apostasy within the Catholic Church talked of *when* it would become the seat of the Antichrist:

"The earth will be struck by calamities of all kinds (in addition to plague and famine which will be wide-spread). There will be a series of wars until the last war, which will then be fought by the *ten kings of the Antichrist* [Revelation 17:12-13], all of whom will have one and the same plan [Revelation 17:13] and will be the only rulers of the world. Before this comes to pass, there will be a kind of false peace in the world. People will think of nothing but amusement. The wicked will give themselves over to all kinds of sin ... this will be the hour of darkness. The Church will suffer a terrible crisis ... *Rome will lose the Faith and become the seat of the Antichrist* ... The Church will be in eclipse, the world will be in dismay."[9]

More recently (1955), *Father Herman Bernard Kramer* wrote that the last pope would rule with a rod of iron the whole world as the Man of Sin.[10]

It was revealed by *Cardinal Mario Luigi Ciappi* (1909–1996) that the last papal leader will lead the Church into apostasy.[11]

• "terrible things are to happen"[12]

The late Malachi Martin (Jesuit priest) notes in his book, *Windswept House*, that the archangel Lucifer was formally "enthroned" in the Roman Catholic Citadel June 29, 1963.

• Purpose:

 1. To raise Lucifer as the true prince over Rome.
 2. To assure "sorcerous inception and embodiment in flesh of that [satanic] immaterial spirit" into a priest who would later become *Petrus Romanus* (the last Peter of Rome). Spiritualism is to be a part of the Catholic Church.

• Shortly thereafter, Pope Paul VI was inaugurated. With knowledge of this event, he noted:
 "The smoke of Satan has entered the Vatican."[13]

Mystic, Roman Catholic theologian and prolific author, *Ronald I. Conte, Jr.,* said (2004) that the final pope "will reaffirm the authority of the Roman Pontiff over the Church" and "will emphasize the supremacy of the Roman Catholic faith and the Roman Catholic Church above all religions and denominations, and its authority over all Christians and all peoples of the world." Conte added that during this pope's reign the "great apostasy" and the "first part of the tribulation during our generation" will begin.[14]

---

8 *Works of the Seraphic Father Saint Francis of Assisi* (1182–1226), Washbourne, 1882 A.D., p. 248.

9 "Apparition of the Blessed Virgin on the Mountain of LaSalette," http://www.thepopeinred.com/secret.htm.

10 Father Herman Bernard Kramer, *The Book of Destiny* (Buechler Publishing Co.; Belleville, IL – 1955), p. 277.

11 John Vennari, "The Fourth Secret of Fatima," *Catholic Family News.*

12 Published Testimony: Cardinal Alonso (1975–1981), *Fatima.org,* http://www.fatima.org/thirdsecret/fralonso.asp.

13 http://www.vatican.va/holy_father/paul_vi/homilies/1972/documents/hf_p-vi_hom_19720629_it.html

14 Ronald L. Conte, "The Future and the Popes,"

Intriguing are the strong efforts the Roman Church has put forth to hide the mystical Third Secret of Fatima (Marian apparitions in 1917 in Portugal).

- The then *Cardinal Ratzinger* said that it was filled with prophecy that would threaten the Catholic faith. Thus – they lied about it.
- The Church feared that it would mark the "beginning of the end times!"
- Which, he said, would "correspond to what has been announced in Scripture!"[15]

Fascinating, isn't it? Keep the Church, keep the world, from knowing what even the devil knows about end-time prophecy. Keep it in such a way that we can control people's beliefs and perceptions!

The late Malachi Martin also had these insights:

"On a syndicated radio broadcast, Father Malachi Martin was asked the following question by a caller: 'I had a Jesuit priest tell me more of the Third Secret of Fatima years ago, in Perth. He said, among other things, the last pope would be under control of Satan … Any comment on that?' Fr. Martin responded, 'Yes, it sounds as if they were reading, or being told, the text of the Third Secret.' In a taped interview with Bernard Janzen, Fr. Martin was asked the following question: 'Who are the people who are working so hard to suppress Fatima?' Fr. Martin responded, 'A bunch, a whole bunch, of Catholic prelates in Rome, who belong to Satan. *They're servants of Satan.* And the servants of Satan outside the Church, in various organizations … It's an alliance. A dirty alliance, a filthy alliance.'"[16]

Satan's Final Expression – Himself

The conflict between Christ and Satan now intensifies. John was warned that at this time Satan will know he has only a short time (Revelation 12:12). He panics, knowing that this is his last chance to conquer or be conquered. "Woe to the inhabiters of the earth and of the sea! For the devil is come down unto you, having great wrath" (12:12). Does he appear as an angry being ready to fight? Is he a bully ready to take on the world or anyone who opposes him? As his poster child, the papacy prepares the way for the devil to personally make his debut. Paul said: "And no marvel; for Satan himself is transformed into an angel of light" (II Corinthians 11:14). Jesus warned of the appearance of a false Messiah (Matthew 24:23-26). Strange demonic powers will soon emerge.

"Satan is striving to gain every advantage. He desires to secure, not only students, but teachers. He has his plans laid. Disguised as an angel of light, he will walk the earth as a wonder-worker. In beautiful language he will present lofty sentiments. Good words will be spoken by him, and good deeds performed. Christ will be personified, but on one point there will be a marked distinction. Satan will turn the people from the law of God. Notwithstanding this, so well will he counterfeit righteousness, that if it were possible, he would deceive the very elect.

Catholic Planet, November 14, 2004; http://www.catholicplanet.com/future/future-popes.htm.

[15] "Joseph Ratzinger as Prefect of the Congregation for the Doctrine of the Faith," *Wikipedia,* last modified November 14, 2011, http://en.wikipedia.org/wiki/Joseph_Ratzinger_as_Prefect_of_the_Congregation_for_the_Doctrine_of_the_Faith.

[16] "Three Secrets of Fatima," *Wikipedia,* http://en.wikipedia.org/wiki/Three_Secrets_of_F%C3%A1tima.

Crowned heads, presidents, rulers in high places, will bow to his false theories."[17]

"We shall be commanded to worship this being, whom the world will glorify as Christ. What shall we do? – Tell them that Christ has warned us against just such a foe, who is man's worst enemy, yet who claims to be God; and that when Christ shall make His appearance, it will be with power and great glory, accompanied by ten thousand times ten thousand angels and thousands of thousands; and that when He shall come, we shall know His voice (RH Dec. 18, 1888)."[18]

"In the last days Satan will appear as an angel of light, with great power and heavenly glory, and claim to be the Lord of the whole earth.... Then will take place the *final fulfillment of the Revelator's prophecy.* 'And they worshipped the dragon which gave power unto the beast: and they worshipped the beast, saying, Who is like unto the beast? who is able to make war with him? And there was given unto him a mouth speaking great things and blasphemies; and power was given unto him to continue forty and two months. [rest of Revelation 13:6-18, also quoted.]"[19] Now we know *when!*

Sequence of Revelation 17 (see graph on next page – not to scale).

The third phase is described in Revelation 13, where the horns of the beast have crowns. The New World Order is in full force! At the end – they all go to *perdition!*

At the end the beast, now dramatically part of Satan's kingdom, ends. That is graphically described in chapter 20, where God's Holy Word notes that after a brief period of deceptive activity, "fire came down from God out of heaven, and devoured them. And the *devil* that deceiveth them was cast into the lake of fire and brimstone, where the *beast* and the *false prophet* are" (20:9-10).

We are in phase two of Revelation 17's beast prophecies. There are seven things that must occur before phase three begins:

1. A geographical "leader" is chosen who is charismatic and whom the world will quickly "wonder at" (13:3)
2. "He" is fully open to satanic influences (13:2)
3. A New World Order must be "activated" by those ten horn symbols, giving "sympathetic power" to the Holy See (17:12-13)
4. Judgment of the Living commences (Rev. 11:1-3 – note that it is before the 42 months/1260 days)
5. Calamities occur that are so severe that mankind cries out to God for help, setting the stage for a religious law (10MR 239)
6. Satan appears as an angel of light (19MR 282)
7. A push to amend or bypass the U.S. Constitution

Observing world and religious events is now urgent, objective and soon to be filled with apocalyptic changes.

---

[17] White, Ellen G.; *Fundamentals of Christian Education,* pp. 471-472.

[18] White, Ellen G.; *The Seventh-day Adventist Bible Commentary,* vol. 6, p. 1105.

[19] White, Ellen G.; *Manuscript Releases,* vol. 19, p. 282 (1902).

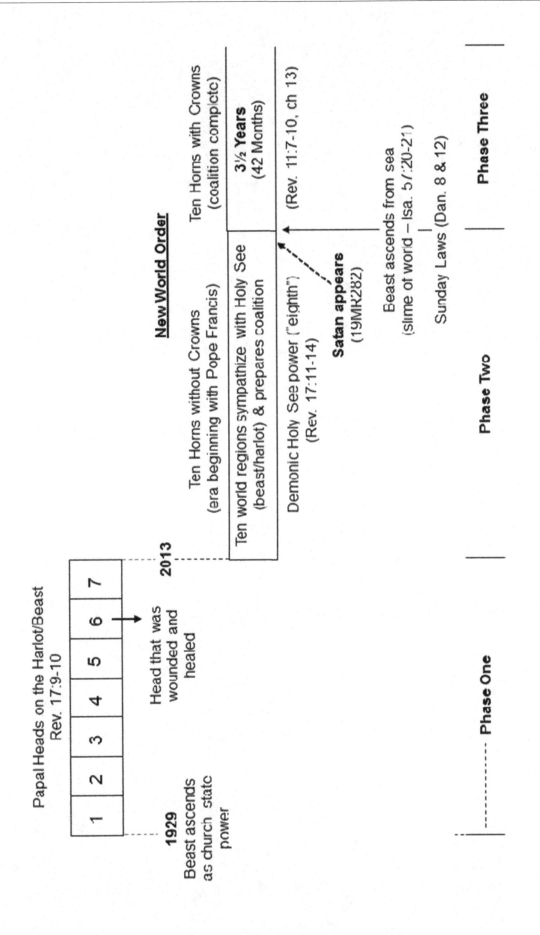

CHAPTER 11

WORLD'S STRANGEST COALITION

"And the ten horns which thou sawest are ten kings, which have received no kingdom as yet; but receive power as kings one hour with the beast. These have one mind, and shall give their power and strength unto the beast" (Revelation 17:12-13).

The seven heads of the beast were described in a unique sequence in verse 10, revealing to us life and death issues regarding its kingdom leaders. The number seven is a metaphor that they acted by divine authority.[1] The symbol of the seven hills disclosed to us that the location of this power is Rome – the center of religious apostasy.

Now another part of the beast is described. The horns give it undisputed power. This echoes the ten horns of the Daniel 7:7-8, 20-25 beast. Then "one of them that stood by" (7:16) – likely an angel told Daniel: "The ten horns … are ten kings" (Daniel 7:24). John is also told:

"And the ten horns which thou sawest are ten kings" (vs 12)

We must look elsewhere in Revelation for clues as to who these are.

Out of the mouths of the dragon, beast and false prophet come "spirits of devils" which go to the *"kings of the earth* and of the *whole world,* to gather them to the battle" (Revelation 16:13-14).

The heads were "kings" of the *Vatican kingdom.* The horns on the beast are kings of *earthly kingdoms* – apparently involving the *whole* earth (cf. 16:13-14, 17:2, 18, 18:3-4, 19:19). We are receiving the story of how Babylon comes to its end (17:1). The above references (16:13-14) precede that "end" (16:19). Satanic powers influence the kings of the whole world. In turn, these ten horns give power and control to or defend that beast when they reside!

Ten is symbolic for the sum total of anti-Christian power.[2] But who might these ten world leaders be? What kingdoms do they rule over? It appears that they collectively rule with the beast in a final global coalition. Since the beast is initially the Vatican – this "Roman Kingdom" will rule the world just before Christ's final parousia.[3] Then it will cooperate with Satan as a final, brief geopolitical power. A vast confederacy is in view.

1. "With whom [the harlot] the *kings* of the earth have committed fornication" (17:2)
2. The woman reigns over "the *kings* of the earth" (17:18)
3. "The *kings* of the earth have committed fornication" with the harlot (18:3).
4. "The *kings* of the earth, who have committed fornication and lived deliciously with her" (18:9)

---

1 Brighton, Louis A.; *Revelation* (Concordia Publishing House, Saint Louis, MO – 1999), p. 450.

2 Thomas, Robert L.; *Revelation 8–22 – An Exegetical Commentary* (Moody Press, Chicago – 1992), p. 300.

3 Beale, G. K.; *The New International Greek Testament Commentary; The Book of Revelation* (William B. Eerdmans Publishing Company, Grand Rapids, Michigan – 1999), p. 878.

5. "And I saw the beast, and the *kings* of the earth, and their armies, gathered together to make war against him that sat on the horse, and against his army" (19:19).

These ten horns represent those kings – clearly anticipated to reign over kingdoms.

This world movement is bonded "deliciously" and appears in prophecy to have a singular end-time objective – to war against Christ and His people. This links to the little horn of Daniel 8:10-11 and is soon to be graphically described in 17:14 and later in 19:19! There is an *issue* that turns the world against Christ and His people. We get amazing clues elsewhere. When Satan makes war against the remnant, John states that they keep the commandments and have the testimony of Jesus (12:17). Then it notes the same for the saints in 14:12 – but, there, they have the "faith of Jesus." They can't be moved. No persecution, coercion or even death alters their commitment to God.

Then it says something most interesting about these kings:

"which have received no kingdom as yet:" (vs 12)

That means that this is a prophecy of ten kings/kingdoms in a coalition to yet emerge future to the king which "is." That is the setting for this prophecy. At the time of Pope John Paul II those kings and kingdoms were yet to develop or be defined.

Then in 13:1 the beast's horns have crowns. They clearly represent kings with kingdoms. Between 17:12 and 13:1 something changes in the world support of the beast; these ten kings and kingdoms

emerge. What happens? What is altered on the world scene?

There is a link between the number "ten" and the number of "kings" that give direct support to the Vatican (and its leaders and church). Has the world been divided into ten regions? Are leaders anticipated over a new world order?

In 1968 The Club of Rome was begun as a think tank to address the long-range challenges of the world (population, environment, trade, food, economics, etc.). Details of its origins and membership are scant. But it is well funded and has a website (clubofrome.org). In 1972 it commissioned a team of individuals at Case Western Reserve University to address many of these issues and to divide the world into *ten regions*. This was called "Regionalized and Adaptive Model of the Global World System."

This is the map they devised:

The United Nations soon revealed its own *ten world divisions* based on food growth and distribution.[4]

---

4   Ten regions by map: Food and Agriculture Organization of the United Nations. General Web site from the UN: http://www.fao.org/index_en.htm Map Index: http;//www.fao.org/DOCREP/005/Y4473E/y4473e0d.htm Actual Map: http://www.fao.org/DOCREP/005/Y4473Ey4473e0d.htm 10 world division map of UN FAO

Soon geography books adapted a socio-political model of **ten world divisions**.[5]

Then in 1997 the World Trade Organization did the same.[6]

In 2000 UNESCO independently divided the world into similar regions.[7]

All these proposed regional areas are similar. The concepts are based on shared resources/wealth and **common good**. That is part of a deep philosophical tenet of the Roman Catholic Church and is outlined in their Catechism.

The Club of Rome celebrated its 40th anniversary on June 15, 2008. Intense networking with world governments, the United Nations and a myriad of organizations was under way. The Club set a "time capsule" for one hundred of its elite members and affiliates to come up with what they *expect* to see on the world scene by 2018.[8] The deadline to have their recommendations submitted was March 16, 2009.

That is most interesting. 2018 is exactly 40 years after the pope that "is" came to power – or – one generation.

The Club of Rome Time Capsule

Is all this coincidental? There are too many things coming together to identify it as chance. With the move toward regionalization of the world into ten regions and with the center of this activity in some "mysterious way" tied to Rome, we are on the verge of something dramatic. Revelation 13 clearly shows those horns with "kingdom power crowns" preceding a 42-month period. Ten geographic world powers will give strength/power to the papacy. Prophecy is precise. These events are moving quickly in that direction. A recent headline:

"Henry Kissinger: The world must forge a new order or retreat to chaos. Not since JFK has there been such a reservoir of expectations. The extraordinary impact of the President … on the imagination of humanity is an important element in shaping a new world order. The new administration could make no worse mistake than to rest on its initial popularity … a new world order is crucial."[9]

<u>"but receive power as kings one hour with the beast." (vs 12)</u>

When this prophecy is fulfilled, these kings/horns will rule over kingdoms with the beast. Who gives them "power," or better translated, "authority"? Throughout this apocalyptic book God permits evil to finish its course and provides Satan and his host one final period to reveal their true character. This is seen elsewhere

---

5   Geography Books Divide the World into Ten Regions: http://w16.239.53.104/search?q=cache: AJUsSWGsx4QJ:www.elon.edu/facstaff/rdobbs/geo131-syllabus.pdf+%22Ten+Regions%22+World+map&hl=en&ie=UTF-8

6   WTO 1997 Recommended Ten World Divisions: http://2a6.239.53.104/search?q=cache:VICK2DsCLawJ:www.intereconomics.com/francois/text9610.pdf+%22Ten+regions%22+World+Free+Trade+GATT&hl=en&start=10&ie=UTF-8

7   UNESCO sees the world as divided into ten regions: http://216.239.53.104/search?q=cache: AdWC0PIMzNUJ:www.unescobkk.org/ips/infoshare/2-1-200/chapter5.pdf+Unesco+%22ten+regions %22+world+geographic&hl=en&ie+UTF-8

8   clubofrome.org/eng/capsule

9   http://www.independent.co.uk/opinion/commentators/henry-kissinger-the-world-must-forge-a-new-order-or-retreat-to-chaos-1451416.html

(Revelation 6:2, 4, 8; 7:2; 9:1, 3, 5; 13:5, 7; 16:8).[10]

"One hour" is also alluded to in the next chapter (18:10, 17, 19) as the time in which "Babylon the Great" comes into judgment by God. This echoes the words, "Then Daniel, whose name was Belteshazzar, was astonished for *one hour*" (Daniel 4:19). This indicates prophetically a very "short time"[11] and must not be interpreted as a timing period. It was the shortest measure of time in the ancient world[12] and was used figuratively.

A final period of *power* of three and a half years (Revelation 11:2, 12:14, 13:5) is alluded to in this coalition.

"In the last days Satan will appear as an angel of light, with great power and heavenly glory, and claim to be the Lord of the whole earth. He will declare that the Sabbath has been changed from the seventh to the first day of the week; and as lord of the first day of the week he will present this spurious sabbath as a test of loyalty to him. *Then will take place the final fulfillment of the Revelator's prophecy.* [Rev. 13:4-18, quoted.]"[13]

Included in her references is the 42 months of Revelation 13:5. This must be literal time since another 1260-year period at the end *after* Satan appears as an angel of light would be unthinkable.

"Ultimately the ten kings are 'purely eschatological figures representing the totality of the powers of all nations on the earth, which are to be made subservient to antichrist.'"[14]

The ten horns symbolize naked might, not sanctioned by any claim of divine authority but through the dragon's authority and power. When they receive their crowns (kingdoms – 13:1), they are still shown as providing support to the beast.

"These have one mind," (vs 13)

This is a fascinating phrase. "One mind" (mian gnomen) is an idiom out of John's era from the political arena.[15] The leaders of these ten areas of the world are of one accord relative to yielding their authority to the papacy! This shocking prophecy reveals an unprecedented tie between church and state. But the "state" concept has here burgeoned into the "world."

"and shall give their power and strength unto the beast." (vs 13)

It is difficult to fathom the extent of support and servitude that this implies! The world appears to give total allegiance to the papacy. They surrender everything to the beast.[16] They not only reign with Rome – they submit to its authority.[17]

We can view these kingdoms as supporting both the papacy and the dragon. However, the former is emphasized because of the vision narrative in Revelation 13.

What provokes this alliance? The next verse describes a war against Christ. But there is a reason behind the war. John was told that three "unclean [deceptive – evil] spirits," "Spirits of devils" "working miracles" go forth to the "kings of the earth" *and* the whole world (Revelation

10 Beale, *op. cit.,* p. 879.
11 Thomas, *op. cit.,* p. 301.
12 Beale, *op. cit.,* p. 879
13 White, Ellen G.; *Manuscript Releases,* vol. 19, p. 282 (emphasis added).
14 Beckwith quote in Mounce, Robert H.; *The Book of Revelation* (Wm. B. Eerdmans Publishing Co., Grand Rapids, Michigan – 1977), p. 319.
15 Aune, David E.; *World Biblical Commentary; Revelation,* Revelation 17–22, vol. 52c (World Books; Publisher, Dallas, Texas – 1997), p. 952.
16 Osborne, Grant R.; *Revelation* (Baker Book House; Grand Rapids, MI), p. 622.
17 Beale, *op. cit.,* p. 880.

16:13-14). Purpose? To draft everyone into earth's final war coalition!

"Evil angels unite their powers with evil men, and as they have been in constant conflict and attained an experience in the best modes of deception and battle and have been strengthening for centuries, they will not yield the *last great final contest* without a *desperate struggle* and all the world will be on one side or the other of the question."[18]

"Fearful sights of a supernatural character will soon be revealed in the heavens, in token of the power of miracle-working demons. The spirits of devils will go forth to the kings of the earth and to the whole world, to fasten them in deception, and urge them on to unite with Satan in his *last struggle against the government of heaven*."[19]

"*A terrible conflict* is before us. We are nearing the *battle of the great day of God Almighty*. That which has been held in control is to be let loose. The angel of mercy is folding her wings, preparing to step down from the throne and leave the world to the control of Satan. The principalities and powers of earth are in bitter revolt against the God of heaven. They are filled with hatred against those who serve Him, and soon, very soon, will be fought the *last great battle between good and evil*.

The earth is to be the battle field – the scene of *the final contest* and the final victory. Here, where for so long Satan has led men against God, rebellion is to be forever suppressed."[20]

The insights advanced above reveal horrific evil coming from the religious world. The Sabbath will be defied. The resulting persecution reflects the war against Christ and His followers.

This coalition reflects the time when the horns (kings) have received their kingdoms (seen with the crowns of Revelation 13). The word for "purpose" or "one mind" ties to Paul's exhortation to the Corinthian church (I Corinthians 1:10). That defines total unity – but, there, it is on God's side.[21]

In 17:17 we will note that the horns and the beast alliance is not forced but by their own volition. It all emerges, however, through divine permission. Why? God is letting Satan and his followers demonstrate to the universe what his character is like when almost totally unbridled. Thus, the world will become divided into two camps. When Christ comes, the "selection" process will be easily defined (Matthew 25:31-33).

All the forces that rule with this antichrist beast will do so for only a short time. Christ's deliverance (Daniel 12:1) and then coming (Revelation 19:16) will rupture Satan's final confederacy.

18   White, Ellen G.; *Selected Messages,* bk 3, p. 425 (emphasis added).

19   White, Ellen G.; *The Great Controversy,* p. 624 (emphasis added).

20   White, Ellen G.; *Last Day Events,* p. 250 and *The Review and Herald,* May 13, 1902 (emphasis added).

21   Thomas, *op. cit.,* p. 301.

CHAPTER 12

A BATTLE THEY'RE GOING TO LOSE!

"These shall make war with the Lamb, and the Lamb shall overcome them: for he is Lord of lords, and King of kings: and they that are with him *are* called, and chosen, and faithful" (Revelation 17:14).

Satan's confederacy is focused on a unified hatred against Christ and His people. It all sounds inconceivable, yet God said that it would occur. Though there are 2.1+ billion Christians in the world, the Sabbath issue will create universal hatred against Jesus and His loyal remnant subjects.

In 12:17 and 13:7 we've been told that the dragon and the beast (Satan and the papacy), with the help of the earth beast, or United States with its apostate Protestantism, will war against the saints.

John has already noted: "And the dragon was wroth with the woman" (Revelation 12:17a). In that review chapter (a prophetic interlude) we are reminded that a point will be reached which won't be pretty. Only a "few" will remain firm – a remnant – what is "left over."

"And they overcame him by the blood of the Lamb, and by the word of their testimony; and they loved not their lives unto the death" (12:11). They do not drink of the abominations from the church's wine cup. God labeled any identity with that drink "infidelity" (17:2, 4). That wine of the "eighth" becomes such an emotional issue, it provokes hatred.

"These shall make war with the Lamb." (vs 14)

This is recounted later: "the beast, and the kings of the earth, and their armies, gathered together to make war against him that sat on the horse, and against his army" (19:19). These "battle" expressions originated with Daniel's apocalyptic prophecies:

The Agressor	The Victor
"horn made war with the saints, and prevailed against them" (Daniel 7:21).	"these will make war with the Lamb, and the Lamb will conquer them" (Revelation 17:14).

As previously noted, this conflict appears in a *commentary insert* that is graphically portrayed in Revelation 16:13-14: "And I saw three unclean spirits like frogs *come* out of the mouth of the dragon, and out of the mouth of the beast, and out of the mouth of the false prophet. For they are the spirits of devils, working miracles, *which* go forth unto the **kings** of the earth and of the **whole world**, to **gather them to the battle** of that great day of God Almighty."

There, they are being influenced and prepared for war; here in 17:14, we are told that their fight is actually against Jesus, Who is victorious!

"But the world at large ... *is* under the control of Satan, Christ's bitterest foe. The gospel presents to them principles of life which are wholly at variance with their habits and desires, and they rise in rebellion against it. They hate the purity which reveals and condemns their sins, and they persecute and destroy those who would urge upon them its just and holy claims. It is in this sense – because the exalted truths it brings occasion hatred and strife – that the gospel is called a sword."[1]

"and the Lamb shall overcome them:" (vs 14)

The Lamb was described for us in 5:6. He had seven horns. This represented a full expression of power. He will conquer and not be conquered. At the end, those "kings of the earth" and the whole world cry to the "rocks and mountains," "hide us from the face of him that sitteth on the throne, and from the wrath of the lamb" (6:16-17). In Daniel 7:21 the little horn (papacy) conquers the saints; in Revelation 19:19-20 the Lamb conquers the beast and its followers.

"for he is Lord of lords, and King of kings:" (vs 14)

This is beautiful language. It draws a great contrast with the arrogant pretense that the beast with the earth's kings make of their powerful positions!

Jesus, the "faithful and true" (Revelation 19:11) has written on His clothes and thigh "King of kings, and Lord of lords" (19:16). Such language is a title of God (Deuteronomy 10:17; Psalm 136:2-3; Daniel 2:37, 47; 4:37). "Jesus Christ" was earlier called "the prince of the kings of the earth" (1:5)! This imposing testimony is made more awe-inspiring when it is recalled that overcomers – you and I – will be given authority over nations and will "shepherd them" (Revelation 2:26-27). Jesus is *the* One who "hath made us kings and priests unto God and his Father" (1:6).

It is hard to fathom the elevated nature of King Jesus. It is impossible to see how a sinner like me/you is slated, in God's redemptive plan, to be one of His administrative assistants!

The prediction of the beast's victory over the saints (Daniel 7:21) is ironically a type of its final defeat by the King of kings.[2] The world defiantly cried, "who is able to make war with him [the beast with the ten horns]?" (13:4). The answer: the "Lamb will conquer them" (17:14).

"Which in his times he shall show, who is the blessed and only Potentate, the King of kings, and Lord of lords" (I Timothy 6:15).

"and they that are with him *are* called, and chosen, and faithful" (vs 14)

Jesus had said that "many are called, but few are chosen" (Matthew 22:14). Those who fight with him are represented as "armies … in heaven … upon white horses, clothed in fine linen, white and clean" (19:14). They were called and chosen because they were faithful to the one called "Faithful and True" (19:11).

Chapter 17 doesn't say that these saints "fought with or for the Lamb." But it is suggested by the little phrase that King Jesus – the fighting Lamb – had an army of subjects at His side. It is almost invitational! If you want to be on the side that wins – be with Jesus! Incredible – the white horse, representing those saints (6:1-2), is seen going out conquering and to conquer (Revelation 6:2).

This is likely the Messianic army of the 144,000.[3] This, intriguingly, ties to another

[1] White, Ellen G.; *The Great Controversy,* p. 46.

[2] Beale, G. K.; *The New International Greek Testament Commentary; The Book of Revelation* (William B. Eerdmans Publishing Company, Grand Rapids, Michigan – 1999), p. 880.

[3] Aune, David E.; *World Biblical Commentary; Revelation 17–22,* vol. 52c (World Books Publisher; Dallas, Texas – 1997), p. 952.

harlot prophecy – the Thyatira church, sympathetic with the wicked Jezebel. The overcomers to that illicit relationship will (Revelation 2:26-28):

Receive power over the nations (from Jesus)

Rule with a rod of iron Get victory over adversaries just as the Father helped Jesus to do

Those "overcomers" are here called the "faithful." This indicates the fulfillment of the human response to Christ's invitation by this select group.[4]

This verse is a vast resource of end-time metaphors.

The Lamb is the King of kings and Lord of lords. He is also the general of heaven's

army. The "called" are with that king at the time of victory (implied) when the dragon went to war against them (remnant) (12:17).

The power of the beasts, the kings and the dragon has been depicted. They have been characterized as brutal, ruthless and unjust within the context of persecution and even martyrdom. The verse now brings hope and assurance. The **end** of repression was prophesied long before.

"*It shall be* for a time, times, and an half; and when he shall have accomplished to scatter the power of the holy people, all these *things* shall be finished" (Daniel 12:7c).

This verse fulfills that prophecy.

4   Thomas, Robert L.; *Revelation 8–22 – An Exegetical Commentary* (Moody Press, Chicago – 1992), p. 303.

CHAPTER 13

ITS POWER BASE – THE WORLD

"And he saith unto me, The waters which thou sawest, where the whore sitteth, are peoples, and multitudes, and nations, and tongues. And the ten horns which thou sawest upon the beast, these shall hate the whore, and shall make her desolate and naked, and shall eat her flesh, and burn her with fire" (Revelation 17:15-16).

"And he saith unto me," (vs 15)

The angel now leaves his discourse about the beast and describes how the harlot will come to her end. This little phrase transitions from one theme to another.

"The waters which thou sawest, where the whore sitteth," (vs 15)

Water in this book can be literal (21:6, 22:1, 22:17) or symbolic (12:15, 16:12). Here, it is obviously symbolic because the whore was sitting or ruling over it in verse 1. The imagery of waters came from Babylon in Jeremiah 51:13 as the city is pictured on many waters – a literal reference to the Euphrates River. Also, in Isaiah 17:12-13 "many waters" represents "many nations."[1]

This harlot portrayal is another evil parody against the Lord who sits enthroned over the flood (Psalm 29:10). Jehovah directed the great deluge in Noah's day.

He governs nature and the earth, and does whatsoever He wills. Here, the harlot is trying to assume that role. This introduces amazing information germane to our grasp of the harlot and the beast!

The ten horns gave it (the Roman Catholic Vatican state – by implication, the Holy See) its world power. Now the Bible says that its church is over the people and nations of the world! As a vendor of deceit, the mingling of church craft and state craft blurs her intentions. Ultimately, the *woman* (the Catholic Church) is on top. At the end, the imagery will focus on the *beast* (Revelation 13), but we now know that that church is its controlling force.

Like a harlot, her clients are "recruited" (cf. Ezekiel 16:15, 25, 31). Her success:

"are peoples, and multitudes, and nations, and tongues." (vs 15)

This grouping expresses universality of the human race.[2] This articulation is noted elsewhere in Revelation, related to what the saints have come out of (5:9, 7:9). It also describes the rebellious population (10:11, 11:9, 13:7, 14:6) as "earth dwellers."

She who dominates the people of the world will be judged. John was initially told that he would see how this happened – but immediately was given the fearful insights of her immoral reign with the beast. Now he comes back to the *rest of the story*. This will not be complete until chapter 18. But – she is destined to hell.

[1] Beale, G. K.; *The New International Greek Testament Commentary; The Book of Revelation* (William B. Eerdmans Publishing Company, Grand Rapids, Michigan – 1999), p. 882.

[2] Brighton, Louis A.; *Revelation* (Concordia Publishing House, Saint Louis, MO – 1999), p. 453.

"And the ten horns which thou sawest upon the beast," (vs 16)

The ten horns had conveyed their servitude power to the Roman Catholic Church in verse 12. This began when the kingdom structure of a final "world order" had not yet materialized. Yet – the prophecy said that they would *unite* for a short time in supreme governance. What now follows appears to occur towards the end of that infatuating union (also towards the final period of Revelation 13's coalition).

This alliance of kings follows a unique prophetic path:

Papal Alliance Forms (17:2-3, 12)

Ten Kings
Fierce loyalty to the papacy
(17:12; 13)
           Collectively

War against the Lamb (17:17)
           Bitterness develops!

Desolating hatred towards the papacy (17:16)

Alliance destroyed (6:15-16, 16:19)

"these shall hate the whore, and shall make her desolate and naked, and shall eat her flesh, and burn her with fire." (vs 16)

This may be one of the most graphic illustrations of the self-destructive nature of evil. The hatred these heinous powers of depravity have for each other was revealed in the fifth and sixth Trumpets. There, torture and death are effigies of their wicked hearts toward each other.

Jesus said of this specific time: "And then shall many be offended, and shall betray one another, and shall hate one another" (Matthew 24:10). This characterizes the driving need to kill and torture by those who are demon possessed (Mark 5:1-20, 9:14-29).

This eschatological war was depicted as Armageddon in chapter 16, where everyone's sword is against his brother (Ezekiel 38:21). That prophecy draws on the country of Gog, typifying the wicked world. This hatred against Rome is a final event that just precedes Christ's second coming. Here are a few prophetic phrases regarding his end:

1. "They shall take away his dominion, to consume and to destroy it unto the end" (Daniel 7:26).
2. "He shall be broken without hand" (Daniel 8:25).
3. "He shall come to his end, and none shall help him" (Daniel 11:45).
4. "He that leadeth into captivity shall go into captivity" (Revelation 13:10a).
5. "These both [beast and false prophet] were cast alive into a lake of fire burning with brimstone" (Revelation 19:20).

Part of this harlot's terminus appears to be the result of a *cause and effect* response of the hatred of world leaders.

"and shall make her desolate" (vs 16)

This desolation is seen again for Babylon the Great in 18:17 and 19, depicting God's judicial response "in one hour." There is a remarkable parallel to a directive Jesus gave: "When ye therefore shall see the abomination of desolation, spoken of by Daniel the prophet, stand in the holy place ... flee" (Matthew 24:15-16).

In Daniel this *desolation* is presented additionally as:

1. "An host was given him against the daily ... by reason of the transgression" ... "transgression of *desolation*" (Daniel 8:12-13) associated with the second rise of the "little horn."

2. "For the overspreading of abominations he shall make it *desolate*" (Daniel 9:27) – associated with the second rise of the little horn papacy of Daniel.

3. "Shall take away the daily ... and they shall place the abomination that maketh *desolate*" (Daniel 11:31) – also associated with the second rise of the vile person (papacy) called the "king of the north."

4. "And from the time that the daily ... shall be taken away, and the abomination that maketh *desolate* set up, there shall be a thousand two hundred and ninety days" (Daniel 12:11).

"and naked, and shall eat her flesh, and burn her with fire" (vs 16)

Intriguing is the gruesome language here portrayed, bringing an end to the Roman Catholic Church! They "strip her naked and consume her with fire" (latter built on Ezekiel 23:25-29, 47; 16:37-41 in which the apostate Jerusalem/Israel is destroyed). "Thou hast walked in the way of thy sister; therefore will I give her cup into thine hand. Thus saith the Lord GOD; Thou shalt drink of thy sister's cup deep and large: thou shalt be laughed to scorn and had in derision; it containeth much. Thou shalt be filled with drunkenness and sorrow, with the cup of astonishment and desolation, with the cup of thy sister

Samaria. Thou shalt even drink it and suck it out, and thou shalt break the sherds thereof, and pluck off thine own breasts: for I have spoken *it*, saith the Lord GOD" (Ezekiel 23:31-34). John's addition of "eat her flesh" is a Jewish expression of "total annihilation."[3]

Here, the "kings of the east" (Revelation 16:12-16), who had joined her in a parody of delivering the world, turn their forces against her. This is the only reference where Babylon the Great, the harlot, the papacy, the Roman Catholic Church, is destroyed by her allies. Elsewhere, we see it occurring by pestilence and plagues (18:8) and from the coming rider on the horse (19:13-15). All symbols "are part of the same sovereign plan of God by which he will bring world history with its depravity to an end."[4]

Another dramatic symbol is presented with the drying up of the Euphrates' waters in 16:12. This amplifies how the religious and economic loyalists throughout the world (17:15) become disenfranchised and cease supporting Lady Babylon. The apostate leaders in another metaphor of Jerusalem are even called harlots (Nahum 3:4-5). Engaging is the portrayal of Israel as a harlot in Jeremiah 2:20-4:30. At the end, her lovers despise her and try to kill her (Jeremiah 4:30).

Recall, these descriptive messages come exactly as the Vial angel promised (Revelation 17:1). This would be the story of how the end of the harlot occurs!

The fulfillment of this destruction is once again depicted in the next chapter:

- "Therefore shall her plagues come in one day, death, and mourning, and famine; and she shall be

---

[3] Osborne, Grant R.; *Revelation* (Baker Book House; Grand Rapids, MI), p. 626.

[4] *Ibid.*

utterly burned with fire: for strong is the Lord God who judgeth her" (Revelation 18:8).

And recently portrayed in 16:12:

- "And the sixth angel poured out his vial upon the great river Euphrates; and the water thereof was dried up, that the way of the kings of the east might be prepared.

Three Destruction Metaphors

"Make her naked" comes from a Laodicean warning where God's apostate people need to buy of Him white garments to "cover their shameful nakedness" (3:18). He warned believers before Babylon's end: "Behold, I come as a thief. Blessed is he that watcheth, and keepeth his garments, lest he walk naked, and they see his shame" (16:15).

Nakedness refers, in desolating language, to exposure of sinful deeds. It also conveys terminal judgment (Hosea 2:3; Jeremiah 10:25; 41:22 (LXX); Micah 3:3; Nahum 3:4-5, 15).

"Shall eat her flesh" builds on Jezebel being eaten by dogs (II Kings 9:36-37) and looks ahead to the end of the wicked (Revelation 19:17-18, 21). It parallels the finality of terrible judgments noted in Ezekiel 23:22-25 as God turns harlot Jerusalem over to Babylonian destruction. The irony is that then it is Babylon that does the destroying, while here Babylon is the destroyed.[5]

"Burn her with fire" reflects the fate of a prostitute in ancient Israel. She was to be "burned in the fire" (Leviticus 20:14, 21:9; Joshua 7:15, 25). This anticipates the lake of fire (20:10).

Harlot Imagery

The fate of unfaithfulness is characterized in the depiction of a prostitute, a harlot. This is so descriptive. God was in love with His people so much and craved to be so intimately a part of them that He said: "Turn, O backsliding children, saith the LORD; for I am married unto you: and I will take you one of a city, and two of a family, and I will bring you to Zion" (Jeremiah 3:14). Thus, infidelity would be a terrible sin and ultimately lead to divine consequences.

There are other parallels to the harlot chicanery in the Old Testament and the Thyatira church![6]

1. Before Jezebel's death, she "colored her eyes and adorned her head" like the harlot of Revelation 17.
2. They were queens (I Kings 16:31; Revelation 17:1-2, 18; 18:7).
3. They seduced people (I Kings 21:25, Revelation 17:2; cf. Revelation 2:20, 22).
4. They were guilty of fornication – symbolizing sinful unfaithfulness (II Kings 9:22; II Chronicles 21:13; Revelation 17:1-2, 5; cf. Revelation 2:20-22).
5. They deceived people by sorceries (mysticism – spiritualism) (II Kings 9:22, Revelation 18:23).
6. They sought greedily for economic prosperity (I Kings 21, Revelation 18:11-19).
7. They persecuted and killed saints (I Kings 18:4, 19:2; Revelation 17:6).
8. A remnant refuses to participate in the harlot's sins (I Kings 18:18a, 19:18; II Kings 9:22; Revelation 17:14b).

---

5   *Ibid.*

6   Beale, *op. cit.,* p. 884.

9. Destruction occurs quickly (II Kings 9:33-35; Revelation 18:10, 17, 19).
10. God judges her followers (I Kings 18:40, II Kings 10:19, Revelation 18:9-11; cf. Revelation 2:23).

Many pictures are painted in the Old Testament of judgment against a prostitute (II Chronicles 21:11-15; Isaiah 1:21-25, 57:3; Jeremiah 2:20, 3:1, 13:27; Hosea 2:2-5, 4:12-18, 5:4, 9:1; Micah 1:7). Disloyalty to God at the end continues in the same descriptive motif. It draws on the most intimate of relationships. They are "prophetic notices" and warnings against supreme apostasy.

What causes the "charm" and allurement of the papacy to end? Changes from love to bitter hatred are recorded elsewhere (II Samuel 13:15). In the end Satan's kingdom will be divided against itself (Mark 3:23-26). The details of the early seductive attraction appear to be:

1. Religious (Revelation 13:13-17) –with apparent demonstration of mystical acts when seen as a *moral leader*
2. She is filled with words of *alluring power* (13:2), apparently not recognized by the world as wrong.
3. Obviously *charismatic* (13:3b)
4. Apparent economic control will be given to her (Daniel 11:43) – monetarily and in trade (Revelation 18:11-19).

5. She *persecutes* the saints (17:6, 18:24), which apparently *assuages her conscience*.

Her end comes. By the world's reaction in Revelation 18:11-19, we get special insight as to what she controls or influences. The terminus appears to be global fear of asset and economic loss.

In contrast is the "outcome of allegiance" to God. In beautiful language as newness, restoration and recreation unfold, when the eradication of sin occurs, there comes the exciting message of "the bride, the Lamb's wife" (21:9). God has been courting humanity for 6000 years. Time and again He has been engaged to be married, but the woman has gone after other "husbands." We are given in Revelation amazing news that an eternal bride is found: "Let us be glad and rejoice, and give honour to him: for the marriage of the Lamb is come, and his wife hath made herself ready" (19:7).

Then in stunning language there is to be a "marriage supper of the Lamb" (19:9)! Those who become saints, a remnant of the "called," will be guests at that mighty event. The harlot loses her "husband." The Lamb gains a bride!

CHAPTER 14

THE GOD FACTOR!

"For God hath put in their hearts to fulfil his will, and to agree, and give their kingdom unto the beast, until the words of God shall be fulfilled" (Revelation 17:17).

Throughout this almost "beyond belief" book, we are often reminded that everything, including Satan's final demonic acts, is tempered by God Himself. Prophecy unfolds within divine parameters. As much as the wicked mind *assumes* freedom and self-will, God has a line that rebellion cannot cross.

"The long-suffering of God is wonderful. Long does justice wait while mercy pleads with the sinner. But 'righteousness and judgment are the establishment of his throne' (Ps. 97:2, margin).... The world has become bold in transgression of God's law. Because of His long forbearance, men have trampled upon His authority.... But there is a line beyond which they cannot pass. The time is near when they will have reached the prescribed limit. Even now they have almost exceeded the bounds of the long-suffering of God, the limits of His grace, the limits of His mercy. The Lord will interpose to vindicate His own honor, to deliver His people, and to repress the swellings of unrighteousness."[1]

There is another stunning matter which this judicial imperative raises:

"For God hath put in their hearts to fulfil his will, and to agree, and give their kingdom unto the beast," (vs 17)

---
[1] White, Ellen G.; *God's Amazing Grace*, 371 (1900).

Does this imply that the wicked will actually patronize God's end-time plans? That's exactly what it means! This must bring at times utter chaos to Satan's emotions and plans. This isn't the first time God has done this – but it will be the last.

Everything noted, therefore, in verses 12-16 reflects God's will – the leaders of the world are in one accord and they all agree to surrender their power to the papal beast.[2] Later, they turn against that institution of deception with violent retaliation – all within the framework of God's terminal plans to bring rebellion to an end. As we penetrate deeper into this verse, it must be construed that these stories unfold not only from *divine permission* but "divine causation, tempered by preserving man's free choice. Through His foreknowledge He permits the exercise of their perverse nature"[3] to reveal another chapter of what evil is like.

Notice how God used even pagan kings anciently to bring about His will:

"Behold, I will send and take all the families of the north, saith the LORD, and **Nebuchadrezzar** the king of Babylon, my servant, and will bring them against this land, and against the inhabitants thereof, and against all these nations round about, and will utterly destroy them, and make them an astonishment, and an hissing, and

---
[2] Aune, David E.; *World Biblical Commentary; Revelation 17–22*, vol. 52c (World Books; Publisher, Dallas, Texas – 1997), p. 958.
[3] Hengstenberg as quoted in Beale, G. K.; *The New International Greek Testament Commentary; The Book of Revelation* (William B. Eerdmans Publishing Company, Grand Rapids, Michigan – 1999), p. 887.

perpetual desolations. Moreover I will take from them the voice of mirth, and the voice of gladness, the voice of the bridegroom, and the voice of the bride, the sound of the millstones, and the light of the candle. And this whole land shall be a desolation, *and* an astonishment; and these nations shall serve the king of Babylon seventy years" (Jeremiah 25:9-11).

"That saith of **Cyrus**, *He is* **my shepherd,** and **shall perform all my pleasure**: even saying to Jerusalem, Thou shalt be built; and to the temple, Thy foundation shall be laid. Thus saith the LORD to **his anointed**, to Cyrus, whose right hand I have holden, to subdue nations before him; and I will loose the loins of kings, to open before him the two leaved gates; and the gates shall not be shut;" (Isaiah 44:28–45:1; cf. Isaiah 6:1-8, 13:5-8; Exodus 4:21, 7:3, 9:12, 10:1, 14:4; II Chronicles 36:22-23; Ezekiel 1:1; Acts 2:23; 4:27-28).

Those pagan kings were addressed as if they were part of God's administration! In time, both Nebuchadnezzar and Cyrus knew that they were acting on the world stage on behalf of God. We aren't given information as to whether the ten kingdoms/kings in this chapter gain such awareness. But whatever their individual wishes might be, their collective response ("to agree") towards the beast will be ardent and passionate. God has even used His enemies to destroy themselves (Judges 7:22, II Chronicles 20:73, I Samuel 14:20, Ezekiel 38:21, Haggai 2:2, Zechariah 14:14). Satan is often used as an instrument to serve His providential purposes?![4] God will give power to people and circumstances to bring about a New World Order. All this is part of His

4   Thomas, Robert L.; *Revelation 8–22 – An Exegetical Commentary* (Moody Press, Chicago – 1992), p. 305.

redemptive strategy to show the universe what evil is finally like.

In 17:13 these kings show that they were of one mind and "purpose" by giving power and authority to the beast. Here, they are of one mind and purpose till the final bestial acts are destroyed.

"until the words of God shall be fulfilled." (vs 17)

These ten kings bond with Rome in some mysterious way until it is no longer useful to them to associate with this religious center. It then becomes abhorrent or repugnant. "God put it in their hearts!" Isn't that amazing?! Divine judicial action begins here through worldly agents.

There is a resolute loyalty to Rome until the issues of prophecy are fulfilled. That appears to be the period of the antichrist's work. It strongly suggests the 42 months of Revelation 13:5. There, it distinctly says: "power was given unto him to continue" for 42 months. This coincides with the period of persecution of the king of the north (Babylon) (Daniel 12:7) and of the Gentiles (ten kings) (Revelation 11:2)!

The words of prophecy (words of God) are fulfilled regarding the harlot and the beast at the end of that three and a half years. At that time God's people are delivered and a special resurrection occurs (Daniel 12:1-2, 6-7).

"They are **all** the prophecies of last events until the overthrow of the false Christ. This statement recalls the sweeping words of the angel in 10:7 regarding the fulfillment of the mystery of God (Lee). The prophecies will reach their goal as God permits wickedness to continue until the cup of iniquity overflows (Walvoord). God's will and God's words dictate that the kingdom of this world be under the control of the beast until the end of the age.

Unification of evil will mark the very end according to the prophetic word."[5]

This leans on a remarkable concept in prophecy. When they are fulfilled, they become truth revealed and vindicate God (Deuteronomy 18:18-22).

"From age to age the Lord has made known the manner of His working. When a crisis has come, He has revealed Himself, and has interposed to hinder the working out of Satan's plans. With nations, with families, and with individuals, He has often permitted matters to come to a crisis, that His interference might become marked. Then He has made manifest that there is a God in Israel who will maintain His law and vindicate His people.

"In this time of prevailing iniquity we may know that the last great crisis is at hand. When the defiance of God's law is almost universal, when His people are oppressed and afflicted by their fellow men, the Lord will interpose."[6]

At the time of deliverance of the saints, the wicked know that they will be lost. In that time of horror and terror, it will be natural to turn against the leaders they had so fiercely defended.

This recalls: "And if Satan rise up against himself, and be divided, he cannot stand, but hath an end" (Mark 3:26). When no hope arrives – division and violence will supervene. Desolation becomes earth's final material blight.

5   *Ibid.*, p. 306 (emphasis added).

6   White, Ellen G.; *Christ's Object Lessons*, p. 178 (1900).

CHAPTER 15

ROME'S FEARFUL FUTURE

"And the woman which thou sawest is that great city, which reigneth over the kings of the earth" (Revelation 17:18).

This begins the final words of interpretation given by the Vial angel – the fourth in a series (17:8, 9-11, 12-14, 18).[1] It also swings open the door for the next chapter, 13, which follows 17 timewise.

"And the woman which thou sawest" (vs 18)

John's first vision of this harlot was when the angel "carried me away" (17:3) into the "wilderness." This focus is a provocative missive! Here's why:

The word for wilderness (*eremon*) is highly symbolic in Biblical typology. It represents a place of refuge and salvation (Isaiah 40:3; Jeremiah 31:2, 8:6; Ezekiel 34:25; Psalm 55:7-8). Intriguingly, the Qumran community understood their presence in the wilderness as having an eschatological fulfillment of Isaiah 40:3 (1 QS 8:12-14, 9:19-21). Revelation 12:6 and 14 are interpreted in that Jewish understanding.[2]

Why are the harlot and the beast first observed in a place of "refuge"? That represents the protective setting that the kings of the world give it as a key component of this prophecy! The leaders of this world – before they even have a kingdom (13:1 – horns with

crowns) – are providing protective support for her detestable beliefs and actions.

John is asked to recall the harlot in that setting. Then comes this incisive statement:

"is that great city." (vs 18)

This label is first tied to Babylon in the second angel's message (14:8). It is a city that is fallen because it made all nations drink of her wine (doctrines – beliefs – teachings). These were positions at variance to the issues presented in the first angel's message (Revelation 14:6-7).

The Babylon concept was first noted without that name but was designated by the words "great city" in chapter 11, where the two witnesses lay dead in its streets (they were silenced). There, several important thoughts are developed (11:7-8).

1. They are "killed" by the beast (same one as later noted in chapters 13 and 17) – which resides in Rome (17:9).
2. There, the beast came out of the abyss (hell) where Satan and his minions are at home (cf. 9:1-2, 17:8) – then it did its heinous acts within that "great city." Later, we are told that the "dragon gave him [the beast] his power" (13:2). They are both represented as originating from the abyss or bottomless pit. Rome/Babylon has leaders from hell!
3. That "great city" has two spiritual (symbolic) names – Sodom

1 Osborne, Grant R.; *Revelation* (Baker Book House; Grand Rapids, MI), p. 628.
2 Aune, David E.; *World Biblical Commentary; Revelation 17–22*, vol. 52c (World Books; Publisher, Dallas, Texas – 1997), p. 706.

(depravity) and Egypt (evil like the wicked world).

Then we learn in 14:8 that the great city is Babylon; then in 17:5 it is also the harlot. That represents an apostate church that rules over Rome – which could be none other than the Roman Catholic Church.

- Thus, in the linguistic ties that thread through these clues we can see emerging a timing association with:
  - The two witnesses (3½-year
  - activity) (11:3) – in great city
  - Persecution (3½-year
  - activity) (11:2) – by beast
  - Second angel's message – great city, Babylon, spiritually fallen
  - Harlot named Babylon with her world support
  - Her "falls" are collectively described in chapters 16, 17:16 and chapter 18.

As noted in Revelation 13, the beast is given 42 months (3½ years) to fulfill its mission. The "great city" designation confirms that final period ties also to the harlot. New insight is now given.

"which reigneth over the kings of the earth" (vs 18)

The woman sat on the seven "hills/mountains" (17:9), denoting her administrative control over Rome. She sat on many "waters" (17:1), which represents power or rule over the people of the world (17:15). The ten horns are ten kings of the world divisions that "receive power with the beast" (17:12). Horns give power and authority to the beast. The world leaders will acquiesce this control over an element of global governance to the harlot that commands the beast. This is to such a degree that the Bible here notes that she has control over the kings of the earth (ten kings implied)!

As we have noted, they will later turn against her. But we now know that that will not occur until all the prophecy, specifically chapters 11–14 and 17–18, is fulfilled. This means that a stunning and fearful series of horrific events lie just ahead, all tied to the Vatican and the Roman Catholic Church.

Those events are portrayed in Revelation 13. We will visit that next and end with a more detailed view of Babylon and the harlot's end in Revelation 18.

CHAPTER 16

FINAL POWER OF THE PAPACY

INTRODUCTION TO REVELATION 13

The harlot – Roman Catholic Church (RCC) – of Revelation 17 is now identified as an end-time agent that persecutes and kills the saints (17:6). These saints are called "chosen" and "faithful" (17:14). The world, divided and controlled by ten kingdoms (horns), will provide power to and reign with the beast (the Vatican kingdom governed by that harlot). That Rome-centered creature was noted to have seven sequenced heads.

The last two of those beast heads are of critical importance to eschatological prophecy. Pope John Paul II, the sixth, was the pope that "is." He was *the* papal head when a crucial alliance occurred between the United States and the papacy. That became a preliminary step in the prophetic groundwork for Revelation 13 to begin. It was then that diplomatic ties were created between the papacy (via Pope John Paul II) and the United States of America (via President Ronald Reagan), referred to as the "Holy Alliance."[1]

Since that papal head died (April 2, 2005), the seventh papal beast head, Pope Benedict XVI, was inaugurated and then resigned February 28, 2013. It will be during the tenure of the "eighth" (referring now to the beast) that the events (see chapter 10) of Revelation 13 occur. Throughout this saga, Satan is active. His driving force is to make the leaders of the world and all "that dwell on the earth" to wonder (17:8) after the Holy See (church

and state). As we will see once again, the power to be given to the papacy is so great that it rules over the peoples and nations of the whole world.

Pope Benedict XVI received and counseled with world leaders on a weekly basis. [*Inside the Vatican* magazine (Ignatius Press; Rome, Italy) reported the details of those visits.] Many of those contacts were significant executive meetings between the papacy and world leaders that had geopolitical overtones.

As one example: "Pope Benedict XVI (December 2006) invited the 83-year-old Henry Kissinger, a Jew and non-Catholic to be a consultant to the Holy See.

Kissinger accepted the position. He, like the Pope, has analyzed the challenges of globalization and is providing special advice in this area. He is an active participant in the Bilderberger meetings where the new world order is a key agenda.

"Veteran Vatican journalist Sandro Magister noted: 'Experts from a variety of disciplines, including the fields of economics, politics and philosophy, are regularly invited to advise Benedict and other Vatican officials on current affairs.'

"Recent individuals who worked with the Holy See have included Paul Wolfowitz, a former President Bush adviser and now president of the World Bank; Michel Camdessus, the former director of the International Monetary Fund; American economist Jeffrey Sachs and Hans Tietmeyer, former governor of Germany's Central Bank.

---

[1] *Time Magazine*, February 24, 1992 (emphasis added).

"The pontifical academies also regularly call on academic luminaries as consultants, such as Nobel laureates Gary Becker, the successor to Milton Friedman at the Chicago School of Economics, and Italian medical researcher Rita Levi-Montalcini."[2]

These are not simply "courtesy visits." Vital world issues are being discussed in an atmosphere of intervention and resolution.

Benedict reached into that power base of world leaders as he brokered globalization plans. Serious Vatican posturing regarding a New World Order officially began in 2001. It was then that the Pontifical Academy of Social Sciences had a Plenary Session on globalization. That was followed by a publication: *Globalization Ethical and Institutional Concerns* (April 25-28, 2001). [ISBN 88-86726-11-2], Vatican City.

Later, under Pope Benedict XVI, a book was published called *Globalization: A Christian Perspective* (September 16, 2006), written by Bishop Giampaolo Crepaldi, secretary of the Pontifical Council for Justice and Peace. He brought together some of the main points made by Popes John Paul II and Benedict XVI on the Roman Catholic Church's leadership interest in geopolitics.

Later, on May 5, 2008, the Pontifical Academy of Social Sciences conducted meetings with the theme: "Pursuing the Common Good: How Solidarity and Subsidiary Can Work Together." The general purpose of those meetings was to "give new meaning and application to the concept of common good throughout the world." "Common Good" is a unique phrase promoted by the Vatican and found in its Catechism. It demands that global decisions must be made in the framework of the good for all humanity. But, it deceptively appeals to the scurrilous plea that Caiaphas made at the trial of Christ, "that it was expedient that one man should die for the people" (John 18:14). That "common good" for Israel would emanate from the death of Jesus. This concept is sinister and has suppressive overtones toward religious liberty.

In June, 2009, the Vatican's International Theological Commission called upon world leaders to consider the … importance in peacefully uniting people of all backgrounds into a common mission based upon "natural law." This concept, via Roman Catholic understanding, leans on "reason" to help pass judgment on the moral worth of various laws. The commission called for a **unified global ethic**. In a major document sent to world leaders entitled "The Search for Universal Ethics: A New Look at Natural Law," they questioned, "Are there objective moral values that can unite men and bring them peace and happiness?" "What are they? How do we recognize them? How do we implement them in personal and community life?"[3]

They noted that "these perennial questions about good and evil are more urgent today than ever, to the extent that men have a greater consciousness of forming a single worldwide community." The Theological Commission also touched upon the Christian community's contribution to universal ethical traditions. [One, which the Vatican has been promoting in the European Union, is to adapt Sunday as a day of universal rest. They want this to be part of the EU Constitution.][4]

"Throughout its history, the Christian community, in elaborating its own ethical tradition – led by the Spirit of Jesus Christ and in critical dialogue with the traditions of wisdom that it met – was also purified and

2   http://ncregister.com/site/article/1370/

3   http://www.zenit.org/article-26149?|=english
4   http://www.ktfministry.org/news/393/ european-bishops-still-pressing-for-sunday-rest]; *The Philadelphia Trumpet,* February 2009.

developed this teaching on natural law as a norm fundamental for ethics." From St. Peter's Square:

> ## "Pope Challenges World Leaders to Make Major Changes to Global Financial System
>
> "VATICAN CITY – Pope Benedict XVI challenged world leaders on Thursday to make major changes to the global financial system, saying short-term answers to the financial crisis weren't sufficient.
>
> "'It's not enough, as Jesus said, to put patches on an old suit,' Benedict said in his New Year's Day blessing to thousands of people huddled under umbrellas in a rain-soaked St. Peter's Square.
>
> "Echoing a similar theme in his New Year's Day homily, Benedict said the crisis should be seen as a test-case about the future of globalization.
>
> "'Are we ready to read it in its complexity as a way for the future and not just an emergency to respond to with short-term answers?' he asked. 'Are we ready to make a profound revision in the dominant development model, to correct it in a farsighted and concerted way?'
>
> "He said the health of the planet required such a correction, as well as what he called the 'cultural and moral crisis' in which the world finds itself.
>
> "Benedict has spoken out frequently about the financial crisis, and he used the Roman Catholic Church's World Day of Peace, celebrated every Jan. 1, to emphasize his belief that the meltdown showed the need for greater solidarity with the poor.
>
> "'Seen in its profundity, the crisis should be seen as a serious symptom that requires intervention at its root,' the pontiff said."[2]

The Roman Catholic Church is positioning itself as a moral force in the globalization moves rapidly going forward. It will succeed as becoming *the* "kingdom" that the world looks to outlined in the prophecy of Revelation 13.

The New World Order is in more than an "idea stage." It is part of a serious strategy to set up global regional units of power that individually handle everything from population control, food production and distribution, defense to economic stability and, as the Pope noted above, to address the "cultural and moral crisis" that is currently plaguing the world.

Beyond the curious numbers of world dignitaries consulting with and admiring Rome come the people who make pilgrimages. The papacy reported that two to three million people saw Pope Benedict XVI during each year of his pontificate.

It is within this backdrop that we are ready to look at what will soon occur during the dynasty of the "eighth" (Revelation 17:11).

In ancient manuscripts, the last verse of chapter 12 of the KJV (vs 17) is part of the Revelation 13 prophecy. By linking these together, chapter 13 is seen as a final chronicle of the dragon's wrath against God's people. He calls into play his agents, and together persecution and death come to those saints.

This becomes possible because of globalization. Here, the ten horns of the beast have crowns!

---

5   Nicole Winfield, Associated Press, January 1, 2009.

CHAPTER 17

EARTH'S LAST BATTLE

RELATES TO GOD'S COMMANDMENTS AND THE BOOK OF REVELATION

"And the dragon was wroth with the woman, and went to make war with the remnant of her seed, which keep the commandments of God, and have the testimony of Jesus Christ" (Revelation 12:17).

Satan's attack against Christ is aimed through His remnant people. His method of engagement centers on the beast that will emerge shortly from the sea.

Revelation 13 is the story of a war against Christ's loyalists. This verse formulates the background of that war. In the fact-filled interlude of Revelation 17, we were already told. "These shall make war with the Lamb, and the Lamb shall overcome them: for he is Lord of lords, and King of kings: and they that are with him are called, and chosen, and faithful" (17:14).

Much of prophecy relates to war between good and evil. Here in Revelation we are informed about the details of those last battles. Satan desperately applies all his skill to defeat these saints.

"He [Satan] is setting his trained agents at work, and moving them to *intense activity*. He is securing his army of human agents to engage in the last conflict against the Prince of life, to overthrow the law of God, which is the foundation of His throne. Satan will *work with miraculous presentations* to confirm men in the belief that he is what he claims to be, — the prince of this world, and that victory is his. He will turn his *forces against those who are loyal* to God, but though

he may cause pain, distress, and human agony, he cannot defile the soul. He may cause affliction to the people of God as he did to Christ, but he cannot cause one of Christ's little ones to perish. *The people of God in these last days must expect to enter into the thick of the conflict;* for the prophetic Word says, 'The dragon was wroth with the woman, and went to make war with the remnant of her seed, which keep the commandments of God, and have the testimony of Jesus Christ.'"[1]

"And the dragon was wroth with the woman," (vs 17)

In 12:12 it is noted that the devil was filled with wrath because he knows his last opportunity to work had come. A "short time" is *oligon kairon*. His final defeat is imminent. Therefore, he turns with hatred against the inhabitants of the earth (12:12). *But* – here it becomes more focused against the woman – His church and all her progeny.

"and went to make war with the remnant of her seed," (vs 17)

The target – the center of hatred – is the last group of people fully committed to God – His last-day "church." The twelfth chapter outlines three distinct defeats of Satan in his war against heaven:

---

[1] White, Ellen G.; *The Seventh-day Adventist Bible Commentary,* vol. 4, p. 1153 (Letter 43, 1895) (emphasis added).

1. He and his minions were cast out of heaven (12:8).
2. The baby Jesus escaped his murderous attempts (12:5) – symbolic of the deliverance of the final remnant!
3. He's been unable to destroy the Christian church (12:15-16). He, however, will be destroyed.

This is Satan's final chance to hurt Christ and His people. He knows prophecy – he has long prepared for this. God now tells us how his frenzied attack against the loyal saints will unfold.

The ideal church was portrayed as the dazzling lady in 12:1-2. That chapter revealed a woman with child, and now we are notified that she has offspring (her seed). The concept of "Mother" Zion bearing children was first introduced in Isaiah 54:1-3; 61:9-10; 65:9, 23 and 66:7-10, 22. The war against those children covers the last 42 months of earth's history (Revelation 13:5). Isn't it interesting that Satan also has an end-time church – the harlot, who is called a mother (17:5). Nothing will he withhold in this last hour to deceive and make it appear that he represents the kingdom of glory. But his heart is evil and those apocalyptic prophecies are not pretty. He would like to annihilate those who support Christ.

This "remnant of her seed" alludes to the 144,000 who are sealed in chapter 7. Now, in spite of the persecution and hatred, a victorious group will emerge, noted in 14:1-5. That incredible editorial is inserted as a commentary of hope.

"It was given unto him [sea beast under Satan's control] to make war with the saints and to overcome them" (13:7). In a previous prophecy, the outer court of the temple was given to the Gentiles (all those not written in the Lamb's Book of Life – 13:8), and they

"tread" (persecuted) the holy city (God's people) for 42 months (11:2). That unveils the final militant activity of the rebellious world against God's people. Then it notes that the beast that ascendeth out of the bottomless pit will make war against God's witnesses and overcome and kill them (11:7). Christ had said that the subjugation of "the holy people" would last for a "time, times and half" (moed, moeds and half – three and a half atonement cycles or three and a half years in context). Then "all these things shall be finished" (Daniel 12:7). Then God's people are delivered – they are free at last! Who are these?

"keep the commandments of God, and have the testimony of Jesus Christ." (vs 17)

God has chosen to define his final army of believers as being obedient to His commandments (entolas) and having the testimony of Jesus, which is given through this book of Revelation. In 19:10 it notes that the testimony of Jesus is the spirit of prophecy. That, in turn, reverts back to 1:2-3 where the "testimony of Jesus Christ" is gotten directly from God. That refers to a divine composite of apocalyptic prophecy (vs 1). In turn, John is told: "Blessed is he that readeth, and they that hear the words of this prophecy, and keep those things which are written therein: for the time is at hand" (Revelation 1:3).

At the end of the three angels' messages the characteristics of the saints are similarly chronicled: "Here is the patience of the saints: here are they that keep the commandments of God, and the faith of Jesus" (14:12).

This faithfulness and obedience to God's requirements were also a key spiritual object of the letters to the churches (2:10, 25-26; 3:3, 10-11).

The context suggests that this "remnant" keep "the commandments which God gave" [this is genitive and refers to the Decalogue] and the "testimony that Jesus bore."[2] The allusions to the power and significance of this testimony (*marturia*) are disclosed in a dramatic series of communiqués. The setting and spelling of this Greek word means "objective information" "is being given in proof" of the prophecies portrayed.[3] The information rises to the level of a legal argument that could be used in a court of law!

The incredible story:

1:2   Gabriel bears record (legal witness) to the **testimony** of Jesus (obtained from God the Father).

1:9   John parenthetically notes that he too had a **testimony** of Jesus, proving the gospel truths (implied) which banished him to Patmos.

6:9   The **testimony** of the end-time martyrs is that of the witnesses of this apocalyptic book (gospel and prophecy).

12:11   God's people overcome Satan by the blood of the Lamb and their **testimony** from these apocalyptic truths (gospel and prophecy).

12:17   God's people – the remnant – keep God's commandments and have the **testimony** of Jesus (contextually, this bond originated with God – 1:2).

19:10   Gabriel holds also to the **testimony** of Jesus, which he affirms is this Spirit of Prophecy.

20:4   John sees individuals who have been martyred for the **testimony** of Jesus and the Word of God.

Thus, the weight of evidence suggests that the "testimony" the saints have is a legally sound, thorough, end-time truth, which originates from Jesus from within this apocalyptic book. It will stir the world. Why is this the object of "war" or satanic wrath? It represents unequivocal evidence that Satan and his minions are wrong – they are deceptive! The "keep" issue will soon expand regarding God's directives – the fight will center on the Decalogue!

One can only imagine the frenzied activity that drives the last few months of Satan's revenge against God. His repugnant hatred will reach a pinnacle of horror. He has rancor toward even the slightest exhibition of faith. God now sees fit to reveal the issues, events and players in earth's final struggle.

The Battle Flow				
Chapter 7	**Chapter 12:1**	**Chapter 17**	**Chapter 13**	**Chapter 14:1-5, 14-17**
There will be a sealed group – 144,000	There will be a pure church	There will be a war against those loyalists	The war	The victors

2   Thomas, Robert L.; *Revelation 8–22 – An Exegetical Commentary* (Moody Press, Chicago – 1992), p. 142.

3   *Freiberg Lexicon* (Bible Works 7 – Revelation 12:17).

CHAPTER 18

SATAN'S ALLY IS READY

"And I stood upon the sand of the sea, and saw a beast rise up out of the sea, having seven heads and ten horns, and upon his horns ten crowns, and upon his heads the name of blasphemy" (Revelation 13:1).

"And I stood upon the sand of the sea, and saw" (vs 1)

Most expositors conclude from the oldest manuscripts that it is the dragon waiting on the seashore for the beast to arise and not John. This is the same beast as in Revelation 17, where the ten kingdoms/horns are not yet configured. From that study, we know that the rise in world power of this papal kingdom accelerated during the time of the sixth head, when a coalition between Rome and the world crescendoed. Finally, the eighth – the beast (the Holy See) reveals himself as a revitalized geopolitical kingdom.

"In the last days Satan will appear as an angel of light, with **great power** and **heavenly glory**, and claim to be the Lord of the whole earth. He will declare that the Sabbath has been changed from the seventh to the first day of the week; and as lord of the first day of the week he will present this spurious sabbath as a test of loyalty to him. **Then will take place** the final fulfillment of the Revelator's prophecy. [Rev. 13:4-18, quoted.]"[1]

This helpful insight adds to the expanding information of Satan's end-time tactics.

1. He knows his time is short (12:12).
2. "having great wrath," he makes war on the remnant of God's people (12:17).
3. Satan then waits for the opportune geopolitical alliance (13:1), the emergence of a blasphemous coalition centered in Rome.
4. There will follow an all-out attempt to annihilate the saints (13:15) – the "dragon was wroth" (12:17)

While appearing as man's benefactor, he is bent on destruction, working through his agents. This was presented in greater detail in the interlude of 17:6, where the woman that controls the beast was drunk with the blood of the saints. Thus, Satan, the dragon, filled with hatred, is seen standing on the seashore *waiting*. As of this writing (2015), that is where he is – waiting for:

1. The ten kingdoms of the world to give the papacy authority (partnership with the kings of the earth) (19:19)
2. The United States (second beast) to provide life and death enforcement power for the tenets of that sea beast

The emergence of the beast means everything to Satan's endgame. This relates to the prophecies of the "little horn" of Daniel 8, the "vile person" of Daniel 11:29-39 and the "king of the north" of Daniel 11:40-45. Its power will extend over a period of time (42 months). That

---

1   White, Ellen G.; *Manuscript Releases,* vol. 19, p. 282 (emphasis added).

encompasses the first five Seals, the end-time persecution of the saints (11:2) and when the two witnesses go out to warn the world of that final time (11:3). Daniel and Habakkuk call this the "appointed time" (Daniel 8:19, 11:35; Habakkuk 2:3). This is when there will be a:

- Conspiracy between Satan and Rome
- Universal success in that partnership, deceiving the world
- Temporary defeat of the saints[2]

This beast (*therion* – ferocious creature) comes out of the sea (alluding to the restless wicked casting onto the shore its slime and filth – Isaiah 57:20-21). It emerges out of the evil world. **But** – another message regarding its arrival has already been presented. It also came out of the abyss (11:7, 17:8) (where demons reside and hate it – Luke 8:31). This defines its very nature as demonic (Luke 9:1; 17:8; 20:1, 3). Satan awaits his partner in evil!

From the wicked populace of the world, who represent rebellion against God, comes this beast. The model for this end-time prophecy alludes to the four kingdom beasts of Daniel 7:3, which arose out of a restless sea.

"a beast rise up out of the sea," (vs 1)

This phrase reveals the emergence or appearance of a kingdom power with key characteristics. We were told in the interlude chapter (17) that this creature was controlled by the Roman Catholic Church.

The word for "rise up" is *anabainon* and refers to the appearance of the beast in

an upward, orderly motion.[3] This suggests that John viewed the designated beast parts in a specific anatomic order. The first part would be the horns – then, the heads. Since this is a continuation of the prophecy which chapter 17 introduces, the imagery is enhanced when seen together.

A wild/ferocious beast makes its debut from the tumult of wicked humanity. This suggests that this power comes into ascendancy when there are terrible world problems (moral conflicts). It appears to arise at a time when it becomes the temporal answer to seemingly irresolvable issues. This is affirmed by the note that the world then *wonders* after the beast. **By looking to the papacy for some answer,** a global issue is affecting everyone everywhere! But, unwittingly at first, the world becomes an accomplice to Satan's wrath and evil.

"having seven heads and ten horns, and upon his horns ten crowns," (vs 1)

The seven heads immediately guide us again to the scarlet colored beast of Revelation 17. Those are specific leaders of the beast kingdom. There, the head that "is," **began** the timing of this prophecy, which ties well with this narrative, where one of the heads was wounded to death and that deadly wound was healed (vs 3). As previously noted, that specifically applied to Pope John Paul II, who was shot in May 1981 and recovered. The beast can only have one head at a time – but it is referred to as the beast with seven heads for clarity.

Those seven heads lead us to the information relative to the horns. In 17:12 they are designated as kings without a kingdom "as yet." This last phrase (*oupo*)

2 Gaebelein, Frank E.; *The Expositor's Bible Commentary,* vol. 12 (Zondervan Publishing House, Grand Rapids, MI), 1984, p. 520.

3 *Freiberg Lexicon* (Bible Works 7 – Revelation 13:1).

means that there would come a time when they **would have** a kingdom or state under their jurisdiction.

It appears, through the imagery of the dragon waiting on the sandy seashore that the delay relates to the development of those kingdoms! *That* is the only change that has occurred from Revelation 17. The time for the two-beast alliance is here, but the support of the ten powers – the crowns – is anticipated, only needing to emerge.

Those crowns or *diademata* are a sign of royalty and rulership. They are not crowns of victory – as when conquering another. They appear prophetically as *all* abruptly present – simultaneously. It suggests that a world movement – a "new world order" – has come into being. The ten horns are not described as sequential – as are the heads. Thus, a new geopolitical system occurs at once.[4]

"and upon his heads the name of blasphemy." (vs 1)

There is an assumption that claiming deity power brings this designation. Is it through a "title" or by his function? Paul outlines these stages (II Thessalonians 2:4), echoing Old Testament messages regarding the antichrist:

1. Opposeth what is called God (Daniel 11:36, 7:25)
2. Exalteth himself above what is called God (Daniel 11:36)
3. Sits in temple as head of all religious elements (Isaiah 14:13)
4. Shows himself that he is God (Isaiah 14:14, Daniel 8:25)

The beast that represents the papacy and also Satan is worshiped and speaks out against God, His church and people. It is noteworthy that the blasphemy is on the heads of the beast. Chapter 17 makes it clear that they represent the leaders of the apostate kingdom/state in Rome. These are the popes since 1929 – beginning with Pope Pius XI. That is a solemn prophetic indictment that we will be required to share soon with the world.

"In the revelation that Christ gave are linked together in a chain of truth the important messages of warning that are to be given to the world before Christ's second coming. The last message of mercy is to be proclaimed where it has never yet been heard. The workers are to labor with such self-denial, such self-sacrifice, that *the message will be borne to those who have not heard it.* Letter 110, 1902, p. 4. (To Dr. David Paulson, July 7, 1902.). White Estate Washington, D.C. April 9, 1956."[5]

The world will need to be warned as to what this prophecy portends. It relates to Satan's final deception. Eternal loss versus eternal life lies immediately ahead for everyone.

"The broken ranks will be filled up by those represented by Christ as coming in at the eleventh hour. There are many with whom the Spirit of God is striving. The time of God's destructive judgments is the time of mercy for those who [now] have no opportunity to learn what is truth. Tenderly will the Lord look upon them. His heart of mercy is touched, His hand is still stretched out to save, while the door is closed to those who would not enter. Large numbers will be admitted *who in these last days*

4 Thomas, Robert L.; *Revelation 8–22 – An Exegetical Commentary* (Moody Press, Chicago – 1992), p. 155 (emphasis added).

5 White, Ellen G.; *Manuscript Releases,* vol. 1, pp. 372-373 (emphasis added).

hear the truth for the first time.–Letter 103, 1903."[6]

The anti-God beast has arrived. Satan is waiting on the beach for the ten-kingdom event. His strongest ally from Rome is ready to act as soon as definitive support comes from this emerging world order.

[6]   White, Ellen G.; *Last Day Events,* p. 182 (emphasis added).

CHAPTER 19

DANIEL AND JOHN FOCUS ON SATAN

"And the beast which I saw was like unto a leopard, and his feet were as *the feet* of a bear, and his mouth as the mouth of a lion: and the dragon gave him his power, and his seat, and great authority" (Revelation 13:2).

God immediately inspires John to disclose important facts about this terrible power.

"And the beast which I saw was like unto a leopard." (vs 2)

This instantly links us to Daniel 7:6 where that Old Testament prophet saw a leopard-like beast that represented the Grecian Empire (323–146 B.C.). That country, in turn, becomes an end-time symbol when it is depicted as a rough he-goat at war with the ram (Daniel 8:5-8, 21). There that Grecian goat represents Satan at war with Christ in a setting called the "time of the end" at an "appointed time" (Daniel 8:17, 19)!

Historically, that goat's initial horn was broken. In an end-time setting, that horn is shown as a little horn that grew to be great (Daniel 8:9-13), representing the papacy. It is then described as a "king of fierce countenance, and understanding dark sentences" (Daniel 8:23). The characteristics of that little horn and its fierce power represent the same power/kingdom as this leopard-like beast in Revelation 13 – same timing – same antichrist – both evil.

Key characteristics of that Daniel narrative discloses that second rise of the little horn as:

1. Starting small and became a massive power (vss 9, 24)
2. It came from the north (vs 9)
3. Persecuted God's people and leaders (vss 10, 24)
4. Filled with deceit (vss 23-24)
5. Magnified himself to the level of Christ (vss 11, 25)
6. Cast God's church down (vs 11)
7. Has a large following (vs 12)
8. Removes the Sabbath (vs 12)
9. Sets up a false sabbath (vs 12)
10. Satan – the he-goat – gives him his power

Already we have seen that blasphemy is a characteristic of this antichrist.

"and his feet were as *the feet* of a bear, and his mouth as the mouth of a lion:" (vs 2)

The story expands with the feet as that of a bear – symbolic of Medo-Persia. Since only the feet are portrayed, it must represent the crushing power of that war machine. The mouth of the lion illustrates the fierceness and power of its blasphemous words, portrayed as Babylon.

Many expositors feel that this beast is a composite of all the beasts of Daniel 7. To a minor degree this is true. However, the bear–lion ties are specific to the *action* of this leopard beast, per se, i.e., feet and mouth. Those symbols allude to *unique characteristics* that God says it displays. From its tie to Daniel, we can see by the description alone:

1. It is a power that will be tied to Satan – the rough he-goat
2. It will think nothing of "crushing" others to achieve its goals.
3. Its words will be self-serving and antichristian.

"and the dragon gave him his power, and his seat, and great authority" (vs 2)

This is another parody where God is really the one who gives power and permits (13:5, 7, 14-15). Yet three things are conveyed by Satan to this beast in a mockery exercise to show what he can wield: power, seat (judicial control of what liberty people have) and authority (jurisdiction over the world) (13:7). He tries to have the last word. This power comes from the "god of this world" (II Corinthians 4:4).

Its authority echoes once again the third beast or leopard of Daniel (7:6). He, too, was given authority to rule!

Since that anti-God authority, judicial power and supremacy relate to the descriptive characteristic of the beast heads – "blasphemy" – many conclude that this is the antichrist or man of sin depicted by Paul to the Thessalonians (II Thessalonians 2:1-12).[1] The ultimate prophetic focus is on the whole beast, historically represented by those papal heads and the ten kingdom horn powers. This also parallels the "king of the north" declaration when "he will magnify himself above every god and will say unheard of things against the God of gods" (Daniel 11:36, Revelation 13:4).

As Jesus shares the Father's throne (3:21), this beast shares the power on the throne of Satan (2:13). Satan had tried to convince Jesus that his dominion was to be coveted (Matthew 4:8, Luke 4:6).[2] He refused it. These moves are now seen as the devil's last attempt to garner followers for that ephemeral kingdom.

[1] Osborne, Grant R.; *Revelation* (Baker Book House; Grand Rapids, MI), pp. 493-494.
[2] Aune, David E.; *World Biblical Commentary; Revelation 17–22*, vol. 52c (World Books; Publisher, Dallas, Texas – 1997), p. 736.

THE "HEAD" – THAT'S HOW WE KNOW!

"And I saw one of his heads as it were wounded to death; and his deadly wound was healed: and all the world wondered after the beast" (Revelation 13:3).

"And I saw" (vs 3)

"I saw" is not in the original text. This is helpful because what follows has already occurred and has been only a point of reference. The dragon has been waiting for the ten kingdoms to give support to the beast (since the period noted in Revelation 17:12-13). Thus – John is not seeing a vision of the wounding of the head and its healing – as many contend. He is identifying this beast as the **one of importance** related to the wounding of one of its papal heads, which was then healed. The beast that begins this whole story in Revelation (17:10) is the one with the head that "is." By number, that head was Pope John Paul II – the sixth leader. This matches the prophecy of a head being wounded!

"one of his heads as it were wounded to death; and his deadly wound was healed:" (vs 3)

The assassination attempt on the sixth pope's life in 1981, from which he recovered, ties this beast with its specific heads to the beast here in chapter 13, which had had a wound that healed. They are the same beast.

The word "wounded" is in the perfect tense. It had occurred in the past in John's narrative. The word for "healed"

is etherapeuthe and is indicative that at some point in time this healing had also occurred. John first described the beast by comparing it to parts of the historical Daniel 7 beasts. Now he characterizes the beast by one of its seven end-time leaders having had a wound that was healed. This, in turn, now reveals its apocalyptic significance.

This is also a parody of Christ dying and coming to life (5:6).

"But there is a difference between the Lamb's recovery and that of the beast. The Lamb really did conquer and defeat death by its resurrection, but the beast's continued existence is not a reversal of his actual defeat. We have seen that the devil's defeat entailed his loss of authority to accuse saints and condemn them to spiritual perdition ... Though he and the beasts are repeatedly mentioned as having 'authority' in ch. 13, they have no authority over the saints and no authority but what God gives them."[1]

The identity of that specific pope/head means everything to our end-time understanding. Most scholars see the picture of the beast rising as eschatological, yet struggle to find an ancient Roman emperor who had a wound that was healed! That's unfortunate because its meaning and the very purpose that God gave this prophecy remains elusive to them.

In "John's description of the beast, there are numerous parallels with Jesus

---

[1] Beale, G. K.; *The New International Greek Testament Commentary; The Book of Revelation* (William B. Eerdmans Publishing Company, Grand Rapids, Michigan – 1999), p. 689.

that should alert the reader to the fact that John is seeking to establish, not a historical identification, but a theological characterization: Both wielded swords; both had followers on whose foreheads were inscribed their names (13;16–14:1); both had horns (5:6; 13:1); both were slain, the same Greek word being used to describe their deaths (*sphagizo,* vv 3, 8); both had arisen to new life and authority; and both were given (by different authorities) power over every nation, tribe, people, and tongue as well as over the kings of the earth (1:5; 7:9; with 13:7; 17:12). The beast described here is the great theological counterpart to all that Christ represents and not the [ancient] Roman Empire or any of its emperors. So it is easy to understand why many in the history of the church have identified the beast with a future personal Antichrist."[2] This *is* that evil power, which is now emerging onto the world scene!

"and all the world wondered after the beast." (vs 3)

The word for wondered (*ethaumasthe*) is the same one as used for the crowds' reaction to Jesus' miracles and teachings (Matthew 8:27, 9:33, 15:31, Mark 5:20).

This "world" that fawns over the papacy is described in 17:8 as those who are "not written in the book of life." The ambassadorial ties between the United States and the Holy See began a high level exchange of diplomats (1983). The world has since accelerated its political interest in Rome, and the papacy now sports 180 (2015) ambassadors from as many different nations. The irony of this is enormous. Note this report:

"AMBASSADOR TO THE HOLY SEE & RELIGIOUS TESTS FOR PUBLIC OFFICE

"America's ambassador to the Vatican is the most unusual and disputed appointment — ambassadorial or otherwise — that a president can make. First and foremost, it isn't really an ambassador to the Vatican city–state but rather an ambassador to the Holy See, which means they are a representative to the pope personally as the head of the Catholic Church. We don't send official representatives to any other religion, so why do we treat the Catholic Church as special and privileged?

"Because this ambassador is an official representative to the pope as head of the Catholic Church, the office has a de facto religious test: only practicing Catholics are even considered, never mind actually appointed. Can you imagine not even considering non-Jews as ambassadors to Israel or non-Hindus as ambassadors to India? Then, because only Catholics are considered as representatives to the pope, we should apparently narrow the religious tests even further by only considering those Catholics whose political and religious views are exactly what the pope prefers."[3]

---

2   Gaebelein, Frank E.; *The Expositor's Bible Commentary,* vol. 12 (Zondervan Publishing House, Grand Rapids, MI), 1984, p. 527.

3   http://atheism.about.com/b/2008/12/11/ ambassador-to-the-holy-see-religious-tests-for-public-office.htm

Pope Francis

This world-wondering prophecy regarding the Roman Church is stunning! World leadership pours into the Vatican each week, where "neutrality" is perceived on global issues. An unprecedented gesture occurred September 8, 2014, when retired Israeli president, Shimon Perez visited Pope Francis. He said, "Perhaps for the first time in history, the Holy Father is a leader not only respected by many people, but also by different religions and their leaders." "In fact," Perez clarified, "he is perhaps the only truly respected leader "in the world today."[4] He then told Pope Francis that he should lead in a coalition of world religions.

There is another issue that this verse entertains! For the world to look in worshipful awe to the papacy – including pagan, Islamic and atheistic regimes – some extreme event or events must convene to turn their attention to this religious power. It is unfathomable to conceive a small sovereign power of 108 acres geographically within another power (Italy) drawing such dependent attention without a "reason."

Most countries now view the Vatican with great favor. There are few conceivable things that might cause the whole world to look at this religious power in such a dramatic way as is unraveled in this prophecy. Looking to a "God"-dependent leader at a time of helplessness might be one. The most important (which Christ said would precede earth's final events), calamities, is anticipated (Matthew 24, Mark 13, Luke 21).

Intriguingly, He noted that after they begin to occur together (distinctly in a defined way), persecution would follow. That's very interesting. Here in Revelation 13 a key focus is the persecution of the saints! Another reason is portrayed – a religious issue! There is a tie between calamities, religious matters and persecution. *This* brings focused attention, *at this time(!),* to the Roman Catholic Church. The world wonders after the beast because it has an apparent answer to the devastating helplessness of the world.

"Satan puts his interpretation upon events, and they think, as he would have them, that the calamities which fill the land are a result of Sunday breaking. Thinking to appease the wrath of God these influential men make laws enforcing Sunday observance.–10MR 239 (1899)."[5] Rome has already urged such laws be developed with civil enforcement.

Stay tuned. This is just the beginning of the unthinkable.

Pope Francis and
Shimon perez

---

4 Perez, Shimon; *Jerusalem Post*, September 9, 2014 (Brian Schrauger).

5 White, Ellen G.; *Last Day Events*, p. 129.

CHAPTER 21

MESMERIZED BY A RELIGIOUS POWER

"And they worshipped the dragon which gave power unto the beast: and they worshiped the beast, saying, Who *is* like unto the beast? who is able to make war with him?" (Revelation 13:4).

In Christ's wilderness retort to the dragon's attempts to get Him to bow down in obeisance, He said: "Thou shalt worship the Lord thy God, and him only shalt thou serve" (Matthew 9:10, Luke 4:8). It's stunning to even imagine that Satan would be so bold and presumptuous as to ask to be worshiped! Yet, it was one of the temptations of Christ. That simple act would make Christ's suffering unnecessary and vindicate Satan's claims against God. Christ refused! Here, a suffering world worships the dragon and the beast! It is a "time of sorrows" (Matthew 24:8). These evil powers promise salvic relief through persecution of the saints – the declared "cause" for its pain and sorrow.

No wonder the sacred record shares the uplifting Messianic praise, "Worthy is the Lamb that was slain to receive power, and riches, and wisdom, and strength, and honour, and glory, and blessing (Revelation 5:12). Why? *He suffered to bring us eventual relief.*

The picture here is fascinating. Satan is worthy of nothing except destruction (Revelation 20:10). Yet, there is a final interlude of time called the "appointed time," when God permits him nearly full independence in the world he claims. This world adores him and his earthly beast representative! Through earth's most sinister deceptions, that allegiance appears Messianic.

"And they worshipped the dragon which gave power unto the beast:" (vs 4)

Why does the world worship the dragon? Satan claimed equality with God (Isaiah 14:13-14, Ezekiel 28:2). Might the world now believe that deceptive claim? He *is* seen as God. A significant issue is unfolding. In Revelation 17:11, when the eighth "head" (beast) becomes apparent, Satan will solidify his power through the papacy. That reality is all unfolded here in Chapter 13.

The weight of evidence suggests that *immediately preceding and during* this period, which has now begun, Satan will make his debut. Thus, we will soon see him worshiped along with the papacy. This takes on the form of actual prostration and suggests intense individual submission.

"Satan has long been preparing for his final effort to deceive the world. The foundation of his work was laid by the assurance given to Eve in Eden, 'Ye shall not surely die.' 'In the day ye eat thereof, then your eyes shall be opened, and ye shall be as gods, knowing good and evil.' [Gen. 3:4, 5.] Little by little he has prepared the way for his master-piece of deception in the development of Spiritualism. He has not yet reached the full accomplishment of his designs; but it will be reached in the last remnant of time. Says the prophet: 'I saw three unclean spirits like frogs; ... they are the spirits of devils, working miracles, which go forth unto the kings of the earth and of the whole world, to gather them to the battle of that great day of God Almighty.' [Rev. 16:13, 14.] Except those who are kept by the power of God, through faith in his Word, *the whole world will be swept into the ranks of this delusion.* The people are fast being lulled to a fatal security, to be awakened only by the outpouring of the wrath of God."[1]

"As the crowning act in the great drama of deception, Satan himself will personate Christ. The church has long professed to look to the Saviour's advent as the consummation of her hopes. Now the great deceiver will make it appear that Christ has come. In different parts of the earth, Satan will manifest himself among men as a majestic being of dazzling brightness, resembling the description of the Son of God given by John in the Revelation. [Rev. 1:13-15.] The glory that surrounds him is unsurpassed by anything that mortal eyes have yet beheld. The shout of triumph rings out upon the air, 'Christ has come! Christ has come!' The people prostrate themselves in adoration before him, while he lifts up his hands, and pronounces a blessing upon them, as Christ blessed his disciples when he was upon the earth. His voice is soft and subdued, yet full of melody. In gentle, compassionate tones he presents some of the same gracious, heavenly truths which the Saviour uttered; he heals the diseases of the people, and then, in his assumed character of Christ, he claims to have changed the Sabbath to Sunday, and commands all to hallow the day which he has blessed. He declares that those who persist in keeping holy the seventh day are blaspheming his name by refusing to listen to his angels sent to them with light and truth. This is the strong,

almost overmastering delusion. Like the Samaritans who were deceived by Simon Magus, the multitudes, from the least to the greatest, give heed to these sorceries, saying, This is 'the great power of God.' [Acts 8:10.]"[2]

Satan has been waiting for his moment. One can't help but muse: "What is in his heart as people bow before him? Is his acceptance one of love and bonding? Or, is that hate-filled mind gratified at their depraved servitude? Likely, the latter. He has garnered more victims.

Fascinating is the timing of this dazzling homage towards Satan. It portrays another of his parodies. It won't be long – three and a half years – that God and Jesus will receive adoration, worship, reverence and adulation. "And every creature which is in heaven, and on the earth, and under the earth, and such as are in the sea, and all that are in them, heard I saying, Blessing, and honour, and glory, and power, be unto him that sitteth upon the throne, and unto the Lamb for ever and ever" (Revelation 5:13). The devil's power will then be at an end.

"There is a limit beyond which Satan cannot go, and here he calls deception to his aid and counterfeits the work which he has not power actually to perform. In the last days he will appear in such a manner as to make men believe him to be Christ come the second time into the world. He will indeed transform himself into an angel of light. But while he will bear the appearance of Christ in every particular, so far as mere appearance goes, it will deceive none but those who, like Pharaoh, are seeking to resist the truth. – 5T 698 (1889)."[3]

The phrase "which gave power unto the beast" is another cue to the bondage that

1   White, Ellen G.; *The Great Controversy,* pp. 561-562 (1888) (emphasis added).

2   *Ibid.,* p. 624.
3   White, Ellen G.; *Last Day Events,* p. 163.

even Satan's host experience. The beast is totally dependent on the dragon's power. In turn, the relationship is one of satanic servitude.

"and they worshipped the beast," (vs 4)

This represents a deification of man. It is a diversion of attention away from God to the worship of a world power and the figure who heads it up.[4] Again, the question from such a dramatic prophecy is: What causes planet earth to give such allegiance to the papacy?

It was previously revealed that it was "blasphemous." The key to this understanding appears to be its convincing exaltation to be like God or perceived like Him: "Who opposeth and exalteth himself above all that is called God, or that is worshipped; so that he as God sitteth in the temple of God, showing himself that he is God" (II Thessalonians 2:4). He is exhibiting a magnetic power that the corrupt world craves, which appeals to their selfish desires.

This echoes the explicit antichrist posturing in Daniel (Daniel 8:11, 25; 11:36-37). There, the description of an end-time, Roman-centered power is similar. Its great sin is rebellion against the Sabbath!

The ten horns' support of the beast alludes directly to Revelation 17:12. Thus, there is not only spiritual identity but civil authority giving obeisance and honor to the papacy. The beast also shares seductive teachings that God calls "abominations" in the harlot's golden cup (17:4). This is identified as the "wine of her fornication." When something God creates or gives that is sacred is discarded for a substitute never sanctioned by heaven, it is an

"abomination" to Him. When the substitute is shared, it is fornication. The Sabbath for Sunday, as we will see, is *the* issue[5] that brings idolatrous worship here. That is why God showed John that its heads were filled with the names of blasphemy!

This apocalyptic book will note such worship again, repeated in 13:8, 12; 14:9, 11; and 20:4. Many scholars say that this worship "is because" the dragon gives it authority.[6] That is, of course, the bottom line. The pope currently receives homage of such intensity, both in his appearance and in liturgy, one could claim that such a worship experience has begun (see the following pictures – this and next page).

There is another fascinating dimension, however. Could there be in this prophecy an allusion to such an assumption of "godlikeness" that the hearts of the world see the pope and papacy as God? (Exodus 20:3, 34:14; Deuteronomy 6:4; Psalm 44:20; Jeremiah 1:16, 11:13). Taking

Giving obeisance to the pope!

4   Thomas, Robert L.; *Revelation 8–22 – An Exegetical Commentary* (Moody Press, Chicago – 1992), p. 160.

5   White, Ellen G.; *The Signs of the Times,* February 22, 1910.

6   Beale, G. K.; *The New International Greek Testament Commentary; The Book of Revelation* (William B. Eerdmans Publishing Company, Grand Rapids, Michigan – 1999), p. 694.

honor due God is not only idolatry but a **supreme** expression of blasphemy. This will be the issue in the last phrase of this verse. But that role will come only if the leaders of the world and its inhabitants see the papacy *as answering a need* that they regard as helpless to solve. Since the words "cup of fornication," "blasphemy," "Babylon" and "war" against the remnant are used in chapters 12 and 17, there is a "spiritual cry" for help that leads to a confederated loyalty to Rome.

"To the very close of time ... [the papacy] will carry forward his work of deception. In both the Old and the New World, the papacy will receive homage in the honor paid to the Sunday institution that rests solely upon the authority of the Romish Church."[7]

Again, what could be the catalyst of helplessness, leading to this affinity to Rome?

"Men in responsible positions will not only ignore and despise the Sabbath themselves, but from the sacred desk will urge upon the people the observance of the first day of the week, pleading tradition and custom in behalf of this man-made institution. *They will point to calamities on land and sea – to the storms of wind, the floods, the earthquakes, the destruction by fire – as judgments indicating God's displeasure because Sunday is not sacredly observed.* These calamities will increase more and more, one disaster will follow close upon the heels of another; and those who make void the law of God will point to the few who are keeping the Sabbath of the fourth commandment as the ones who are bringing wrath upon the world. This falsehood is Satan's device that he may ensnare the unwary."[8]

Will this issue spread to encompass the world?

"The so-called Christian world is to be the theater of great and decisive actions. Men in authority will enact laws controlling the conscience, after the example of the papacy. Babylon will make all nations drink of the wine of the wrath of her fornication. Every nation will be involved. Of this time John the Revelator declares: [Rev. 18:3-7; 17:13, 14, quoted]. 'These have one mind.'"[9]

The Sabbath–Sunday issue was opened as an end-time matter in Daniel 8, 9 and 12. Those are predominantly end-time prophecies. Here in Revelation 13 is the description of how they will all be fulfilled!

Can you imagine, even in a small way, the world's reaction to massive devastating calamities that paralyze segments of the earth? Since Satan has already appeared, a word from him as to cause and effect will point the finger of guilt at Sabbath keepers.

"Satan puts his interpretation upon events, and they think, as he would have them, that the calamities which fill the land are a result of Sundaybreaking. Thinking to appease the wrath of God these influential

7   White, Ellen G.; *The Great Controversy,* p. 578 (1988).

8   White, Ellen G.; *The Southern Watchman,* June 28, 1904 (emphasis added).

9   White, Ellen G.; *Last Day Events,* pp. 136-137.

MESMERIZED BY A RELIGIOUS POWER

men make laws enforcing Sunday observance."[10]

The "worship of the beast" resides in bringing allegiance and honor to an institution of the papacy. Sunday worship becomes an issue so intense it forms the basis for "a legal war" against the saints who keep the commandments of God. They are the focus of "cause."

Sylvester I, 314–335 A.D., was the first bishop of Rome to call himself "pope." He decreed the first Sunday law (ecclesiastical), defining it as the Lord's Day. Constantine, Roman Emperor and friend, decreed the first civil Sunday law with strong anti-Semitic lines (Appendix II, p. ~178).

Thus, the institution of Sunday as a worship day came from Rome – first that church, then that empire. This concept of assumed authority to change one of the ten commandments will mature as this unholy power in prophecy continues. The papacy and the Roman Catholic Church are given obeisance through a blasphemous institution – a false worship day.

The helpless experience from destructive calamities will bring this key reactant issue against God's remnant.

"saying, Who _is_ like unto the beast? who is able to make war with him?" (vs 4)

"Who is like unto" is another parody relating to God! (Exodus 8:10, 15:11; Psalm 71:19; 89:8; Isaiah 44:7; Micah 7:18). The honor or worship given the papacy and its heads only belong to God.

This, once again, was prophesied by Daniel in 8:10-13, 22-25, 11:31. There, the beast power is seen as persecuting God's

people. That "war" is at first successful (Revelation 13:7). "Who can challenge that power?"

The question, "Who can defeat him?" was already answered in a _commentary insert_ in Revelation 12:11: "And they overcame him by the blood of the Lamb, and by the word of their testimony; and they loved not their lives unto the death."

The saints will declare victory over the dragon. Then God's wrath will bring the beast and his image into final judgment (14:10-11).

"These shall make war with the Lamb, and the Lamb shall overcome them: for he is Lord of lords, and King of kings: and they that are with him are called, and chosen, and faithful" (17:14). Thus, from the saints' vantage ground, they cry: Who can deliver us from the power ... of the beast?[11] It will be "the Lamb."

In the context of this chapter, the worship "factor" will also be seen as "making an image" to the beast. In ancient Rome "worship" could even be towards a symbol representing a revered person or being. It is done "on behalf of" not necessarily to.[12] It is a form of idolatry.

The "image" and "mark" of the beast will come front and center stage in the verses ahead, appealing to such idolatrous loyalties. The worship of the papal standard will be seen as worshiping the papacy.

The irony is picturesque. Those who arrogantly cry in defiance, "Who is like unto our god?" "Who is able to make war against him?" will soon cry another final desperate wish: "I must escape your God." "And said to the mountains and rocks, Fall on us, and hide us from the face of him

---

10 _Ibid.,_ p. 129 and _Manuscript Releases,_ vol. 10, p. 239 (1899).

11 Aune, David E.; _World Biblical Commentary; Revelation 17–22,_ vol. 52c (World Books; Publisher, Dallas, Texas – 1997), p. 742

12 _Ibid.,_ p. 741.

that sitteth on the throne, and from the wrath of the Lamb" (Revelation 6:16).

Then they ask rhetorically, "For the great day of his wrath is come; and who shall be able to stand?" (Revelation 6:17). Their sad lives and rebellion will then end.

God fills every prophecy with clocks. This narrative is no exception. Let's now see if we can tell "what time" all this will happen!

CHAPTER 22

THE PREDESTINED TIME PERIOD

"And there was given unto him a mouth speaking great things and blasphemies; and power was given unto him to continue forty *and* two months (Revelation 13:5).

In the previous verse the world is so enamored by the beast that they ask "power-related" questions. Who can match anything like the papacy? Who can stand up to him? Little do they know that they will soon be crying when they see Jesus' face, "Who shall be able to stand?" (6:17). This will occur shortly after the noted 42 months ends.

A new part of this saga now unfolds. Here is another reason the world wonders after this church/state (defined in Revelation 17).

"And there was given unto him" (vs 5)

The papacy is given permission by God to reveal who she really is. This is one of His amazing judicial acts just before the second coming. The character of Satan and his minions is to be fully expressed. The papal exhibition of power appeals to the selfish motives of man's heart – more on that later.

Satan had tried to kill the Christ child (12:4-5), he had fought the very kingdom of God in heaven (12:7), he made accusations against God's people (12:10), then came persecution of the saints (12:14-15). This chapter fills in details of that hatred towards God's people. The sacred record says, however, that they (the remnant – the saints) will "overcome" him by the blood of the Lamb" (12:11).

In the context of Satan's knowledge that his "time was short," God gives him one more chance to reveal his side of the conflict. The war that is waged against the church is God contained. How do we know? *There is a time limit!* Elsewhere, we see similar expressions of controlled "permission" (6:4, 8; 7:2; 9:5).

"a mouth speaking great things and blasphemies;" (vs 5)

This mouth looks like a lion's (13:2). Though Christ is the "Lion of the tribe of Juda" (5:5), the focus here is on the mouth of this apostate power. This relates to a prior warning by Peter: "Be sober, be vigilant; because your adversary the devil, as a roaring lion, walketh about, seeking whom he may devour" (I Peter 5:8).

The "speaking" echoes the little horn of Daniel (7:8), where it proclaimed "great things." The blasphemous words were "boasting" (Daniel 7:11, 20) "against the Most High" (7:25). A similar theme comes from the evil king of the north: "And the king shall do according to his will; and he shall exalt himself, and magnify himself above every god, and shall speak marvellous things against the God of gods, and shall prosper till the indignation be accomplished: for that is determined shall be done" (Daniel 11:36). This mouth is slandering the name of God and demanding the nations give him worship instead of the Father. "Speaking" also suggests that a legal net is being cast around the world's inhabitants – decrees, laws, are being created against heaven.

Throughout Revelation the word "great" is used often to relate to acts of God (e.g., 8:8, 10; 12:14; 18:21; 20:11). Also, "great" voices refer to angelic anthems of honor and praise (e.g., 1:10; 5:2, 12; 7:2, 10; 8:13; 10:3).[1] There are places, however, where Satan and his agents attempt to usurp that "greatness."

- Speaking "great" things – suggesting it is making demands or giving orders that belong only within God's patronage
- "Great" dragon (12:3, 9) – the supreme power of evil – Satan
- Forces of evil claiming greatness (16:19, 17:1, 19:2)
- Babylon – that "great city" (e.g., 14:8) – center of apostasy

Is there a way that God's name and honor can be slandered in relationship to the Decalogue? The emphasis of the "remnant" keeping the commandments (12:17), as do the "saints" (14:12), raises a question of contrasting loyalties. Since the sin of the little horn (papacy) is against the Sabbath (Daniel 8:13), this "speaking" out against God of this Rome-centered church must have resistance to that holy day. Intriguingly, the Sabbath commandment identifies *which God* belongs to His people – the Creator God. It is also God's mark or sign of re-creation (Exodus 31:13, 16-17). If a law(s) is made to change that worship day – the *identity* of God would be marred. That *is the* matter at hand in this chapter.

A change in that sacred day would be blasphemy. We see unraveling how Satan and the papacy act when given the chance. A hopeful theme from Daniel, which John draws on beautifully, is the sovereignty of God over world governments (Daniel 4:17, 25, 32).[2] Though experiencing horrible things just ahead, God's people know that in the end He conquers.

"to continue forty *and* two months." (vs 5)

This clearly states that the papacy has been granted this limited amount of time to work. It will be a frantic period of hateful activity as was noted in Daniel's "little horn" visions (chapters 7 and 8). This period of time represents the last half of the 70th week of the Daniel 9 prophecy. Since the probation for the Jewish people ended at the Cross (Matthew 21:43, 23:36-39), the final purpose of the 490-year mission is yet to be accomplished. John's prophecy notes that there *will* be a remnant (12:17) and saints (14:12).

A final prophetic application to this time period was noted by E. G. White.[3]

This 42-month period is closely associated with Daniel 7:25, 12:14 and Revelation 11:2-3. In Daniel it also notes that the little horn not only speaks great words against the Most High but thinks to "change times and laws." The issue of redefining God through a change in the Sabbath comes forward again.

Three and a half years is a predestined eschatological period of time.[4] It is important to note that the beast with crowned horns coalition is in place before this 42-month period begins!

1   Osborne, Grant R.; *Revelation* (Baker Book House; Grand Rapids, MI), p. 499.

2   Thomas, Robert L.; *Revelation 8–22 – An Exegetical Commentary* (Moody Press, Chicago – 1992), p. 161.

3   White, Ellen G.; *Manuscript Releases,* vol. 19, p. 282.

4   Aune, David E.; *World Biblical Commentary; Revelation 17–22,* vol. 52c (World Books; Publisher, Dallas, Texas – 1997), p. 743.

CHAPTER 23

OUT OF HIS TERRIBLE MOUTH

"And he opened his mouth in blasphemy against God, to blaspheme his name, and his tabernacle, and them that dwell in heaven" (Revelation 13:6).

Some time ago John was describing Christ (called "another mighty angel") as crying with a loud voice. Then he added, "as when a lion roareth" (10:1, 3). In another parody of Christ, the beast here is opening its lion-like mouth. The beast is speaking in an official or authoritative manner. Since the world wonders after the papacy, this message is addressed to them.

"And he opened his mouth in blasphemy against God," (vs 6)

The name of blasphemy was on its heads (13:1) as on its scarlet colored body (17:3). It is the epitome of desecration of holiness and profanity against heaven.

This description (addressed in Revelation 17) is a crushing indictment against:

- The Vatican state
- The pope as its leader

Its ability to communicate heresy is supreme. The world listens and commensurates.

Clearly, this characteristic is not an incidental expression but a permanent part of the beast's nature. He is Satan's mouthpiece.[1] He resembles the "king of the north" of Daniel 11:36-45. God revealed the consequence of this type of sin: "He that blasphemeth the name of the LORD, he shall surely be put to death, *and* all the congregation shall certainly stone him: as well the stranger, as he that is born in the land, when he blasphemeth the name *of the LORD*, shall be put to death" (Leviticus 24:16).

The "teaching" authority of the beast is expressed through its mouth. This is an allusion to Daniel 7:8, 11 and 20. "I considered the horns, and, behold, there came up among them another little horn, ... I beheld then because of the voice of the great words which the horn spake" (Daniel 7:8b, 11a).

This "blasphemy" enhances the idea that it deceives and draws loyalty from the world through pretense. Daniel 7:25 noted: "And he shall speak *great* words against the most High, and shall wear out the saints of the most High." Then in Daniel 11:32 and 36 (NAS): "by smooth [deceitful] words he will turn to godlessness those who act wickedly." Tragically, the world listens!

"to blaspheme his name, and his tabernacle, and them that dwell in heaven." (vs 6)

To blaspheme God's name is to slander Him. It is a usurpation of that name by claiming it or posing as His holy representative, demanding obeisance due only to God. In the Lord's prayer the sacred honor conveyed to God is expressed in "hallowed be thy name" (Matthew

---

[1] Thomas, Robert L.; *Revelation 8–22 – An Exegetical Commentary* (Moody Press, Chicago – 1992), p. 162.

6:9, Luke 11:2). That honor only goes to divine beings! It is a violation of the third commandment (Exodus 20:7, Deuteronomy 5:11) to blaspheme.

The "little horn" of Daniel 8:9-12 grew till it reached the "host of heaven" (the goal of the tower of Babel).[2] Then it set itself up to be as great as the "Prince of the host." Next, truth was cast to the ground. Both reflect the behavior of the antichrist right at the end against God.

The next imprecation is against the tabernacle or those "who inhabit heaven." There is not an "and" in the Greek (like the NIV correctly conveys – 13:6) between these last two phrases. The tabernacle represents those who are *citizens of heaven*. In 12:12 those who "dwell in heaven" represent saints who could be either on earth or in heaven.[3] This is in contradistinction to those who "inhabit the earth" (13:8, 12).

The antichrist tries to come in and control the church – our spiritual lives – in apostasy. But God's great plan, as later noted by John: "And I heard a great voice out of heaven saying, Behold, the tabernacle of God is with men, and he will dwell with them, and they shall be his people, and God himself shall be with them, and be their God" (21:3). We become one with Him. The tabernacle is more than a place – it is Divine fellowship with His glorified people.

Blaspheme against God's tabernacle replicates a similar travesty in Daniel 8:10-13 where the little horn papacy causes some of the host of heaven and some of the stars to fall to the earth, causing, then, the place of the sanctuary to be cast down.[4] Paul equates the church as in

heaven (Ephesians 2:6, Colossians 3:1). The beast does everything to displace that fellowship with God through deceit and persecution. False standards that mock God are placed before the people. One unites by coercion and control, the other through love and friendship.

Two end-time warnings of abominable temple intrusions are noted in the New Testament.

- "When ye therefore shall see the abomination of desolation, spoken of by Daniel the prophet, *stand in the holy place*, (whoso readeth, let him understand:)" (Matthew 24:15).
- The "man of sin" will be revealed "Who opposeth and exalteth himself above all that is called God, or that is worshipped; so that he as God *sitteth in the temple of God,* [here now is the key] *showing himself that he is God*" (II Thessalonians 2:4).

The pope and his "Holy See" attempt to redefine what Christianity means by recharacterizing God. By such an act, he/she symbolically enters the temple precincts by demanding worship of its institution or leader. This arrogance is blatantly portrayed in the Catholic catechism: "26. Basing itself on Scripture and Tradition, the Council teaches that *the Church,* a pilgrim now on earth, *is necessary for salvation:* the one Christ is the mediator and the way of salvation; he is present to us in his body which is the Church. He himself explicitly asserted the necessity of faith and Baptism, and thereby affirmed at the same time the necessity of the Church which men enter

2 Osborne, Grant R.; *Revelation* (Baker Book House; Grand Rapids, MI), p. 500.
3 *Ibid.*
4 Beale, G. K.; *The New International Greek*

Testament Commentary; The Book of Revelation (William B. Eerdmans Publishing Company, Grand Rapids, Michigan – 1999), p. 697.

through baptism as through a door. Hence they could not be saved who, knowing that the Catholic Church was founded as necessary by God through Christ, would refuse either to enter it or to remain in it."[5]

The Holy See redefines salvation, man's way to God's throne, what the church represents and claims blasphemous power of its leaders – which belong only to God!

This institution is described in Daniel 7:25, speaking as an "eschatological fiend" who not only speaks out against God but equates himself with God.[6]

---

[5] *Catechism of the Catholic Church,* #846 (Catholic Book Publishing Co., New York).

[6] Beale, *op. cit.,* p. 696.

WARRING AGAINST GOD'S LOYALISTS

"And it was given unto him to make war with the saints, and to overcome them: and power was given him over all kindreds, and tongues, and nations" (Revelation 13:7).

"And it was given unto him to make war with the saints, and to overcome them:" (vs 7)

This prophecy was first conveyed in Daniel 7:21, where the little horn would make war against the saints and prevail. That timing is also just before Christ comes, and judgment comes in favor of the saints (Daniel 7:22). Its end-time setting is again noted in Daniel 8:10, where resistance comes during an "appointed time."

Then in the story of the two witnesses, the beast that ascended out of hell is prophesied to "make war against them" (Revelation 11:7) during a three-and-a half-year period (Revelation 11:3). The beast does succeed in its "shall overcome them, and kill them." In an "interlude" the woman who controls the beast was "drunk with the blood of the saints, and with the blood of the martyrs" (17:6). This is a solemn message.

"Overcoming" the saints is a ghastly insight into the hatred and violence that will fall on God's faithful at the end. But – their spiritual well-being remains unblemished. Their physical lives are alone threatened. This group of loyal saints represents those who escape into the wilderness (12:14), a symbol of God's spiritual care and protection. Not all are martyred – but that

possibility is a God-permitted act at this time.[1]

Thus, the beast is given license to make war as is the dragon (12:17). We are again alerted by these words: "And it was given." God is letting Satan exhibit to the universe what he is really like when given freedom to "be himself."

"Of those who honor Jesus, and keep the commandments of the Lord, Christ has said, 'Marvel not if the world hate you.' We can expect no better treatment from the world than the treatment given to the law of God. Those who vindicate the law of God by keeping the commandments, will be targets for the wrath of the dragon, and opposition to righteousness will not end until evil is destroyed; for as long as human nature is under the control of the enemy of all righteousness, enmity to the righteous will be manifested through the children of men. The offense of the cross has not ceased by any means. Satan has his most efficient batteries masked under pretensions to godliness, and he will cause them to open fire upon the followers of Jesus Christ. The servants of God must expect that they will be reviled, misrepresented, maligned, persecuted, and oppressed; for all who 'will live godly in Christ Jesus shall suffer persecution.' The people of God will stand firm to the faith only through the grace of God. 'The dragon was wroth with the woman, and went to make war with the remnant of her seed, which keep the commandments of God,

---

[1] Thomas, Robert L.; *Revelation 8–22 – An Exegetical Commentary* (Moody Press, Chicago – 1992), p. 163.

and have the testimony of Jesus Christ.' The great rebel against God is leading his armies to the conflict; but let the followers of Christ bear in mind the fact that he can bruise only the heel, while those who are loyal to Christ by their fidelity and piety shall bruise the head of the serpent. While men are making void the law of God, we must pray, as did David, 'It is time for thee, Lord, to work; for they have made void thy law.' Through Christ believers will gain the mastery, and inch by inch they will contest the ground, and obtain the victory."[2]

"With God's presence and favor, His people are safe, although they may suffer persecution for the truth's sake. His goodness and the riches of His grace are their protection and salvation."[3]

"and power was given him over all kindreds, and tongues, and nations." (vs 7)

God permits – but the direct endowment here of sovereign might comes directly from Satan! Can you imagine unleashing the devil's murderous hatred as a world power? The imagery is stunning and demands the closest ties to Jesus. The list of kindreds, tongues and nations has been used before (5:9, 7:9, 10:11, 11:9, 14:6, 17:15) and always refers to the wicked, unbelieving world.

"We know that we are of God, and the whole world lieth in wickedness" (I John 5:19).

The beast – the papacy, with the last pope – will achieve what no other power in earth's history has accomplished – coercive control. This was its original commission from Satan (13:2b). The scope of that mission is unique in world history. Amazing will be this religious power, wielding a final scepter over earth!

A great note of hope is submitted in the first prophecy of this horrendous power in Daniel. Its subversive oppression continues "until the ancient of Days came and pronounced judgment in favor of the saints of the Most High, and the time came when they possessed the kingdom" (Daniel 7:22 – NAS). The little horn antichrist that waged war is now vanquished.[4]

The beast "conquered" the saints by silencing them (Revelation 11:7) through persecution and martyrdom (13:7). But – that power is short-lived (42 months).[5]

They have victory over the beast (15:2). This replicates the victory that Christ had over Satan. When the saints share the "fellowship of His suffering" (Philippians 3:10), they ultimately share in His victory and finally take possession of the kingdom.

2   White, Ellen G.; *The Signs of the Times,* November 14, 1895.
3   White, Ellen G.; *Sermons and Talks,* vol. 2, p. 329.
4   Steinmann, Andrew E.; *Daniel* (Concordia Publishing House, St. Louis, 2008), p. 372.
5   Osborne, Grant R.; *Revelation* (Baker Book House; Grand Rapids, MI), p. 501.

CHAPTER 25

WORSHIP BEAST VS WORSHIP GOD

"And all that dwell upon the earth shall worship him, whose names are not written in the book of life of the Lamb slain from the foundation of the world. If any man have an ear, let him hear" (Revelation 13:8-9).

"And all that dwell upon the earth shall worship him." (vs 8)

A sweeping description of who these people are was just given (vs 7):

- All kindred
- All tongues } They are the wicked from the entire world.
- All nations

In Revelation 17:2 the kings of the earth have an illicit relationship with Babylon – Roman apostate Christianity. The world follows her.

This almost unbelievable prophecy reveals a universal loyalty to the pope/

Vatican! In the way this "future tense" message is written, "This cannot ... refer to any situation in the past or present but must refer to the eschatological future when the rule of the beast will include the entire known world."[1]

Amazing is this dossier. The beast has nearly universal success in attracting worshipers. This will be the ultimate achievement of Satan. It will resonate as a new world order and the pinnacle of ecumenism.

It is fascinating that the word "him" is *auton*. This confirms that the beast must be a person as well as a kingdom. The focus in chapter 17 was first on the heads and then the beast. That sequenced into this Revelation 13 beast imagery!

"whose names are not written in the book of life of the Lamb slain from the foundation of the world" (vs 8)

The grammar is actually singular ("whose name is."). The world is worshiping the wrong "god," resulting in its *individuals* being eliminated from that heavenly citizenship book. This book is noted five other times (3:5; 17:8; 20:12, 15; 21:27) and refers to a divine registry of those destined for the heavenly kingdom. Here, the way it is expressed suggests that a judicial decision has made their eternal destiny "permanent."[2] The beast worshipers are inhabitants of the earth and will not be inhabitants of heaven.

The Lamb's book is a coveted place to have one's name recorded and retained. In the Old Testament it was recognized as the place where the names of the righteous are kept (Psalm 69:28, Daniel 12:1). The latter was noted initially to be the record of all of "Daniel's people," which expanded that designation to the universal church. Then Michael will deliver "every one whose name is found written in the book."

That book is the "Lamb's Book of Life." It was His blood that won the victory over

---

[1] Aune, David E.; *World Biblical Commentary; Revelation 17–22*, vol. 52c (World Books; Publisher, Dallas, Texas – 1997), p. 746.

[2] Thomas, Robert L.; *Revelation 8–22 – An Exegetical Commentary* (Moody Press, Chicago – 1992), p. 164.

the dragon on behalf of the saints (12:11). They, in turn, washed their robes in that blood (7:14). Their names belong there!

When the beast comes to its end (16:19, 17:8), the world will then wonder in a different way. They are identified as those not written in the Book of Life but had been there at "the foundation of the world." This unique message reveals a plan of redemption that encompasses everyone. Each individual was chosen by that restoration plan and written in the book. "Forasmuch as ye know that ye were not redeemed with corruptible things, *as* silver and gold, from your vain conversation *received* by tradition from your fathers; But with the precious blood of Christ, as of a lamb without blemish and without spot: Who verily was foreordained before the foundation of the world, but was manifest in these last times for you" (I Peter 1:18-20). God does have the authority to remove that name.

Moses understood that language! The very first Biblical account occurred after the golden calf incident. God's wrath was about to explode and, in a beautiful rendition of devotion to wayward Israel, Moses offered his life *if their lives could not be spared* – "blot me out of the book you have written" (Exodus 32:32-33).[3] God also made it clear to the Sardis Church that only the "overcomers" will be clothed in white raiment and He will then not blot them out of the Book of Life (Revelation 3:5). That suggests that there is a period of probation before judgment.

Some have concluded that the names of the wicked were eliminated at creation based on: "and they that dwell on the earth shall wonder, whose names were not written in the book of life from the foundation of the world, when they behold

the beast that was, and is not, and yet is" (Revelation 17:8).[4] This does not agree with other insights regarding that book. This verse (because of 13:8 here) is believed to really mean "whose names have been recorded in the Book of Life since the creation of the world."[5]

As observed above, Peter did note that before the world was made the blood of the Lamb was anticipated (I Peter 1:19-20). Jesus spoke of a kingdom prepared from the creation of the world.

The heart-wrenching rendition of eternal loss is found in these prophecies by the simple statement, "not found written in." Because it is called the "Lamb's Book," it is a pre-creation list of all who might identify with the blood of that Lamb!

Names can be blotted out of that record. The saints, in turn, have their sins blotted out and names retained!

"The sins of the overcomers will be blotted out of the books of record, but their names will be retained on the book of life. The True Witness says, 'He that overcometh, the same shall be clothed in white raiment; and I will not blot out his name out of the book of life, but I will confess his name before my Father, and before his angels.' [Revelation 3:5]. When the conflict of life is ended, when the armor is laid off at the feet of Jesus, when the saints of God are glorified, then and then only will it be safe to claim that we are saved and sinless. True sanctification will not lead any human being to pronounce himself holy, sinless, and perfect. Let the Lord proclaim the truth of your character."[6]

---

3   Osborne, Grant R.; *Revelation* (Baker Book House; Grand Rapids, MI), p. 504.

4   Aune, *op. cit.*, p. 747.

5   Aune, *op. cit.*, p. 940 (cf. Ephesians 1:4).

6   White, Ellen G.; *The Signs of the Times,* May 16, 1895.

"If any man have an ear, let him hear." (vs 9)

Many scholars believe that this refers to the next verse. But in all the churches (Revelation 2–3) it is a *summation thought* to study and learn what the meaning was of the message just presented.

CHAPTER 26

A JUDICIAL MANIFESTO

"He that leadeth into captivity shall go into captivity: he that killeth with the sword must be killed with the sword. Here is the patience and the faith of the saints (Revelation 13:10).

There is vast conflict as to what this verse means. The best view is simply to see it as a *commentary insert*, providing two divine missives:

1. A statement regarding God's justice
2. An affirmation comment to the loyal saints

"he that killeth with the sword must be killed with the sword" (vs 10)

This serves as a warning to all persecutors (16:6; 18:2-3, 5-8, 20; 19:20). God's people will be put into prison and even face martyrdom – but – He will deal with the perpetrators and persecutors. Clearly, the saints will join Jesus in the "fellowship of suffering" (Philippians 3:10). This corresponds to Matthew 26:52: "Then said Jesus unto him, Put up again thy sword into his place: for all they that take the sword shall perish with the sword." This is called "the law of retribution." It reveals that God is just. But it is His judicial prerogative that He exercises at a precise time.

God had advised those in Smyrna: "Fear none of those things which thou shalt suffer: behold, the devil shall cast some of you into prison, that ye may be tried; and ye shall have tribulation ten days: be thou faithful unto death, and I will give thee a crown of life" (Revelation 2:10). **Opposition and persecution to death** have always been part of the risk of God's faithful. John was on the prison Island of Patmos because of his "testimony" (1:9). In the revealing apocalyptic prophecy Jesus gave to His disciples just before the Cross, He noted that "you will be handed over and persecuted and put to death" (Matthew 24:9). The beautiful spirit of Esther before her daring appearance before King Ahasuerus, "If I perish, I perish" (Esther 4:16), is to be ours!

Why does it become so cruel? The moral integrity of God's government is being threatened. God is looking for subjects who will remain devoted and unwavering, even to the point of death. They will be rewarded. That loyalty is simply described in the rest of the verse.

"Here is the patience and the faith of the saints." (vs 10)

Since persecution and trial are part of the end-time prophecy that God permits to happen, this amazing phrase is addressed to the "holy ones." This suggests that they recognize the inevitable events and God's sovereign will.[1] "Who, when he was reviled, reviled not again; when he suffered, he threatened not; but committed *himself* to him that judgeth righteously" (I Peter 2:23).

That, in turn, is represented by the "faith" of the saints. *Pistis* – faith – is a noun that constantly anticipates action. The endurance (*hypomone*) characterizes that action. Such patience God commended

---

[1] Thomas, Robert L.; *Revelation 8–22 – An Exegetical Commentary* (Moody Press, Chicago – 1992), p. 168.

in the churches of Ephesus, Thyatira and Philadelphia (2:2-3, 19; 3:10).

Some expositors elaborate on the word "Here." The Greek is *hode* and can be interpreted as "moreover" or "this demands."[2] They see an ethical/legal issue related to the saints. "In spite of the rage lashing from the dragon and the beast, the faithful will have patience and trust."

This was previously alluded to (12:17) and once again will be asserted at the end of the third angel's message (14:12).

The saints are characterized, defined and even described by "not loving their lives even to the point of death" (12:11) and by trusting God to ultimately defeat evil (6:11). The example of John the Baptist is a clarion lesson that rivets how the saints respond. In many ways his imprisonment and death are a painful and difficult story. But – John will be in the kingdom. Nothing exceeds that in importance. Such loyalty vindicates holiness and God's character.

---

[2]   Osborne, Grant R.; *Revelation* (Baker Book House; Grand Rapids, MI), p. 506.

CHAPTER 27

THE BEAST LIKE SATAN

"And I beheld another beast coming up out of the earth; and he had two horns like a lamb, and he spake as a dragon" (Revelation 13:11).

A second beast comes onto the end-time scene. This creature will be noted as a member of the false trinity in 16:13, labeled the "false prophet" (cf. 19:20, 20:10). The timing of its *emergence* is not clear from the record. But – when it speaks as a dragon on behalf of the first beast, it is distinctly after the rise of that sea beast. Both are identified as savage, brutal and blood-thirsty. The earth beast functions as a facilitator and enforcer of a unique geopolitical "law" of the sea beast.

"And I beheld another beast coming up out of the earth;" (vs 11)

"And I beheld" or "I saw" marks this as a new scene within the vision story. This new creature is also identified as *therion* or a ferocious beast, just like the first creature. Since it is later identified as a "false prophet," its barbarous actions relate to *religious matters*. That is an alarming concern. It raises a chilling reality that a civil power will wield oppressive force in support of ecclesiastical issues.

Like the first beast, this beast **"ascends"** or **"rises up."** This is a determined debut into end-time history. Interesting is another parallel to Daniel 7. The four beasts there initially ascended out of the sea (7:3). Thus, there is a "sea" application. Could there be an "earth" application? That is introduced later in

Daniel's chapter when it says, "These great beasts, which are four, *are* four kings, *which* shall **arise** out of the earth" (Daniel 7:17). Daniel 8 with the ram, he-goat and little horn embellishers that new end-time motif. That is a unique distinction and suggests a parallel application at the end of time when those kingdoms have key symbolic meanings.

The meaning of the "earth" has been a problem to scholars. The gamut of ideas presents many complex possibilities. There is, however, a wonderful key. The first beast comes out of the sea; the second from the earth. These are "opposites" or contrasting images. It is anticipated, then that they bring contrasting origins or beginnings. Since we are told what water and sea represents in prophecy, the earth would depict the opposite.

	Arises from Sea	Arises from Earth
Rev. 17:15	Peoples, multitudes, nations, tongues	Undeveloped area, void of masses of people, nations and languages
Is. 57: 20-21	Wicked, restless, dirty	Peaceful, without problems or evil (at least initially)

The beast is a kingdom or nation that emerges "lamb-like" in an area of the world void of many people and seeks to do good. This beast first represents the historical beginning of a nation that quickly moves right up to the very end. The United States of America fits its origins exquisitely. It began by pilgrims migrating from Europe to escape religious oppression from Catholicism. Its civil structure was based on two principles: Protestant Christianity and the concept of Republicanism.

"We hold these truths to be self-evident, that all men are created equal, that they are endowed by their Creator with certain unalienable Rights, that among these are Life, Liberty and the pursuit of Happiness."[1]

Patrick Henry (May 29, 1736 – June 6, 1799), who was a prominent figure in the American Revolution, known and remembered for his "Give me Liberty, or give me Death" speech, said: "It cannot be emphasized too strongly or too often that this great nation was founded, not by religionists but by Christians, not on religions, but on the gospel of Jesus Christ."[2]

"and he had two horns like a lamb, and he spake as a dragon." (vs 11)

Those two horns representing those great ideals are never mentioned again.

But a paradox suddenly emerges. A religious nation with two lamb-like horns, symbolizing its two key foundational precepts that would lead to its greatness, changes to become satanic! The sea beast had a mouth like a roaring lion, spewing out anti-God words. The earth beast spews out of his mouth utterances like Satan.

How does the dragon speak? The Bible actually records some of his words!

The Garden of Eden, Satan's challenge over Job and Christ's temptations in the wilderness provide a key framework of how that master of evil will be portrayed at the end of time! (See following table.)

The Dragon Spoke – The Dragon Will Speak

Garden of Eden:
"Now the serpent was more subtle than any beast of the field which the LORD God had made. And he said unto the woman, *Yea, hath God said, Ye shall not eat of every tree of the garden?* And the woman said unto the serpent, We may eat of the fruit of the trees of the garden: But of the fruit of the tree which *is* in the midst of the garden, God hath said, Ye shall not eat of it, neither shall ye touch it, lest ye die. And the serpent said unto the woman, *Ye shall not surely die: For God doth know that in the day ye eat thereof, then your eyes shall be opened, and ye shall be as gods, knowing good and evil"* (Genesis 3:1-5).

---

[1] *Declaration of Independence* adopted by Congress July 4, 1776.
[2] Henry, Patrick; Virginia Convention speech, March 23, 1775.

"Satan represented to the holy pair that they would be gainers by breaking the law of God. Do we not today hear similar reasoning? Many talk of the narrowness of those who obey God's commandments, while they themselves claim to have broader ideas and to enjoy greater liberty. What is this but an echo of the voice from Eden, 'In the day ye eat thereof' – transgress the divine requirement – 'ye shall be as gods'?
Satan claimed to have received great good by eating of the forbidden fruit, but he did not let it appear that by transgression he had become an outcast from heaven." – Ellen G. White, *Patriarchs and Prophets,* p. 55.

"The only one who promised Adam life in disobedience was the great deceiver. And the declaration of the serpent to Eve in Eden–'Ye shall not surely die'–was the first sermon ever preached upon the immortality of the soul. Yet this declaration, resting solely upon the authority of Satan, is echoed from the pulpits of Christendom and is received by the majority of mankind as readily as it was received by our first parents. The divine sentence, 'The soul that sinneth, it shall die' (Ezekiel 18:20), is made to mean: The soul that sinneth, it shall not die, but live eternally. We cannot but wonder at the strange infatuation which renders men so credulous concerning the words of Satan and so unbelieving in regard to the words of God." – Ellen G. White, *The Great Controversy,* p. 533.

"Satan beguiles men now as he beguiled Eve in Eden by flattery, by kindling a desire to obtain forbidden knowledge, by exciting ambition for self-exaltation. It was cherishing these evils that caused his fall, and through them he aims to compass the ruin of men. 'Ye shall be as gods,' he declares, 'knowing good and evil.' Genesis 3:5. Spiritualism teaches 'that man is the creature of progression; that it is his destiny from his birth to progress, even to eternity, toward the Godhead.' And again: 'Each mind will judge itself and not another.' 'The judgment will be right, because it is the judgment of self.... The throne is within you.' Said a spiritualistic teacher, as the 'spiritual consciousness' awoke within him: 'My fellow men, all were unfallen demigods.' And another declares: 'Any just and perfect being is Christ.' – Ellen G. White, *The Great controversy,* p. 554.

"The **law of God**, through the agency of Satan, **is to be made void**. In our land of boasted freedom, religious liberty will come to an end." – Ellen G. White, *Evangelism,* 236 (1875) (emphasis added). This is the final work of this earth beast.

Chiding God Over Job:

"And the LORD said unto Satan, Whence comest thou? Then Satan answered the LORD, and said, *From going to and fro in the earth, and from walking up and down in it.* And the LORD said unto Satan, Hast thou considered my servant Job, that *there is* none like him in the earth, a perfect and an upright man, one that feareth God, and escheweth evil? Then Satan answered the LORD, and said, *Doth Job fear*

God, and escheweth evil? Then Satan answered the LORD, and said, *Doth Job fear God for nought? Hast not thou made an hedge about him, and about his house, and about all that he hath on every side? thou hast blessed the work of his hands, and his substance is increased in the land. But put forth thine hand now, and touch all that he hath, and he will curse thee to thy face*" (Job 1:7-11).

"Job is brought before us as a man whom the Lord permitted Satan to afflict. The enemy stripped him of all he possessed; his family ties were broken; his children were taken from him. For a time his body was covered with loathsome sores, and he suffered greatly. His friends tried to make him see that he was responsible, by his sinful course, for all his afflictions. But he denied the charge, declaring, 'Miserable comforters are ye all.' By seeking to prove Job guilty before God, and deserving of punishment, his friends brought a grievous test upon him, and placed God in a false light; but Job did not swerve from his loyalty, and God rewarded his faithful servant." – Ellen G. White, *The Signs of the Times,* June 21, 1899.

"The great controversy between good and evil will increase in intensity to the very close of time. In all ages the wrath of Satan has been manifested against the church of Christ; and God has bestowed his grace and Spirit upon his people to strengthen them to stand against the power of the evil one. When the apostles of Christ were to bear his gospel to the world and to record it for all future ages, they were especially endowed with the enlightenment of the Spirit. But **as the church approaches her final deliverance, Satan is to work with greater power.** He comes down 'having great wrath, because he knoweth that he hath but a short time.' Rev. 12: 12. He will work 'with all power and signs and lying wonders.' 2 Thess. 2:9. For six thousand years that master-mind that once was highest among the angels of God, has been wholly bent to the work of deception and ruin. And **all the depths of Satanic skill** and subtlety acquired, all the cruelty developed, during these struggles of the ages, **will be brought to bear against God's people** in the final conflict. And **in this time of peril** the followers of Christ are **to bear to the world the warning of the Lord's second advent;** and a people are to be prepared to stand before him at his coming, 'without spot, and blameless.' 2 Pet. 3:14. At this time the special endowment of divine grace and power is not less needful to the church than in apostolic days." – Ellen G. White, *The Great Controversy,* Author's Preface (emphasis added).

"You will be given opportunity to say, 'Though he slay me, yet will I trust in him' (Job 13:15). Oh, it is so precious to think that opportunities are afforded us to confess our faith in the face of danger, and amid sorrow, sickness, pain, and death." – Ellen G. White, *Selected Messages,* bk 1, p. 117 (emphasis added).

Temptation in the Wilderness – One:

"And the devil said unto him, *If thou be the Son of God, command this stone that it be made bread*" (Luke 4:3)."

"In the *last great conflict* of the controversy with Satan those who are loyal to God will see *every earthly support cut off*. Because they refuse to break His law in obedience to earthly powers, they will be *forbidden to buy or sell*. It will finally be decreed that they shall be put to death. See Rev. 13:11-17. But to the obedient is given the promise, 'He shall dwell on high: his place of defense shall be the munitions of rocks: bread shall be given him; his waters shall be sure.' Isa. 33:16. By this promise the children of God will live. When *the earth shall be wasted with famine, they shall be fed*. 'They shall not be ashamed in the evil time: and in the days of famine *they shall be satisfied*.' Ps. 37:19. To that time of distress the prophet Habakkuk looked forward, and his words express the faith of the church: 'Although the fig tree shall not blossom, neither shall fruit be in the vines; the labor of the olive shall fail, and the fields shall yield no meat; the flock shall be cut off from the fold, and there shall be no herd in the stalls: yet I will rejoice in the Lord, I will joy in the God of my salvation.' Hab. 3:17, 18" – Ellen G. White, *The Desire of Ages*, pp. 121-122.

"For he shall give his angels charge over thee, to keep thee in all thy ways" (Psalm 91:11).

Temptation in the Wilderness – Two:

"Then the devil taketh him up into the holy city, and setteth him on a pinnacle of the temple, And saith unto him, *If thou be the Son of God, cast thyself down: for it is written, He shall give his angels charge concerning thee: and in their hands they shall bear thee up, lest at any time thou dash thy foot against a stone*" (Matthew 4:5-6).

"Satan thought to take advantage of Christ's humanity, and urge Him beyond the limits of trust into the sin of presumption. But while manifesting perfect trust in his Father, He refused to place Himself in a position which would necessitate the interposition of his Father to save Him from death. He would not force Providence to his rescue, and thus fail to give man an example of perfect trust and submission." – Ellen G. White, *The Bible Echo*, November 15, 1892.

"But faith is in no sense allied to presumption. Only he who has true faith is secure against presumption. For presumption is Satan's counterfeit of faith. Faith claims God's promises, and brings forth fruit in obedience. *Presumption also claims the promises, but uses them as Satan did, to excuse transgression.* Faith would have led our first parents to trust the love of God, and to obey His commands. Presumption led them to transgress His law, believing that His great love would save them from the consequence of their sin. It is not faith that claims the favor of Heaven without complying with the conditions on which mercy is to be granted. Genuine faith has its foundation in the promises and provisions of the Scriptures." – Ellen G. White, *The Desire of Ages*, p. 126.

Temptation in the Wilderness – Three:

"And the devil, taking him up into an high mountain, showed unto him all the kingdoms of the world in a moment of time. And the devil said unto him, *All this power will I give thee, and the glory of them: for that is delivered unto me; and to whomsoever I will I give it. If thou therefore wilt worship me, all shall be thine*" (Luke 4:5-7).

"If man sacrifices righteous principles and truth because he can thus avoid persecution and trial in this life, he may obtain the friendship of the world, but will lose the favor of God. He barters his eternal welfare for trifling considerations. But he that obeys the requirements of Christ, neither looking nor planning for his own convenience, preferring even to sacrifice his temporal life rather than turn from the light of truth will secure the reward of the future immortal life. Jesus has said, 'He that loveth his life shall lose it; and he that hateth his life in this world shall keep it unto life eternal.'" – Ellen G. White, *The Signs of the Times,* March 21, 1878.

"As the crowning act in the great drama of deception, Satan himself will personate Christ. The church has long professed to look to the Saviour's advent as the consummation of her hopes. Now the great **deceiver will make it appear that Christ has come.** In different parts of the earth, Satan will manifest himself among men as a majestic being of dazzling brightness, resembling the description of the Son of God given by John in the Revelation. Revelation 1:13-15. The glory that surrounds him is unsurpassed by anything that mortal eyes have yet beheld. The shout of triumph rings out upon the air, 'Christ has come! Christ has come!' **The people prostrate themselves** in adoration before him, while he lifts up his hands, and pronounces a blessing upon them, as Christ blessed his disciples when he was upon the earth. His voice is soft and subdued, yet full of melody. In gentle, compassionate tones he presents some of the same gracious, heavenly truths which the Saviour uttered; he heals the diseases of the people, and then, in his assumed character of Christ, he claims to have changed the Sabbath to Sunday, and commands all to hallow the day which he has blessed. He declares that those who persist in keeping holy the seventh day are blaspheming his name by refusing to listen to his angels sent to them with light and truth. This is the strong, **almost overmastering delusion."** – Ellen G. White, *The Great Controversy,* p. 624.

"But although Satan may work diligently, we need not be discouraged; for the Captain of the Lord's host has said. 'All power is given unto me in heaven and in earth;' 'Lo, I am with you alway, even unto the end of the world;' 'Be of good cheer, I have overcome the world.'" – Ellen G. White, *The Review and Herald,* July 23, 1889.

All these issues are deceptive areas that Satan uses and exercises through the earth beast. In their boldest religious tyranny, the Protestants of America will bring falsehood and traitorous beliefs to the world. Intriguingly, as will soon unfold, the issue of force will follow, especially over a single doctrine. This beast becomes the voice of Satan the dragon. (Matthew 7:15 –"Beware of false prophets, which come to you in sheep's clothing, but inwardly they are ravening wolves.").

"It is apparent that the second beast captures organized religion in the service of the first beast."[3] If this understanding is correct, and we believe it is, Protestants of America will increasingly become more favorable to Rome.

"History is sacrificed on the altar of ecumenism as an oblation to Rome. No sacrifice is too great to further the 'unity' movement that is drawing the non-Catholic church back under the pope. Recently the Duchess of Kent, seven Anglican bishops, and more than 700 English clergymen converted to Catholicism. The same historical revisionism is being practiced by American evangelical leaders who dishonor the memories of those who preserved the gospel with their blood....

"Eugene Daniels, World Vision International's senior adviser for church relations, recently said, 'We discovered that we could work with the Catholic Church in terms of the spiritual needs of the people in much the same way that we have traditionally worked with the Protestant churches.' Other major evangelical ministries that have been working with Catholics as fellow Christians include the Billy Graham Evangelistic Association, Charles Colson's Prison Fellowship, InterVarsity Christian Fellowship, Campus Crusade for Christ, Full Gospel Businessmen's Fellowship, Youth With A Mission, Wycliffe Bible Translators, and others. Obviously this recent development, *peculiar to our generation,* is extremely significant and is gaining momentum as Rome increases its campaign to present itself as 'evangelical'....

"On Trinity Broadcasting Network, the largest Christian television network, network founder Paul Crouch and popular televangelist and faith healer Benny Hinn declared that Roman Catholic doctrine is no concern, for, after all, Catholics 'love Jesus.' ... On another program Crouch told two priests and a leading Catholic laywoman who were guests:

"'In the essentials our theology is basically the same: some of these even so-called doctrinal differences ... are simply matters of semantics. One of these things that has divided us [referring to transubstantiation] all of these years shouldn't have ... we were really meaning the same thing but just saying it a little differently....

"'So I say to the critics and theological nitpickers,' 'Be gone, in Jesus' name!' Let's come together [with Rome] in the spirit of love and unity.... [Audience applause.]"[4]

Shocked? I hope you are! But there's more – far more. Two familiar examples:

"I don't know anyone more dedicated to the great fundamental doctrines of Christianity than the Catholics." – W. A. Criswell, former president, Southern Baptist Convention.

"I've found that my beliefs are essentially the same as those of orthodox Roman Catholics." – Billy Graham.[5]

---

3   Thomas, Robert L.; *Revelation 8–22 – An Exegetical Commentary* (Moody Press, Chicago – 1992), p. 174.

4   Hunt, David; *The Woman Rides the Beast* (Harvest House Publishers; Eugene, OR – 1994) pp. 402-403, 405 (emphasis added).

5   *Ibid.,* p. 388.

Perhaps the concern of true Christians (called here in chapter 13, "saints") is best expressed in these words from Mary Ann Collins, a former Catholic nun, writing with deep concern about Catholic issues:

"The Pope is called 'Holy Father' and the Catholic Church is called 'Holy Mother Church.' According to 'The Catholic Encyclopedia," the idea of freedom of religion is wrong. People are not supposed to use their own personal judgment to determine their religious beliefs. 'According to Canon Law (the official laws governing the Roman Catholic Church), Catholics are required to **submit their minds and wills** to any declaration concerning faith or morals which is made by the Pope or by a church council. They are also required to avoid anything that disagrees with such declarations. And they can be coerced if they don't comply.'

"'The Catholic Church teaches that only the Magisterium of the Catholic Church (the Pope and the bishops in communion with him) has the right to interpret Scripture. People like us are not allowed to interpret Scripture for ourselves. We have to check it out with Church authorities.' (This is online.)

"'Catholicism teaches that Catholics are supposed to "receive with docility" any directives given to them by Catholic Church authorities. Catholicism teaches that there is no salvation apart from the Catholic Church, its sacramental system, the priesthood, and the Pope.'

"The Bible says, 'Be ye not unequally yoked together with unbelievers' (2 Corinthians 6:14). By Biblical standards, the Catholic Church presents a Gospel that is badly distorted. It is salvation by 'Jesus plus.' Jesus plus the Catholic Church. Jesus plus the sacraments. Jesus plus good works. Jesus plus Catholic tradition.

"This is contrary to Scripture. The Apostle Paul said that requiring people to be circumcised nullifies the grace of God, with the result that people are not saved. It is such a serious thing that 'Christ is become of no effect unto you' and you 'are fallen from grace.' In other words, Jesus Christ no longer does you any good (Galatians 5:1-4).

"If just being required to add circumcision nullifies the grace of God, then what happens when you are required to add the sacraments and the Pope and Catholic tradition and good works and the Catholic magisterium? [The 'magisterium' is the official teaching authority of the Roman Catholic Church].

"Catholics have faith in the Catholic Church. (Their faith in Jesus Christ is through the Catholic Church, rather than directly in Jesus Himself.) Their rule of faith is the 'Catechism of the Catholic Church' and other official Catholic documents. This includes the Catholic Bible, as interpreted by the Catholic magisterium."[6]

"This imagery and background suggest deception within the covenant community itself. Whereas the first beast speaks loudly and defiantly against God, the second beast makes the first beast's claims sound plausible and persuasive. False teachers in the church are encouraging compromise with the culture's idolatrous institutions, which are all associated in some way with the Roman cult."[7]

This apostasy is intensified and nourished through the driving power of the earth beast. What now follows empowers Rome and reveals the tragic decadence the Protestant America will sink to.

---

[6] http://www.CatholicConcerns.com

[7] Beale, G. K.; *The New International Greek Testament Commentary; The Book of Revelation* (William B. Eerdmans Publishing Company, Grand Rapids, Michigan – 1999), p. 708.

CHAPTER 28

WORLD IS FORCED INTO BLASPHEMOUS WORSHIP

"And he exerciseth all the power of the first beast before him, and causeth the earth and them which dwell therein to worship the first beast, whose deadly wound was healed" (Revelation 13:12).

In verses 1-8 the messages are in the aorist tense – as if occurring in the past but anticipated in the future. Verse 11 is in the imperfect tense, suggesting something that occurred which continues into the future. The rest of the chapter, beginning with this verse, is in the present tense. These make a storyline of the growing intensity of the antichrist work with his supporters. We have stepped into the future and observed what will happen in "real time" soon.

"And he exerciseth all the power of the first beast before him," (vs 12)

No wonder he speaks like the dragon. The devil gave them both power. This beast operates with the same sovereign authority as the sea beast – but works on his behalf.[1] The United States will function in servitude to the mandates of Rome. It will soon appear that it becomes an effective agent to persecute those resisting a Catholic Church mandate.

The "exercise" of its power comes "independent" of the first beast, but in concert with it. It actually means "in the presence of"[2] and suggests that he

is acting on Rome's behest and even under its authority. One author suggests that this conveys a "priestly role" (by the beast) over the false prophet.[3] That is fascinating and suggests that there is a religious supervision over this civil power. Since it is called a "false prophet," it too is "performing" a religious mission.

"and causeth the earth and them which dwell therein to worship the first beast," (vs 12)

Eight times the word "causeth" (*poieo*) is used in this prophetic discourse (vss 12-16). It means "to make" – "to force." This emphasizes the incredible power of this beast – the "false prophet" – on behalf of the papacy. It is coercive.

This means that it enforces some legal injunction. It functions as a police state over an item of conscience and has almost military-like power over the world. The sea beast, though blaspheming God, is worshipped by the world (vss 3-4). Now we are told one reason why. The earth beast is forcing the world to do so! The papal power has its own way through its accomplice wielding force and terror. From Daniel 8–12 we are informed that it is over a Sabbath issue. The earth beast "causeth" obeisance to this papal god and not the Creator God.

The expression here of forcing the "earth" veers from other ways the "world"

1   Thomas, Robert L.; *Revelation 8–22 – An Exegetical Commentary* (Moody Press, Chicago – 1992), p. 174.
2   Beale, G. K.; *The New International Greek Testament Commentary; The Book of Revelation* (William B. Eerdmans Publishing Company, Grand

Rapids, Michigan – 1999), p. 708.
3   Aune, David E.; *World Biblical Commentary; Revelation 17–22*, vol. 52c (World Books; Publisher, Dallas, Texas – 1997), p. 758.

is alluded to, for instance, "all the world wondered after the beast" (vs 3). There, it suggested all the wicked world. Here, the tyranny of the earth beast over the "earth" covers everyone – good and bad[4] – everyone who dwells there.

"whose deadly wound was healed." (vs 12)

This verse is very different from those concerning the mortal wound of the head (vss 3-4, 17:10). There, it was **the head** that was wounded and healed. Here, it is **the beast** that had had a deadly wound which was healed. There are two views of this phrase – both could apply; however, the second is unlikely. This phrase refers to the first beast (from the sea).

View One:

The papacy had its ecclesiastical power curtailed in 1798 – not its "kingdom" power.

In 1796 **French Republican** troops under the command of **Napoleon Bonaparte** invaded Italy and defeated the papal troops. Pius VI sued for peace, which was temporarily granted on February 19, 1797. New violence in Rome was blamed on the papacy, leaving a new pretext for the invasion of Rome. **General Berthier** marched into that city, entering it unopposed on February 10, 1798, and proclaimed it a **Roman Republic**. He demanded the Pope renounce his temporal authority. Upon his refusal he was taken prisoner on February

Pope Pius VI

20, 1798. He died on August 29, 1799, having then **reigned longer than any other pope.**

This is a historical resumé of the loss of ecclesiastical leadership by a mortal wound that would quickly be healed. That would be addressed in the "woman" imagery, which was riding/directing the beast as presented in chapter 17! There must be another **prophecy-specific** issue related to the "kingdom" part or "beast," per se, as alluded to in this verse! There is!

During Napoleon's conquest the Papal States, comprising much of the peninsula of Italy, were seized. They were then restored in June, 1800, under the new Pope, Pius VII. The French again invaded in 1808, and this time the States of the Church were annexed to France. With the fall of the Napoleonic system in 1814, the Papal States were restored once again.

Italian **nationalism** had been stoked during the Napoleonic period but dashed by the settlement of the **Congress of Vienna** 1814–1815), which left Italy divided. In 1848, nationalist revolutions began to break out across Europe; in 1849, a **Roman Republic** was declared for Italy. In the years that followed, Italian nationalists saw the Papal States as the chief obstacle to Italian unity. In 1860, with much of the region already in rebellion against Papal rule, the Papal States were all formally annexed and a unified Kingdom of **Italy** was declared. Those States were reduced to a small papal region immediately surrounding and including Rome.

---

[4] Thomas, *op. cit.,* p. 174.

Pope Pius IX, under whose rule the Papal States passed under secular control, was now isolated in Rome. The City was declared the capital of Italy in March of 1861. King **Victor Emmanuel II,** the new ruling head of Italy, sent a personal letter to Pius IX offering a face-saving proposal that would have allowed the peaceful entry of the Italian Army into Rome, under the guise of offering protection to the pope. The Pope's reception of San Martino, the courier **(September 10, 1870),** was unfriendly. Pius IX had violent outbursts toward Martino. He threw the king's letter on a table and said he would never let Rome be invaded by the armies.

That same day, **September 10**, Italy declared war on Rome. The **city was**

Pope Pius IX

captured on **September 20, 1870**. Rome was annexed to the kingdom of Italy.

This kingdom or "beast" was now mortally wounded. It would later rise from the ashes of war to once again become a church/state, fulfilling the Revelation 13 and 17 prophecies (see deeper discussion under chapter 17). That wouldn't occur until the Lateran Treaty/Packs of 1929.

The Lateran Pacts of that year contained three sections – the **Treaty of Conciliation** (27 articles), which established Vatican City as an independent state, restoring the civil sovereignty of the pope as a monarch, the **Financial Convention** annexed to the treaty (3 articles), which compensated the Holy See for loss of the papal states, and the **Concordat** (45 articles), which dealt with the Roman Catholic Church's ecclesiastical relations with the Italian State.

An **agreement between the Italian Republic and the Holy See** amended the Lateran Pacts in 1985, which gave the Holy See more independence as a church and a state. Thus, the prophecy of the **beast** here in Revelation could not be fulfilled until 1929 *and* cannot be completed until the United States forces others, in some legal manner, to give deference and allegiance to the papacy!

This means that we are in the middle of the time between 1929 and the very end, just before the papacy comes to its end (Daniel 7:25-26 – "little horn" will cease at the termination of a 42-month period; Daniel 8:9-12, 25 – "little horn" will be broken without hands; Daniel 11:40-45 – the "king of the north" will come to his end,

and none shall help him; Revelation 17:14 – the "beast," "ten horns" and "harlot" are then overcome by the Lamb).

In this setting, some world-wide catalyst will bring focused power to the papacy. Civil and religious tyrannical control of the United States over some legal issue will be the "cause" of forced allegiance to Rome.

Therefore – the papal beast kingdom was wounded (1870) and then healed (1929).

View Two:

Satan is often seen as the beast that was wounded and then arose in power. He was seen as an angel "perfect in beauty" (Ezekiel 28:12). He was cast to this earth (Revelation 12:9): "And the great dragon was cast out, that old serpent, called the Devil, and Satan, which deceiveth the whole world: he was cast out into the earth, and his angels were cast out with him."

Christ had declared that the prince of this world would be "cast out" (John 12:31), alluding to the Cross when Christ had victory over death and this world. But there will come a time – a very brief time at the end of this world – when the devil will be granted powers he has never exhibited before. He will impersonate Christ. "And no marvel; for Satan himself is transformed into an angel of light" (II Corinthians 11:14).

At that time the "mortally wounded dragon" will appear to be healed. It is then that he will make war with the saints (12:17). His power to persecute, kill and control will rise to levels never before permitted. Then will be executed the terrifying events outlined in this incredible chapter!

Thus, the "first" beast can be seen as having a dual meaning. Contextually, however, the greater emphasis is on the papacy.

We will now see unfolding the prophecy addressing the time when Satan *and* his agents have nearly unbridled power.

CHAPTER 29

DECEPTIVE WONDERS

"And he doeth great wonders, so that he maketh fire come down from heaven on the earth in the sight of men, And deceiveth them that dwell on the earth by *the means of* **those miracles which he had power to do in the sight of the beast;" (Revelation 13:13-14a).**

"And he doeth great wonders," (vs 13)

The pronoun "he" apparently refers to the "false prophet" or earth beast. But, in a revealing commentary, John is later shown three unclean spirits – like frogs – coming out of the mouths of the dragon, beast and false prophet. Then it describes them as *spirits of devils* – evil angels – *working miracles* "which go forth unto the kings of the earth and of the whole world, to gather them to the battle of that great day of God Almighty" (Revelation 16:14). Three distinct powers are appealed to with specific missions. All are deceptive, undermining the purity of truth. "Out of their mouths" suggests that they are all making legislative proclamations or edicts for the world.[1] Here the earth beast is singled out, the sea beast and dragon having already been addressed. Together they form a false trinity.

Through *demonic power*, the three "creatures" of Revelation 13 do miracles before the whole world. Making fire come down from heaven is specific to this earth beast. Paul talks, however, of the eschatological antichrist as "him whose coming is after the working of Satan with all power and *signs and lying wonders*" (II Thessalonians 2:9). That would relate to the sea beast. Later in Revelation it specifically notes that the earth beast – the false prophet – "wrought *miracles* before him" (19:20).

An earmark of this false trinity will be miracles! Here, in context with verse 12, fire coming down from heaven is focused on the false prophet, but Satan and the sea beast are part of this cunning chicanery.

Expositor White uses this verse many times in her works. She makes allusions to "Satan," the "false prophet" and many "agencies" performing their wonders: "In Revelation we read concerning Satan: 'And he doeth great wonders, so that he maketh fire come down from heaven on the earth in the sight of men, and deceiveth them that dwell on the earth by the means of those miracles' ... [Rev. 13:13-17 quoted]."[2]

"The final struggle will be waged between those who keep the commandments of God and the faith of Jesus and that *apostate power* [the earth beast or false prophet] which will deceive all who dwell upon the earth. 'And he doeth great wonders, so that he maketh fire come down from heaven on the earth in the sight of men, and deceiveth them that dwell on the earth by the means of those miracles' [Rev. 13:13]"[3]

"The deceiving power of Satan will continually increase to the very end. Through his *agencies* he will do great

---

1   Osborne, Grant R.; *Revelation* (Baker Book House; Grand Rapids, MI), p. 591.

2   White, Ellen G.; *Selected Messages,* vol. 3, p. 393.
3   White, Ellen G.; *The Review and Herald,* August 31, 1897 (emphasis added).

wonders, 'so that he maketh fire come down from heaven on the earth ... by the means of those miracles [Rev. 13:13].'"[4]

Thus, she applies this verse, to the false prophet, to agencies such as the papacy and the dragon as it contextually unfolds.

"so that he maketh fire come down from heaven on the earth in the sight of men," (vs 13)

This is *the deceptive sign* that will attract the world. When Elijah called fire down from heaven (I Kings 18:38, II Kings 1:10), it was to validate and vindicate the true God. Here, the deceptive blasphemous beasts and Satan do this to "affirm" their words and validate their spiritual authority.[5]

"This is not a religious act but a public-relations performance intended to enhance the worship of the false trinity."[6] In the Septuagint it is noted that Nebuchadnezzar extolled the "God of heaven" for "doing signs and great wonders" (Daniel 4:37a).[7] Such a display here is devised to bring praise to the being that is "in the sight of men." No wonder God calls this earth beast a "false prophet."

This echoes a fascinating theme written by Moses: "If there arise among you a prophet, or a dreamer of dreams, and giveth thee a sign or a wonder, And the sign or the wonder come to pass, whereof he spake unto thee, saying, Let us go after other gods, which thou hast not known, and let us serve them; Thou shalt not hearken unto the words of that prophet, or that dreamer of dreams: for the LORD your God proveth you, to know whether ye love the LORD your God with all your heart and with all your soul" (Deuteronomy 13:1-3).

Christ had warned that counterfeit signs would accompany false christs at the end (Matthew 24:24-25). How can one know that it is false? The *truth* related to these prophecies will be the means to unlock that emotional time. For starters, Jesus compared the false end-time appearances of "Christ" as being at variance to His dramatic coming.

"Wherefore if they shall say unto you, Behold, he is in the desert; go not forth: behold, *he is* in the secret chambers; believe *it* not. For as the lightning cometh out of the east, and shineth even unto the west; so shall also the coming of the Son of man be" (Matthew 24:26-27).

The next chapter is filled with information regarding the falsehood of the beasts here recorded. Authenticity of truth is now to be riveted in our hearts through relentless study of God's word! "Beloved, believe not every spirit, but try the spirits whether they are of God: because many false prophets are gone out into the world. Hereby know ye the Spirit of God: Every spirit that confesseth that Jesus Christ is come in the flesh is of God: And every spirit that confesseth not that Jesus Christ is come in the flesh is not of God: and this is that *spirit* of antichrist, whereof ye have heard that it should come; and even now already is it in the world" (I John 4:1-3).

"The time is coming when *Satan* will work miracles right in your sight, claiming that he is Christ; and if your feet are not firmly established upon the truth of God, then you will be led away from your foundation. The only safety for you

---

4   White, Ellen G.; *The Review and Herald,* June 4, 1894 (emphasis added).

5   Brighton, Louis A.; *Revelation* (Concordia Publishing House, Saint Louis, MO – 1999), p. 359 (emphasis added).

6   Osborne, Grant R.; *Revelation* (Baker Book House; Grand Rapids, MI), p. 514.

7   Beale, G. K.; *The New International Greek Testament Commentary; The Book of Revelation* (William B. Eerdmans Publishing Company, Grand Rapids, Michigan – 1999), pp. 708-709.

is to search for the truth as for hidden treasures. Dig for the truth as you would for treasures in the earth, and present the word of God, the Bible, before your Heavenly Father, and say, Enlighten me; teach me what is truth. And when his Holy Spirit shall come into your hearts, to impress the truth into your souls, you will not let it go easily. **You** have gained such an experience in **searching the Scriptures,** that **every point is established**. And it is important that you continually search the Scriptures. You should store the mind with the word of God; for you may be separated, and placed where you will not have the privilege of meeting with the children of God. Then you will want the treasures of God's word hidden in your hearts, and when opposition comes around you, you will need to bring everything to the Scriptures."[8]

Everything Satan does is an invitation to the saints to defect from God's ranks.

"And deceiveth them that dwell on the earth by *the means of* those miracles which he had power to do in the sight of the beast;" (vs 14).

In Christ's words to His disciples in that great end-time discourse, He warned,

"Take heed that no man deceive you" (Matthew 24:4). People will be fooled into believing lies as though they were God's truths. Stunning is this prophecy! The whole earth will become victims of these satanic delusions.

Satan was branded the "deceiver of the whole world" (12:9) and later will be called the "deceiver of the nations" (20:3, 8, 10). Here, he and false apostate Protestantism in the United States continue that end-time trajectory.

Intriguingly, several old manuscripts say that "he deceives **mine**" (verse 14), suggesting that the main submissive prey are those inside the church![9]

"By *the means of* those miracles which he had power to do in the sight of the beast" (vs 14a) suggests that the sea beast gives approval to what the earth beast is doing.[10] In essence, it functions as the servant of the papacy. "True prophets receive their inspiration and commissions as they stand before the presence of the Lord (11:4). Likewise, the false prophet receives his inspiration and commission as he acts 'in the presence of the beast.'"[11]

[8]   White, Ellen G.; *The Review and Herald,* April 3, 1888 (emphasis added).

[9]   Beale, *op. cit.,* p. 710.
[10] Thomas, Robert L.; *Revelation 8–22 – An Exegetical Commentary* (Moody Press, Chicago – 1992), p. 177.
[11] Beale, *op. cit.,* p. 710.

CHAPTER 30

THE POWER OF AN IMAGE

"saying to them that dwell on the earth, that they should make an image to the beast, which had the wound by a sword, and did live. And he had power to give life unto the image of the beast, that the image of the beast should both speak, and cause that as many as would not worship the image of the beast should be killed" (Revelation 13:14b-15).

"saying to them that dwell on the earth," (vs 14)

This is a repeated phrase and rivets the horrendous issue that everyone is commanded to follow – no exceptions.

"that they should make an image to the beast, which had the wound by a sword, and did live." (vs 14)

Ferreted out of the false trinity coalition, this is the beast that survived military action – "by a sword." We were reminded of that in verse 12c (cf. 17:8, 11). God is championing precision in understanding. That beast kingdom is identified through its progressive history!

The spotlight is on the papacy in its 1798/1870 frays. The earth beast now *compels* the world to make an "image" to *that* sea beast – the Holy See. What now follows is so oppressive that this earth beast, the United States, mutates to be coercive and tyrannical.

An "image to the beast" echoes Daniel 3:1-6 and the ninety foot high golden image Nebuchadnezzar had made, likely of himself. He was king and kingdom (Daniel 2:38-40). The image was representative of both. His subjects were commanded to worship it on pain of death.

This is the first of several apocalyptic references to this "image" (13:15; 14:9, 11; 15:2; 16:2; 19:20; 20:4). The image-worship command in Daniel's day was idolatrous and rejected by his three companions. This end-time global worship requirement is enforced by the false prophet and follows a similar storyline. It relates to religious homage towards something in the Roman Catholic Church. The world's worship and allegiance will be demanded. It exalts or glorifies some "creation" of the Vatican – the papacy. Unquestionably, it will be clear what it is and means. It is a *facsimile* of something they want honored. Is it some idolatrous asset in the Holy See that is copied? Or – could it be replicating something the Roman Church established to be honored?

Let's look deeper. *The sea beast:*

1. Blasphemies God, His church and His people (vs 6). That is done by giving the world abominations from her cup (17:4) – something spiritually illicit.
2. Accepts the worship of man and "sets up" an abomination. Jesus said that there would be such an end-time abomination described in Daniel related to a false Sabbath (Matthew 24:15; cf. Daniel 8:12-13, 9:27, 11:31, 12:11).
3. Accepts the creation of an image that represents all that power and

139

blasphemy. It is to be worshiped – even by the wicked world (vss 14-15).

Resistance to that worship (just like Daniel's friends) develops a spirit of hatred against God's people who are identified by their faith and obedience (vs 7, 12:17) in:

1. Keeping God's commandments and
2. Having the testimony of Jesus

The remnant defy that image and its worship. They only identify with God's *original*. What is that "idol" or image which is to be honored?

There are two Biblical Greek words for an image or statue:

1. *agalua* – most often refers to a *statue* or an idol. The image of Mary is one example.
2. *eikon* – is a descriptive *symbol* of a god or even a deified emperor. It refers to a representation of something living or original.[1]

Eikon is used here in Revelation to describe the worship of something that the papacy fashioned. It is in the "doctrinal" likeness of the original, a defined conformity to a special religious dogma.[2]

What *one* "belief" could embrace the power and glory of the sea beast? Revolting against the Decalogue Sabbath by erecting a false Sabbath! The true Sabbath honors the Creator God; the false Sabbath the papacy. That is actually what the papacy has done for centuries. But now it becomes a required liturgical act for everyone. A new law will coerce

its worshipers, just as Daniel outlined (chapters 8, 11-12). The words "saying," "speak" and "cause" all reveal this!

Rebellion against the fourth commandment curses who God is – it's blasphemy. A false sabbath is already worshiped by half of the world, and it defies God's saints who keep the Decalogue which originally had the Sabbath in stone. Again, that supports what we already observed in Daniel. The great abomination or sin against God which leads to desolation pointedly relates to defiance of His sanctifying day (Daniel 8:12-13; cf. Exodus 31:13). God firmly revisited that in Ezekiel's vision when He noted the men worshiping the sun, facing the east (the rising sun) as the greatest abomination or sin (Ezekiel 8:15-16).

The image to/of the beast is transcendent. It is theologically descriptive. It defies what God established and honors a false day of worship. The nation of the United States forces the world to set up a false day of worship to honor Rome, which already made the first civil and religious laws, exacting the same allegiance in 321 A.D. The false prophet copies the papacy by forcing others to follow that Catholic dogma!

"But the stern tracings of the prophetic pencil reveal a change in this peaceful scene. The beast with lamb-like horns speaks with the voice of a dragon, and 'exerciseth all the power of the first beast before him.' The spirit of persecution manifested by paganism and the papacy is again to be revealed. Prophecy declares that this power will say 'to them that dwell on the earth, that they should make an image to the beast.' [Rev. 13:14.] The image is made to the first or leopard-like beast, which is the one brought to view in the third angel's message. By this first beast is represented the Roman Church, an ecclesiastical body clothed with civil power, having authority to punish all

---

[1] Aune, David E.; *World Biblical Commentary; Revelation 17–22*, vol. 52c (World Books; Publisher, Dallas, Texas – 1997), p. 761.
[2] *Thayer Lexicon* on *eikon*.

dissenters. The formation of this image is the work of that beast whose peaceful rise and mild professions render it so striking a symbol of the United States. Here is to be found an image of the papacy. When the churches of our land, uniting upon such points of faith as are held by them in common, shall influence the State to enforce their decrees and sustain their institutions, then will Protestant America have formed an image of the Roman hierarchy. Then the true church will be assailed by persecution, as were God's ancient people. Almost every century furnishes examples of what bigotry and malice can do under a plea of serving God by protecting the rights of Church and State. Protestant churches that have followed in the steps of Rome by forming alliance with worldly powers have manifested a similar desire to restrict liberty of conscience. In the seventeenth century thousands of non-conformist ministers suffered under the rule of the Church of England. Persecution always follows religious favoritism on the part of secular governments."[3] That's what this prophecy is all about.

"And he had power to give life unto the image of the beast." (vs 15)

Since laws which suppress God's people are about to be enacted, most conclude that "he" is the false prophet, earth beast or the United States.

The conveyance of life is *dounai pneuma*, which simply means "gives it breath." It symbolically makes this image have the ability to function, as though it were alive, the true, the original. The image "makes a statement." Since it replicates the sea beast's claim to have authority to

change God's law, whatever it says will be like its lion mouth – roaring (everyone hears), ferocious (will threaten) and destructive (its teeth will harm).

How has the papacy dealt with the Sabbath/Sunday issue?

Pope Sylvester I wrote the first ecclesiastical Sunday law (314 A.D.): "If every Sunday is to be observed joyfully by the Christians on account of the resurrection, then every Sabbath on account of the burial is to be execration [loathing or cursed] of the Jews."[4] Constantine's civil Sunday law followed seven years later (321 A.D.).

Is there anything contemporary that might be "copied" relative to this? Pope John Paul II wrote a major encyclical called *Dies Domini* advocating the observance of sacredness of Sunday:

"Point 66. *In this matter, my predecessor Pope Leo XIII in his Enclyclical Rerum Novarum spoke of Sunday rest as a worker's right* **which the State must guarantee**."

"**Point 67.** Therefore, also in the particular circumstances of our own time, *Christians* **will naturally strive** *to ensure that* **civil legislation respects** *their duty to keep Sunday holy." Dies Domini* 5/31/1998.

It may seem that this pope was peaceful and would not be involved in coercive measures to enforce religious duty. But, in 1983 he changed several areas of the Canon Law of the Church, which governs the religious and civil life of Rome.

"The figure of John Paul II is almost apocalyptic in grandeur. Underneath the facade, however, is an iron fisted hold on people in terms of law. Like Pope Gregory VII (1073-1085), who resolved never to rest until he had subjected all authority and power, both spiritual and temporal, to the

---

3   White, Ellen G.; *The Spirit of Prophecy,* vol. 4, pp. 277-278.

4   Quoted by S. R. E. Humbert, Adversus Graecorum calumnies 6, in Patrologie Cursus Completus, Series Latina, ed. J. P. Migne, 1844, p. 143.

'chair of Peter,' so also the present Pope is determined to build such an empire, by both Church and civil law. John Paul II has been adamant in his efforts to update the laws of the Roman Catholic Church. Since the days of Gregory VII, Popes have seen the necessity of making iron and inflexible church laws before attempting to control their subjects and others by compulsion, if necessary. In 1983, John Paul II's revision of the 1917 *Code of Canon Law* added to the Roman Catholic laws, for example, '**The Church has an innate and proper right to coerce** offending members of the Christian faithful by means of penal sanctions.'

"Examination of these added laws shows them to be even more absolute and totalitarian than those of the past. In his law the Pope, in clearer terms than any cult, enunciates the necessity of suppressing one's God given faculties, especially the mind and will. 'A religious *respect of intellect and will,* even if not the assent of faith, is to be paid to the teaching ... [of] the Supreme Pontiff ...' The consequences of not submitting are also spelled out in his law, 'The following are to be punished with *a just penalty:*

consistent with the supernatural end of the Church.'[5]

"John Paul II knows right well how to enforce his will in law. In few things is his genius more conspicuous than in this." There are no checks and balances in Catholic Canon Law. Note the following:

"'The Church's governmental system is vastly different from the notion of a balance of powers. In fact, the three functions are situated in the same office.... *Unlike the American system, ecclesiastical law does not arise from the will of the governed, nor does the Church's juridical structure rely on a system of checks and balances to maintain its effectiveness* ... The Code promotes this system through a hierarchical structure that is more vertical than horizontal. *Ultimately, the highest judge, the pope, is also the highest legislator and administrator.*"[6]

That spirit, dogma and judicial rancor are what the "image" is all about.

What does it speak? In prophecy "speaking" usually means a law or decree is brought into effect. *If* this image of the papacy relates to the Sabbath – and evidence is strong that it does – this law relates to that same

---

The enforcement of a papal "religious duty" by any civil power is making an "image to the beast." The false sabbath issue is *the* issue (noted in their documents) that conveys civil or religious penalties if resisted! This directive began with Pope John Paul II – the "head" that "is." Obedience to that rule is nothing short of worshiping the beast.

---

1. a person who teaches a doctrine condemned by the Roman Pontiff ...' Specific penalties are also decreed, 'The law can establish other *expiatory penalties* which deprive a believer of some spiritual or temporal good and are

issue. A false sabbath law – based upon its history – is anticipated. But this law is more than a religious Catholic membership

5 Bennett, Richard; www.biblebelievers.com/bennett/ bennett_john_paul2.html
6 *Ibid.,* "The Accomplishments of John Paul II, *EndTime Issues...,* Nov. 2003 (emphasis added).

requirement. It is for all inhabitants of earth. Horrifying and terrifying – it will eventually have a death penalty!

God gives life – this image leads to removal of life. God only can remove life eternally – this image is given life to act and "function." Interesting!

"and cause that as many as would not worship the image of the beast should be killed." (vs 15)

The golden idol worship of Nebuchadnezzar is seen once again. Obeisance or death confronted Shadrach, Meshach and Abednego. Worshiping this "image" or false sabbath will soon lead to threatened loss of life.

This prophecy surrounds a key issue – who/what is worshipped? The United States forces the world to worship a false sabbath. God says "worship only me, the Creator God of the seventh-day Sabbath."

This is not an annihilation of the righteous. The woman's escape into the wilderness (12:14) conveying spiritual protection to God's people. The dragon still spews a flood at her, suggesting persecution will reach her precincts. The great multitude which no man could number (7:9) reveals that there is a vast group of tribulation survivers (7:13-15). That also means that those who have no ability to buy or sell will successfully pass through this time (13:17-18).[7]

This imagery fulfills the devilish threat of making war on the saints spoken of in verse 7.

7. Thomas, Robert L.; *Revelation 8–22 – An Exegetical Commentary* (Moody Press, Chicago – 1992), p. 179.

CHAPTER 31

THE "MARK OF THE BEAST" MARKS THE BEAST

"And he causeth all, both small and great, rich and poor, free and bond, to receive a mark in their right hand, or in their foreheads:" (Revelation 13:16).

The power of the once Protestant United States, now in apostasy, has entered a time of imposing oppression. Its leaders have created religious laws with enforcement teeth that complement the careless masses. It intimidates and terrorizes the saints, who disagree with its required religious dictums. This country's strong arm of coercive moves continues with another stunning step:

"And he causeth all, both small and great, rich and poor, free and bond," (vs 16)

There are many ways that this apocalyptic book expresses "the whole world."

- "And the kings of the earth, and the great men, and the rich men, and the chief captains, and the mighty men, and every bondman, and every free man, hid themselves in the dens and in the rocks of the mountains" (Revelation 6:15a,b).
- "The nations were angry" (11:18).
- "The whole world wondered" (13:3)
- "All that dwell on the earth shall worship" (13:8)

This verse (16) is another expression, showing how extensive its universal control has become – "causeth all."

This is the ninth time the word *poiei* ("causeth" – makes, **forces**) is used. It is riveted into the reader's understanding that this nation of freedom and democracy, beginning like a lamb, changes into a suppressive government. What is inconceivable is that this hand of despotism finally encircles the world! The inclusive language encompasses every individual!

"to receive a mark in their right hand, or in their foreheads:" (vs 16)

This echoes a contrast to the sealing of the saints:

- Servants of God are sealed – in foreheads (7:3) (Christ's name – 22:4). They escape God's wrath.
- Wicked world marked – in forehead or hand (13:16) (Babylon – 666). They escape the beast's wrath.[1]

God is seemingly revealing that this marking is a final act that will bring a judicial response from the One who separates the good and the bad – the sheep and the goats (Matthew 25:32-33). This comes into sharp focus in the third angel's message (14:9-11). Those who are charmed by the papal image and are enticed into receiving his mark are addressed in another more serious manner – their names will be absent from the Book of Life:

---

1   Thomas, Robert L.; *Revelation 8–22 – An Exegetical Commentary* (Moody Press, Chicago – 1992), p. 180.

- Those who **worship** the beast will not have their names in that citizens' record (13:8).
- The "dwellers on the earth" are the wicked who **wonder** after the beast and are not found in that book (17:8).
- Soon, in graphic language, those not in that book will be burned with fire (20:15).

We can, therefore, assume that those who are lost are *enamored* by the beast, participate in *worshiping his image* and have that mark. What is that *mark*? Speculation is limited only by the imagination. Very helpful concepts introduced by expositor White regarding God's seal help us in a dramatic comparison:

"I saw Satan would work more powerfully now than ever he has before. He knows that his time is short and that the sealing of the saints will place them beyond his power; he will now work in every way that he can and will try his every

insinuation to get the saints off from their guard and get them asleep on the present truth or doubting it, so as to prevent their being sealed with the seal of the living God."[2]

"Just as soon as the people of God are sealed in their foreheads – it is not any seal or mark that can be seen, but a settling into the truth, both intellectually and spiritually, so they cannot be moved – just as soon as God's people are sealed and prepared for the shaking, it will come."[3]

The mark is "certainly the satanic counterpart to the sealing of the saints by God in 7:2-4."[4]

If we assume, therefore, that the seal of God is an opposite delineation of the "mark" (and that does appear to be valid), the picture in the box below emerges.

Since life and death power resides in the earth beast *related to that mark,* one is **tempted to conclude** that some "record" or "stamp" identifies those who will resist or accept those religious laws. That leads to "adding" speculative ideas to His word. The

	Seal of God	Mark of the Beast
Forehead	Fully identify with Christ	Fully identify with Babylon – 666
Hand		Pretend to accept it to avoid penalties
Invisible	Invisible	Invisible (assumed)
Settling in	Of truth intellectually and spiritually	Of falsehood intellectually and spiritually
Places	Saints beyond Satan's power	Wicked beyond Christ's power
Loyalty to	Christ is defined by his Sabbath, the Creator's 7th	Beast is defined by his Sabbath, the Babylonian 6th (doesn't reach 7th)

2   White, Ellen G.; *Manuscript Releases,* vol. 8, p. 220 (1850).
3   White, Ellen G.; *Last Day Events,* pp. 219-220 (1902).
4   Osborne, Grant R.; *Revelation* (Baker Book House; Grand Rapids, MI), p. 517.

mere obedience/ disobedience of enforced civil codes will quickly reveal who is on the Lord's side.

The sealing of the saints of Ezekiel 9:4 by Yahweh was by the Hebrew letter tau placed on their foreheads. That indicated that they belonged to Him. They were saved. The mark of the beast/dragon means that they belong to him – their destiny is sealed. They are lost.

How do we deal with the legal language that the beast makes the world receive a mark that sounds literal? Even the inkhorn (*tau*) mark of Ezekiel appears like an authentic "literal" branding of some sort! That literal assumption adds another dimension to the imagination, detracting from the deeper issues being conveyed. Most scholars feel that it is incorrect to take it literally.[5]

"That the mark of the name is figurative and not literal is evident from the 'blasphemous names' on the head of the beast (13:1), which figuratively connote false claims to earthly divine kingship.

"No evidence, however, can be cited from the ancient world where a *charagma* is placed on a *person,* let alone on the 'right hand' or on the 'forehead,' though a seal (*sphragis*) was customarily put on slaves and soldiers."[6] *Charagma* is the Greek word for that "mark."

This "mark" and God's "seal" both represent the final imagery of where eternal loyalty is given. It relates to one's response to a *religious dictum,* which epitomizes either loyalty to God or Satan. It is a "citizenship certificate" as to what kingdom a person has entered. It is a legal symbol, a metaphorical passport into a dominion. Once issued – it is irrevocable.

What then is a specific *sign* of God's *seal* or *mark*?

1. Sabbath is a *sign* forever that God is Lord (Exodus 31:13, Ezekiel 20:20)
2. Sabbath is a *sign* forever that He sanctifies them (31:13)
3. Keeping it holy is *God's key* life and death issue (31:14)
4. Keeping it preserves man's *perpetual covenant* with God (31:16)
5. It is a *sign* to God of man's friendship (31:17)

The actual mark or seal is depicted in two ways:

1. As a family name and title deed to the saved (Revelation 3:12)
2. Identifies who their king is! (Ezekiel 9:4, Revelation 7:2-3, 22:4)

The latter is what is alluded to in this chapter and echoes those wonderful themes described in Exodus. Keeping the Bible Sabbath is a *sign* (our *mark*) of who our Leader is – Creator God!

If the mark of God on the saints and the mark of Satan from the papacy are opposites (and they are), then we must see the Sabbath revealing dramatic polarization.

God's Mark	Beast's Mark
True Sabbath	False sabbath
Voluntary acceptance	Forced acceptance
God's law	Man's law

---

[5] Beale, G. K.; *The New International Greek Testament Commentary; The Book of Revelation* (William B. Eerdmans Publishing Company, Grand Rapids, Michigan – 1999), p. 716.

[6] *Ibid.* (emphasis added).

The malignant spirit of the earth beast deepens. Wherever there is a law, and a "marking" issue, there has to be a punishment for those who breach it. Amazing – that's what happens next!

The incredible details related to this end-time Sabbath apostasy are detailed in Daniel 8–12. There, the rebellion, laws forcing the will, persecution and hatred against the true Sabbath are presented.

CHAPTER 32

ECONOMIC SANCTIONS UNLESS MARKED

"And that no man might buy or sell, save he that had the mark, or the name of the beast, or the number of his name" (Revelation 13:17).

"And that no man might buy or sell," (vs 17)

This does not describe a financial depression, it characterizes *economic sanctions*. The United States will impose repressive measures based on resistance to religious issues. This signals a desperate situation, a last-ditch effort to solve global problems, now perceived to be "spiritually" associated. This act is coersive and reflects one aspect of persecution against the saints. Jesus notes that this suppressive spirit begins when a "time of sorrows" has come to the world (Matthew 24:8). Mark, who first recorded this warning, noted a collection of calamities that would lead to this state of affairs.

The full meaning of what this period of sorrows represents is not conveyed. Apparently a dire situation has fallen upon the earth, and its inhabitants see nowhere to turn but to God. They follow the advice of the papacy – and laws forcing Sunday worship become tyrannical and cruel.

"save he that had the mark, or the name of the beast, or the number of his name." (vs 17)

This distinguishing "stain" is the world's badge of honor. It will take a while, but they will discover it was satanically inspired!

This mark is on the forehead or right hand (vs 16). Intriguingly, the name of Christ – the Lamb – is on the forehead of the redeemed (22:4). The "mark of the beast" is held out as relentless pressure to conform to Rome and not to God. "You will suffer unless you yield."

The clearest rendition of the phrase "the mark, or the name of the beast, or the number of his name" *is* "the mark, *which is* the name ... or the number called himself."[1] This means that the "mark" is characterized by these two features.

Mark of the Beast

Name   and/or   Number

The NIV and NET Bibles word it this way:

"... so that they could not buy or sell unless they had the mark, which is the name of the beast or the number of its name." (Revelation 13:17 – NIV).

"Thus no one was allowed to buy or sell things unless he bore the mark of the beast – that is, his name or his number" (Revelation 13:17 – NET).

The number will be described in the next verse. The name can be defined through the context of the beast and the woman who rides that creature.

- The beast was full of the names of blasphemy (17:3).
- The beast's heads had on each one the name of blasphemy (13:1).

---

[1] Tischendorf New Testament (8th edition), Greek (emphasis added).

- The harlot's name was on her forehead, "mystery, Babylon the great, the mother of harlots and abominations of the earth" (17:5).

Whatever the earth beast/United States is forcing on earth's inhabitants, one can deduce several points from Revelation 17 and 13:

1. Its name signifies blaspheme against God.
2. It relates to issues associated with Babylon.
3. Whatever it shares and symbolizes, God has called it "abominations of the earth."

These clues again take us to Daniel where many agencies are blaspheming God. A specific area where Jesus wanted us to focus was the "abominations that lead to desolation" (see Appendix III). Those horrible sins called transgressions (be•pesha) are shown to be against God's true Sabbath. He is honored as the "Creator God" by our keeping the seventh day holy. The issue of a false sabbath defies God and His authority. The abomination is blasphemy against Him; and through its number, we will discover that it is Babylon association is a fearful element. God has warned that is fallen – "come out of her" (Revelation 18:2, 4).

The ultimate "name" is best seen as duplicating the "name" on the harlot's head – Babylon. Everything that this prophetic word alludes to is what the "mark of the beast" stands for. It is symbolized/epitomized by a false sabbath. The anti-Creator sabbath!

CHAPTER 33

THAT MYSTICAL NUMBER – 666

"Here is wisdom. Let him that hath understanding count the number of the beast: for it is the number of a man; and his number *is* Six hundred threescore *and* six" (Revelation 13:18).

"Here is wisdom." (vs 18)

The literature is filled with strange, entertaining and imaginative claims as to what this verse means. John's opening words are instructive and a warning: *hode he sophia* – "here is wisdom." This demands extraordinary understanding (I Corinthians 2:14).

When Daniel was receiving those amazing last-day timing visions, he heard Christ tell him: "Those who are wise will understand" (Daniel 12:10). What kind of reasoning or thought process relates to Scriptural wisdom? It is uniquely associated with end-time prophecy that God's Spirit helps to clarify. An incredible link is found in Mark 13:14 and Matthew 24:15 to those visions in Daniel. We are instructed to go where he prophesied that the "abomination that causes desolation" would be found. Then Jesus, in an aura of urgency, said: "Let the reader understand" (Mark 13:14). Contextually, the messages can be understood. In Daniel they can't be understood until the "time of the end" (es qes) (Daniel 12:4, 9). They are now clear! Where is that spirit-filled "wisdom" found? Daniel 12 is front and center. It is linked to this numeric mystery.

God made a remarkable promise through the apostle James: "If any of you lack wisdom, let him ask of God, that giveth to all men liberally, and upbraideth not; and it shall be given him" (James 1:5).

These verses require a special endowment of the Holy Spirit to grasp and understand. Careless speculation will dishonor God and confuse the solemn issues He is conveying.

"In other words, this is seen as a critical point of the passage, and John is calling for his readers to exercise extreme care and divinely guided wisdom in interpreting this number. It also means that he expected his readers to understand it, pointing further to the solution as centered in first-century rather than twentieth-century symbolism."[1]

"Thoughtful investigation and earnest, taxing study are required to comprehend it. There are truths in the word which are like veins of precious ore concealed beneath the surface. By digging for them, as the man digs for gold and silver, the hidden treasures are discovered. *Be sure that the evidence of truth is in the Scripture itself.* One scripture is the key to unlock other scriptures. The rich and hidden meaning is unfolded by the Holy Spirit of God, making plain the word to our understanding: 'The entrance of Thy words giveth light; it giveth understanding unto the simple.'"[2]

"All over the field of revelation are scattered the glad springs of heavenly truth, and peace, and joy. They are within the reach of every seeker. The words of

---

1 Osborne, Grant R.; *Revelation* (Baker Book House; Grand Rapids, MI), p. 519.
2 White, Ellen G.; *Fundamentals of Christian Education,* p. 390.

inspiration, pondered in the heart, will be as streams flowing from the river of the water of life. Our Saviour prayed that the minds of the disciples might be opened to understand the Scriptures. And whenever we study the Bible with a prayerful heart, the Holy Spirit is near to open to us the meaning of the words we read."[3]

"Let him that hath understanding count the number of the beast:" (vs 18)

Those earnestly seeking God's Spirit to guide them can enter into the realm of actually calculating or ascertaining the meaning of the beast's number. Recall that the mark of the beast was either its name or its number. They are related. This verse opens up that number.

The name and especially the number are symbols for the antichrist or anti-Christian powers in which 666 is a specific numeric symbol tied to Babylon. It is adopted by humanity who are in total rebellion against God. It represents "incompleteness, incompleteness, incompleteness," whereas seven is the complete or perfect number in the book.[4]

"Counting" the number, an idiomatic expression, means to solve the numeric code. "Figure out, interpret, come to an understanding."[5]

This is *the* numeric identity with the beast. Since the number six falls short of the perfect number seven, it represents an imperfect number. The horrible beast is being guided by and supports the harlot, noted in Revelation 17:3. This lady is identified not only as an apostate church located in Rome but as "Babylon the Great" (17:5). She represents all of the apostasy outlined in the Bible related

to that city. Intriguingly, *Babylon had a numeric system tied to the number six.*

In the next chapter God is informing the world that "Babylon has fallen." God finally acts toward that abominable apostasy, and the Record says that the "great Babylon came in remembrance before God, to give unto her the cup of the wine of the fierceness of his wrath" (16:19). It is then broken into three parts.

Those parts represent the false trinity who are all acting like God – trying to be honored and perceived as God: (1) the dragon – Satan, (2) the sea beast – papacy and (3) the earth beast – false prophet – apostate Protestantism. The triple six identifies each of these agencies as in rebellion. They never honor God's sacred seven. They maintain an allegiance to a false sabbath – thus, they fall short of God's divine plan.

"for it is the number of a man;" (vs 18)

The Greek word interpreted as "man" is *anthropou.* It has many allusions to man, humanity or mankind. Several translators have worked through its context in this book and feel it is better to use: "it is man's number" (NIV), referring to mankind in general. John uses the same word in 21:17, where the New Jerusalem is being measured according to the "measurements" of *anthropou* or mankind. Most expositors feel that this relates to a "human measurement" (NAS, NET) or "mankind's measurement." That new city was measured by the benchmark system man uses. There, the measurement of a "cubit" was used. Thus, it is *not* the number of *a man* but a measurement of mankind!

"and his number *is* Six hundred threescore *and* six." (vs 18)

---

[3]   White, Ellen G.; *Our High Calling,* p.205.

[4]   Osborne, *op. cit.,* p. 520.

[5]   *Freiberg Lexicon* on Revelation 13:18.

Man's measuring system developed in Babylon was based on sixty and sixes. Ours is based on ten. Nebuchadnezzar's image was 60 cubits high and 6 cubits wide (Daniel 3:1). The sun was worshiped. They created a "sun dial" to tell time. Sixty degrees were assigned to each sixth of a circle – thus, 360 degrees came to represent a full circle.

The Babylonians became far advanced in astronomy and mathematics. In turn, out of their mystical worship of celestial objects, they developed a complex belief system tied to astrology. That system was directly associated with the number of 666. To protect them from many angry celestial gods, they created amulets to wear around the neck with a matrix of 6x6 or 36 squares. In each square was a number. In either direction (horizontally or vertically), when the columns were added up, they equaled 111 – then times 6 columns equaled 666 on each side. On the next page are photographs of amulets.

Notice the sun god Shamash on one side. Tied to their sun worship was the mystical number 666.

Adam and Eve were created on the sixth day. Without the seventh day of rest they would have been imperfect. The idea of incompleteness "is also evident from writings that interpreted the seven days of Genesis 1, by way of Psalm 90:4, as representing seven thousand years of world history (*Barnabas* 15; Irenaeus, *Adversus Haereses* 5.28.3; cf. *b. Sanhedrin* 97a). The sixth thousand was to be the time of antichrist, immediately preceding the Messiah's victorious millennial reign (cf. *Barnabas* 15). Against the background of this chronological reckoning of world history, Irenaeus (*Adversus Haereses* 5.28.2) understood 666 'as a summing up of the whole of that apostasy that has taken place during six thousand years.' This idea of 'six' is also present in the sixth seal, the sixth trumpet, and the sixth bowl, which all depict actions or reactions of the beast's followers. The seventh in each series depicts (in various expressions) the consummated kingdom of Christ. Each series is incomplete without the seventh."[6]

The weight of evidence suggests that the seventh-day Sabbath will be pivotal in this great time of rebellion against God. The sacred seven found deep in God's prophetic numbering system is rejected. Babylon, the symbol for satanic power working on man, becomes a system that God urgently calls His people out of. They have established a false worship day – Sun-day – based on the apostate number of 666. That numeric "sign" relates to the false trinity that divinely comes to her end (Revelation 16:19).

6   Beale, G. K.; *The New International Greek Testament Commentary; The Book of Revelation* (William B. Eerdmans Publishing Company, Grand Rapids, Michigan – 1999), p. 722.

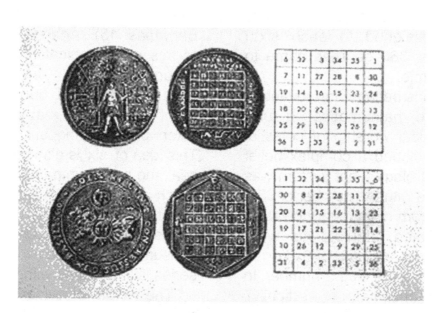

CHAPTER 34

PREPARATION FOR EARTH'S FINAL WARNING

Revelation 18 is part of the interlude that began in the previous chapter. It fills in terminal details of events going all the way back to the first Trumpet. Its greatest focus is on the delusive, subordinate course the world takes toward Babylon – headed by the papacy. A bizarre, almost schizophrenic, reaction is depicted towards it:

1. The **world** laments that Babylon has fallen, seemingly because of what it had hoped to gain from the relationship (this chapter).
2. The **world** hates the "whore" (Babylon) and will soon make her desolate (Revelation 17:16).

The destruction of Babylon (17:16; cf. 16:19) – specifically the harlot – is now enlarged into a full vision. This really completes the angelic promise that John would see the terminal judgment of this evil church (17:1). What now follows is an overarching theme of the final end of Babylon/ Rome.[1]

The storyline enters the stage by John witnessing another flying angel.

"And after these things I saw another angel come down from heaven, having great power; and the earth was lightened with his glory" (Revelation 18:1).

<hr/>

[1] Osborne, Grant R.; *Revelation* (Baker Book House; Grand Rapids, MI), p. 631.

"And after these things I saw" (vs 1)

These are words John frequently uses to announce a transition between two visions or prophecies.

"another angel come down from heaven," (vs 1)

The last **messenger** angels were what is deemed the "three angels" in Revelation 14. They were flying *"in the midst of heaven"* [14:6, 14:8 (implied), 14:9 (implied)]. This angel appears to come down from heaven!

There is, however, another angel with unique parallel language that appears to be the precursor to this angel. Both **come down** from heaven – both cry with a **loud voice:** "And I saw another mighty angel come down from heaven, clothed with a cloud: and a rainbow *was* upon his head, and his face *was* as it were the sun, and his feet as pillars of fire: And he had in his hand a little book open: and he set his right foot upon the sea, and *his* left *foot* on the earth" (Revelation 10:1-2).

Could this be a sequencing cue? This appears to be an important consideration. This is part of the timing imagery embedded in these prophecies (see box – next page).

That first "angel" is identified as Christ (10:1). There, the description of His Being unquestionably represents a divine person who has descriptive parallels to Revelation 1:13-18 and Daniel 10:5-6. In the former vision He was like the "Son of man" (Revelation 1:13) and self-declared as the

Babylon's fall but how horrendously evil it is.

Angel with Loud Cry (Rev. 10:1-2, 11:2-3)	Angel with Strong Voice (Rev. 16:19, 18:1-2, 8-9, 24; Dan. 12:6-7)
Seven warning thunders Prepare – eat the Word	Warning: Babylon filled with demons
Time will soon no longer be delayed	Prepare – come out
Judgment of the living begins	Last chance – time about to end
A 3½-year period begins	In one hour executive judgment comes A 3½-year period ends

- Clearly – this sets the stage to detail what is about to happen in the third angel's message (14:9-11).
- An end to Babylon – this harlot, the world has been enamored with, is presently anticipated.

There is a terminal flow of redemptive information in this chapter. It begins with an urgent cry to prepare – the opportunity to respond is still open. It ends when God's judicial act has brought Babylon to its end. Probation will have closed.

everlasting (vss 17-18).

The imagery in Revelation 18 appears to draw on two very distinct areas!

1. The information contained in the little open book of Revelation 10 becomes part of the message to "prophesy again" to the whole world (10:11). It is then carried throughout the earth by His two witnesses (11:3-71).
2. The second messenger angel in Revelation 14:8: "And there followed another angel, saying, Babylon is fallen, is fallen, that great city, because she made all nations drink of the wine of the wrath of her fornication."

However, in linking both areas, a final call is suggested. The onset of the last three and a half years has been entered (11:3). Not only is there the warning of

- Babylon is fallen (vs 2) – last warning to man
- Sins have reach to heaven (vs 5)
- Plagues have started (vs 8)
- Babylon will be utterly burned with fire (vs 8-9)
- With violence the great city Babylon is thrown down (vs 21)

The record of its fall was in 16:19. We now have unfolded the final sequence of prophetic events in that drama. The story of how terrible this city/beast acts is graphically shown in Revelation 13. The angel's warning as to what God's expectations are and how much at variance Babylon is (Revelation 14) to the divine plan are portrayed. Then God's ominous wrath as to its final end comes.

Now, here, it must be close to the *final end* of that three-and-a-half-year period. This "angel" "coming down" means that it has a message directly from heaven for God's witnesses. The last thunder warning voices are about to sound.

"having great power; and the earth was lightened with his glory." (vs 1)

This power (*exousian*) or authority means that it will complete its mission. Nothing will stop it. This parallels the announcement regarding the two witnesses where nothing would stop them until "they shall finish their testimony" (11:7a).

The word "earth" foretells that the whole world – all its inhabitants – will hear this final appeal.

The intriguing expression lies in the phrase "lightened with his glory." No celestial angelic being has glory (*doxes*). This "angel" is symbolic of Christ giving His witnesses their last call, conveying divine glory through the heavenly oil! Since the parallels to 10 and 11 are strong, those witnessing saints reflect the glory described there (10:1) as Jesus' face like the sun.

There's more – far more. Though the details cannot be fully elucidated here, this prophecy was first given by Ezekiel. Though there was a minor application then to the Babylonian issues for the Jewish people, a great eschatological story is portrayed in those ancient prophecies!

"Most agree that Ezek. 43:2 is echoed here, 'The land was radiant with his glory.' In Ezek. 43 the measurements of the temple have been completed (42:15-20), and now a solemn procession occurs as Yahweh enters the restored temple through the east gate (43:1). Here the glory of God once more returns to the temple (43:2-9) and illumines the whole earth (43:2). In that narration, Israel is reminded of the past and warned of future judgments if she persists in her sin (43:3, 7-9). The twin motifs of Yahweh's glorious presence and the warnings of judgment are also present here, and it is likely that John intended these parallels to Ezek. 43. Some (Beale 1999:893, following Sweet 1979: 266) also believe that this anticipates Rev. 21:10-11, the New Jerusalem that is also based in part on Ezek. 40–48. 'The desolation of Babylon thus prepares the way for God to dwell in the new creation.'"[2]

The final cry, which will soon unfold here by John, is there recorded: "Now let them put away their whoredom" (Ezekiel 43:9). That "replacement city for Babylon," the New Jerusalem, is called in Ezekiel by a most fascinating name:

- "And the name of the city from that day shall be, The **Lord is there**" (Ezekiel 48:35).
- "And I saw no temple therein: for the Lord God Almighty and the Lamb are the temple of it" (Revelation 21:22).

2   Beale, G. K.; *The New International Greek Testament Commentary; The Book of Revelation* (William B. Eerdmans Publishing Company, Grand Rapids, Michigan – 1999), p. 893.

CHAPTER 35

THE DEVIL'S PRISON HOUSE

"And he cried mightily with a strong voice, saying, Babylon the great is fallen, is fallen, and is become the habitation of devils, and the hold of every foul spirit, and a cage of every unclean and hateful bird" (Revelation 18:2).

"And he cried mightily with a strong voice," (vs 2)

Such voices represent important warnings or announcements preceding major redemptive events! Elsewhere, such warning markers are called "loud voice" or "great voice." They are authoritative and represent the certainty of the message[1] and its universal application. They are often final warnings to those who may have delayed commitment to God.

- First voice as it were a trumpet (4:1; cf. 1:10) – Feast of Trumpets final warning call – judgment is about to begin
- Throne then thunder – judgment underway (Revelation 4:2, 5)
- "Loud voice" (5:2) asking who is worthy to begin the time of the end
- "Loud voice" (7:2) – protect the sealing or making up of God's kingdom
- "Loud voice" (7:10) – kingdom made up – praise

---

[1] Beale, G. K.; *The New International Greek Testament Commentary; The Book of Revelation* (William B. Eerdmans Publishing Company, Grand Rapids, Michigan – 1999), p. 893.

- "Loud voice (10:3) – announcing the appointed time will soon begin (during that judgment)
- "Loud voice" (14:7) – the hour of God's judgment has begun
- "Loud voice" (14:9) – warning that executive judgment is about to occur
- "Loud voice" (14:15) – announces the harvest will soon occur
- "Great voice" (16:1) – announcing that probation has closed
- "Strong voice" (18:2) – interlude – last warning call (likely begins one year before probation closes at a typological *Shemita* starting at Trumpets)
- "Loud voice" (19:17) – announcing that all the wicked will die at His coming

"saying, Babylon the great is fallen, is fallen," (vs 2)

This repeats the second angel's herald (14:8) and echoes Isaiah: "And he answered and said, Babylon is fallen, is fallen; and all the graven images of her gods he hath broken unto the ground" (Isaiah 21:9b). Its judicial end will find its idols destroyed. Since the antichrist has idolized herself, she too comes to an end.

This will be elaborated on in verse 7, but its message is graphic in the NIV: "Give her as much torture and grief as the glory and luxury she gave herself. In her heart she boasts, 'I sit as queen; I am not a widow, and I will never mourn.'"

A similar allusion is made in Zephaniah: "This *is* the rejoicing city that dwelt carelessly, that said in her heart, I *am,* and *there is* none beside me: how is she become a desolation, a place for beasts to lie down in! every one that passeth by her shall hiss, *and* wag his hand" (Zephaniah 2:15).

"As it fell in times past, so will it be destroyed in the future. Part of the reason for using 'Babylon' is that the readers will know what God did to the first Babylon and be quick to recognize that in giving Rome that title he will once again carry out his judgment of that city. The aorist tense denotes the certainty of future fulfillment. It is the prophetic way of declaring that the great purpose of God in triumphing over evil is a fait *accompli.*" [2]

"and is become the habitation of devils, and the hold of every foul spirit, and a cage of every unclean and hateful bird." (vs 2)

This book is filled with "sets of three" expressions or bits of information. This is one and is called an "apocalyptic trilogy."

The *first expression* describes the Roman Catholic Church – the harlot woman ("Babylon the Great" – Revelation 17) – as the "habitation of devils."

"And Babylon shall become heaps, a dwellingplace for dragons, an astonishment, and an hissing, without an inhabitant" (Jeremiah 51:37).

This is the opposite of Christians, who are said to be the dwelling place of God: "In whom ye also are builded together for an habitation of God through the Spirit" (Ephesians 2:22).

The *second expression* reveals the consequences of being inhabited with Satan's minions – she contains or retains every "foul spirit."

The *third expression* is that this "demon-possessed" church is now graphically portrayed as a cage or prison of every "unclean or hateful bird." The word for "bird" is the usual expression for a cardinal, robin or sparrow. But the description of "unclean" (*akathartos*) and "hateful" (*miseo*) together means a morally detestable angel or evil spirit (same as a demon – 16:13-14).[3]

This is enormously fascinating. The beast came out of the abyss (where Satan's angels reside – 11:7, 17:8), showing the nature of its origins. Satan's angels came out of the abyss (9:2), revealing who they were (depicted as locust with scorpion tails). Now we discover that they have a new home – this stunning apostate church! This is one of the amazing graphic images in this book. Satan's spirits or angels are so much a part of the papacy and its supporting elements, it is described as a prison house![4]

Summary Line!

- Demon possession is in the Church of Rome (by implication, also residing in her "daughters" or apostate Protestantism).
- God's last cry is for people to come out of *demon possessed churches.*

---

2   Mounce, Robert H.; *The Book of Revelation* (Wm. B. Eerdmans Publishing Co., Grand Rapids, Michigan – 1977), p. 325.

3   Ford, J. Massingberde; *The Anchor Bible* (Doubleday, New York), 1975, p. 678.

4   *Ibid.*

CHAPTER 36

GUILT EVERYWHERE

"For all nations have drunk of the wine of the wrath of her fornication, and the kings of the earth have committed fornication with her, and the merchants of the earth are waxed rich through the abundance of her delicacies" (Revelation 18:3).

The reason that Babylon – that great city – the harlot – is filled with demons is now revisited (from chapter 17). In a myriad of ways God re-examines apostasy to unmask and then disclose why Satan is now controlling the "Christian world."

"For all nations have drunk of the wine of the wrath of her fornication," (vs 3)

This comes from:

Revelation 13:3: The *world* wondered after Babylon's leader and even worshiped her.

Revelation 14:8: "she made" (forced) all *nations* to drink (Revelation 17:2, 4).

The imagery is one of:

* The strength of sexual seduction (force)
* Providing enjoyment/fascination
* No limit to her methods

She is the mother of other harlots. She has a trade – a business. She replicates herself until the whole world is involved with her illicit behavior.

What standard is this labeling against? God's laws and His declarations. If anyone is involved with her, he is marked – by God. That is why the previous verse describes how she is "marked." She is demon possessed. God has a response to this – He'll make her drink of His wine! (Revelation 14:10; cf. Jeremiah 25:15-18, 27-28; Isaiah 51:17; Zechariah 12:2).

Fornication/adultery/immorality = religious apostasy.

"For they shall eat, and not have enough: they shall commit whoredom, and shall not increase: because they have left off to take heed to the LORD" (Hosea 4:10).

"Lift up thine eyes unto the high places, and see where thou hast not been lien with. In the ways hast thou sat for them, as the Arabian in the wilderness; and thou hast polluted the land with thy whoredoms and with thy wickedness" (Jeremiah 3:2).

"and the kings of the earth have committed fornication with her," (vs 3)

This now refines the intensity of the illicit relationship. The leaders of the world have joined with her in acts of apostasy against God. This reviews:

* Revelation 17:12-13: Ten horns, which *will be* kings, gave their authority and strength to the beast.
* Revelation 13:1: The horns have crowns; they are now kings ready to work treachery with the beast.

That power is so great that it is over all kindreds and tongues, and nations (13:7)!

Can you imagine world powers that are demon possessed? Then it notes that they make war against the remnant (12:17) or saints (13:7).

In the Old Testament God's people are seen as a wife to God (Yahweh)

[Leviticus 17:7, Numbers 14:33, Deuteronomy 31:16; cf. Jude 2:17 (apocryphal), I Chronicles 5:25, Psalm 73:27, Hosea 1:2]. Tyre is a metaphor for apostasy, described as a "prostitute" selling herself to the "kingdoms of the earth" for profit (Isaiah 23:17). That imagery, in turn, shows its commercial or financial benefit to Tyre. In Daniel 11:43 it is noted: "But he shall have power over the treasures of gold and of silver." In verses 9-19 of this eighteenth chapter the world grieves over Babylon when it comes into judgment. Much of that lament relates, intriguingly, to loss of commercial interest!

"and the merchants of the earth are waxed rich through the abundance of her delicacies." (vs 3)

These were wholesale dealers[1] referred to four times in this chapter. They dealt in large quantities of "merchandise" and grew wealthy from their trade (vss 15, 23).

In Roman history, merchants used wealth to control the world, much like armies. This becomes the elite class and part of the civil bureaucracy. Commerce –

finances – will become centered in Rome.

1. **The people of the world**
2. **The leaders of the world**
3. **The commerce of the world**

} Associated with the Roman Church – the apostate woman

} When she comes to her end, the economic value ceases; their wealth then vanishes.

Much of this prophecy relates to a lament found in Ezekiel 27 over Tyre.

Thus, we have fascinating indictments from the divine Court.

The world supports some falsehood that the devil creates. Thus, a religious issue is promulgated. In this vast coalition – an economic network is established. There appears to be financial rewards ("delicacies") that come to the earth from this global alliance. It is a bond of "common cause," a new world order.

Since mankind is universally morally bankrupt, this verse sets the tone for the last call to repentance (vs 4) before destructive judgments (vss 5-6). The outcome? "Go to now, *ye* rich men, weep and howl for your miseries that shall come upon *you*" (James 5:1).

In ways that are not clear, the actual power of the woman Babylon or sea beast works to enrich merchants, kings and herself.[2] This is portrayed by the terms "lived deliciously."

This lifestyle is self-indulgent and is insolently and luxuriously based on a religious bond that unites their coalition. God sees it as a lewd act, an adulterous accord. This chapter ties to an Old Testament metaphor likened to end-time Babylon: "And Ephraim said, Yet I am become rich, I have found me out substance: *in* all my labours they shall find none iniquity in me that *were* sin" (Hosea 12:8). He was an apostate whose tribe led to Israel's fall.

1 Osborne, Grant R.; *Revelation* (Baker Book House; Grand Rapids, MI), p. 637.

2 Thomas, Robert L.; *Revelation 8-22 – An Exegetical Commentary* (Moody Press, Chicago – 1992), p. 319.

CHAPTER 37

GOD'S EMERGENCY CALL

"And I heard another voice from heaven, saying, Come out of her, my people, that ye be not partakers of her sins, and that ye receive not of her plagues. For her sins have reached unto heaven, and God hath remembered her iniquities" (Revelation 18:4-5).

"And I heard another voice from heaven." (vs 4)

There is disagreement as to "who" the voice is. The allusions to God's witnesses, to an angel or to Christ or even God Himself, have been proposed. Because He will address those saints still in Babylon as "my people," and then in the next verse we will hear God the Father speak, it suggests that it is a message from His throne (cf. 10:4, 8; 14:2).

"saying, Come out of her, my people," (vs 4)

Here and 21:3 are the only places that the remnant are addressed as God's people. What a wonderful divine missive to know that we can be His — in the truest sense of family language.

Since Babylon is about to be destroyed, "get out of it." The call is an urgent cry to His saints to escape to protect yourselves before it's too late.

"that ye be not partakers of her sins, and that ye receive not of her plagues." (vs 4)

Paul had a similar concern for young people (II Timothy 2:22): "Flee also youthful lusts: but follow righteousness, faith, charity, peace, with them that call on the Lord out of a pure heart."

The sins of Babylon lead to God's wrath and, in a unique chiasm, are drawn together.[1]

Lest you share
In her sins
And her plagues
Lest you receive

This arrangement heightens the cause and effect relationship between the sin and the plagues.[2]

- If you share in her sins
- You will share in her plagues

Similar language is used for Sodom and Gomorrah (Genesis 19:15, 17, 26) and with ancient Babylon (Isaiah 48:20; Jeremiah 50:8-9, 51:6, 9, 45; Zechariah 2:6-7).

All this "summons to escape" echoes Paul's exhortation to the Corinthians: "Wherefore come out from among them, and be ye separate, saith the Lord, and touch not the unclean *thing*; and I will receive you" (II Corinthians 6:17).

This has become a spiritual call to the last generation of believers. It is when one

---

1. Aune, David E.; *52C World Biblical Commentary; Revelation 1-5* (World Books; Publisher, Dallas, Texas), 1997, pp. 991-992 (special order in the Greek).
2. Osborne, Grant R.; *Revelation* (Baker Book House; Grand Rapids, MI), p. 639).

must 'renounce their rights as citizens of the world"[3]

The nature of the separation command is urgent. One perceives that execution of God's judicial wrath will quickly follow. The tension of human emotion is heightened with:

"For her sins have reached unto heaven," (vs 5)

This unique expression means that those sins have judicially touched the court of heaven. A *God response* is anticipated. It is now an active case before the bar.

- It echoes the apostate people who built the tower of Babel (Genesis 11:4) that reached "to the heavens." That's when God reacted.
- God denounced ancient literal Babylon and said that her "judgment" (sins) reached to the "skies" or, literally, to the "clouds" (Jeremiah 51:9, 53). Babylon will fall (Jeremiah 50:35–51:58).

Ezra was filled with gratitude at God's gracious intervention in permitting the Jewish people to return to their native land. But the daring sins of many leaders "overwhelmed" him with "righteous indignation" and "grief at their ingratitude."[4]

He "unburdened" his heart to God and prayed: "O my God, I am ashamed and blush to lift up my face to thee, my God: for our iniquities are increased over our head, and our trespass is grown up unto the heavens" (Ezra 9:6). The phrase "unto the heavens" is a metaphor, which emphasizes

the magnitude of how great those sins were (cf. Genesis 11:4; Deuteronomy 1:28, 9:1; II Chronicles 28:9).[5] Ezra fears that God will react, and he pleads for mercy.

"In the OT and later Jewish writings being 'lifted up' was an idiom for an extreme degree of corporate sin (Jon. 1:2, Ezra 9:6, 1 Esdras 8:75, 4 Ezra 11:43)."[6]

Babylon's sins are characterized as having come up to God "glued" together in one big corpus ("chunk"). A coalition of wrong has finally reached a critical mass. God must now execute justice.[7]

The verdict? Plagues – the Seven Vials.

"and God hath remembered her iniquities." (vs 5)

This interesting expression *usually* means He commands everyone to remember their relationship with Him (Revelation 2:5, 3:3). Here, God is recalling Babylon's sins. Again, it anticipates divine action. It is a reminder, indicating that God doesn't forget. A line has been crossed. The time has come for Him to respond.

When God remembers His people, He responds (Psalm 105:8-11, 111:5-6; Ezekiel 16:60). When He comments on His perception of wickedness (as in the days of Noah – Genesis 5:5-6), He is going to react judicially (Psalm 109:14; Hosea 8:3, 9:9).

"Thus saith the LORD unto this people, Thus have they loved to wander, they have not refrained their feet, therefore the

---

3   Mounce, Robert H.; *The Book of Revelation* (Wm. B. Eerdmans Publishing Co., Grand Rapids, Michigan – 1977), p. 327, quoting Augustine De Civ De; 18.18.

4   White, Ellen G.; *Prophets and Kings,* p. 620.

5   Aune, David E.; *World Biblical Commentary; Revelation 17–22,* vol. 52c (World Books; Publisher, Dallas, Texas – 1997), p. 992.

6   Beale, G. K.; *The New International Greek Testament Commentary; The Book of Revelation* (William B. Eerdmans Publishing Company, Grand Rapids, Michigan – 1999).

7   Thomas, Robert L.; *Revelation 8–22 – An Exegetical Commentary* (Moody Press, Chicago – 1992), p. 321.

LORD doth not accept them; he will now remember their iniquity, and visit their sins" (Jeremiah 14:10).

Here in Revelation the final end of Babylon is graphically portrayed: "And the great city was divided into three parts, and the cities of the nations fell: and great Babylon *came in remembrance* before God, to give unto her the cup of the wine of the fierceness of his wrath" (16:19).

- The term for "sin" in 18:5 is *adikemata,* and refers to rebellion against God.
- It is elsewhere an elevated description legally of serious "crimes" (Acts 18:14, 24:20).[8]

God's anger (wrath) tied to 14:10 is over Sabbath issues. In 16:19, it is over organized defiance against His authority.

8   Osborne, Grant R.; *Revelation* (Baker Book House; Grand Rapids, MI), p. 640.

BASICS OF DIVINE JUSTICE

"Reward her even as she rewarded you, and double unto her double according to her works: in the cup which she hath filled fill to her double" (Revelation 18:6).

This reflects a legal term called *lex talionis* (*Latin*) – the law of retribution. We looked at that briefly in 13:10. Since her sins have now reached heaven, God must act proportionately. This verse reveals the legal standard by which He will render sentencing.

The Bible is filled with courtroom scenes, pronouncements by judges and execution of justice. One simple example of God's justice is found in Matthew 25:

- When Jesus comes the second time He will be sitting on a throne.
- All nations will be gathered before Him.
- He "sets" (judicial language) the sheep on the right – He "sets" the goats on the left.

There on His throne (courtroom bench), accompanied by His attendants, He judicially separates the righteous and the wicked. The sheep are "sentenced to eternal life." The goats are separated for everlasting fire prepared for the devil and his angels. Two groups, two sentences – both eternal and irrevocable, all related to their works (Revelation 20:12-13).

We are now going to take a glimpse into a little area of God's judicial mind.

"Reward her even as she rewarded you," (vs 6)

"The whole scene could be likened to a universal courtroom, in which a class-action suit takes place. Plaintiffs in this suit are Christians together with all those killed on earth (18:24); the defendant is Babylon/Rome, who is charged with murder in the interest of power and idolatry; and the presiding judge is God. As announced previously in 14:8, Babylon/Rome has lost the lawsuit and therefore its associates break out in lamentation and mourning, while the heavenly court and Christians rejoice over the justice they have received."[1]

This verse is an audition of the sentence against Babylon. This provides insight into God's character. We see a few pages from His law books. With amazing patience He has permitted the case to proceed slowly over an extended time for loyalties to change. That's divine *mercy*. The execution of the sentence is severe and final. That's divine *justice*.

This is "retributive justice" and is considered an equitable, even respectable, legal response. This echoes an Old Testament judicial warning regarding Babylon: "Call together the archers against Babylon: all ye that bend the bow, camp against it round about; let none thereof escape: *recompense her according to her work;* according to all that she hath done, do unto her: for she hath been proud

---

[1] Schussler-Fiorenza (1991:99) as quoted in Osborne, Grant R.; *Revelation* (Baker Book House; Grand Rapids, MI), p. 640.

against the LORD, against the Holy One of Israel." (Jeremiah 50:29; cf. Psalm 137:8).

Is such a forensic decision fair? This verse unequivocally signals its divine origin (cf. Psalm 28:4, Proverbs 24:12, Isaiah 3:11, Lamentations 3:64, Romans 2:6, II Corinthians 11:15, II Timothy 4:14).

"He that leadeth into captivity shall go into captivity" (Revelation 13:10a).

"And thine eye shall not pity; *but* life *shall go* for life, eye for eye, tooth for tooth, hand for hand, foot for foot"

(Deuteronomy 19:21).

"and double unto her double according to her works:" (vs 6)

In the Old Testament the "payback" for a wicked deed was often double the loss:

- Stealing an animal, stealing in general, illegal possession of a beast (Exodus 22:4, 7, 9)
- Double restitution was a principle taught by the prophets (Isaiah 40:2; Jeremiah 16:18, 17:18)
- There were at times calls for a seven-fold retaliation (Psalm 79:12)

At first this all seems excessive and certainly uncharacteristic of an honorable God! There is, however, a deeper issue related to this prophecy and its timing.

Many scholars see this, eschatologically, as a terminal summary action, when all sin cases are finally closed.[2]

That would mean a "full recompense" rather than twice the penalty. Osborne notes that Klein (1989:177) assumed that these two Hebrew words originally meant "equivalent." God will judge "fully" for all they have done (cf. Isaiah 40:2; Jeremiah 16:18, 17:18; Matthew 23:15; I Timothy 5:17). This would be "according to the deeds" – *the* basis of God's final judgment (Psalms 28:4, 62:12; Isaiah 59:18; Jeremiah 17:10; Romans 2:6; II Corinthians 11:15; I Peter 1:17; Revelation 2:23, 20:12-13, 22:12).[3]

This is not divine "revenge" but "just requital."[4]

"in the cup which she hath filled fill to her double." (vs 6)

This refers to the cup the harlot forced on the world, filled with the wine of her fornication (apostasy).

Thus, since she (Babylon) seduced the world into drinking the cup of sin, she must drink the cup of God's wrath "full strength" (14:10).

2   Beckwith, Ladd, P. Hughs, Ford, Sweet, Klein; 1989, Krodel, Chilton, Mounce, Thomas, quoted in Osborne, Grant R.; *Revelation* (Baker Book House; Grand Rapids, MI), p. 641.
3   Thomas, Robert L.; *Revelation 8–22 – An Exegetical Commentary* (Moody Press, Chicago – 1992), p. 324 (emphasis added).
4   Mounce, Robert H.; *The Book of Revelation* (Wm. B. Eerdmans Publishing Co., Grand Rapids, Michigan – 1977), p. 328.

CHAPTER 39

THE MISTRESS OF THE WORLD

"How much she hath glorified herself, and lived deliciously, so much torment and sorrow give her: for she saith in her heart, I sit a queen, and am no widow, and shall see no sorrow" (Revelation 18:7).

After a judicial edict in the last verse, God now critiques what He means by sin or iniquity. He now discloses the basis of the judgment He will execute.

"How much she hath glorified herself, and lived deliciously," (vs 7)

The glory of "herself" contrasts with the saints who glorified God [part of the last invitation to the world (14:7 – "give glory to him; cf. 15:4, 19:1)]. This is a divine issue and draws on many similar Biblical notices:

- "I [Satan] will be like the most High" (Isaiah 14:14).
- He shall stand up against the Prince of princes" (Daniel 8:25) (antichrist – little horn).
- "He shall exalt himself, and magnify himself above every god" (Daniel 11:36) (antichrist – vile person).
- "Exhalteth himself above all that is called God" (II Thessalonians 2:4) (antichrist – man of sin).

Living "deliciously" (*estreniasen*) alludes to her living in luxury and unlimited indulgence in sensory desires. By other intimations, fornication and immorality are suggested. Opulent living, having all she wants and a life of indulgence represent the deepest of spiritual issues. They belie the sin of self-sufficiency and pride. In Christ's parable of the sower, He noted the seed that fell among thorns.

"And these are they which are sown among thorns; such as hear the word, And the cares of this world, and the deceitfulness of riches, and the lusts of other things entering in, choke the word, and it becometh unfruitful" (Mark:4:18-19).

Babylon – a "harlot" – has a lust for things besides God. Though she is portrayed as religious, it's all a facade. Now we see that her love of the world and its "treasures" has a disastrous end. This institution/city/Rome is a stunning metaphor for apostasy, and belies the sad commentary of ancient Israel **and** the Christian church at the end.

"Moreover the LORD saith, Because the daughters of Zion are haughty, and walk with stretched forth necks and wanton eyes, walking and mincing *as* they go, and making a tinkling with their feet: Therefore the Lord will smite with a scab the crown of the head of the daughters of Zion, and the LORD will discover their secret parts" (Isaiah 3:16-17). Everything is open to God. There are no secrets.

All her acts are found to be the "antithesis of holiness."[1] Her secrets are laid bare.

Now God, acting on His previously noted judicial principle, says:

"so much torment and sorrow give her:" (vs 7)

---

[1] Osborne, Grant R.; *Revelation* (Baker Book House; Grand Rapids, MI), p. 642.

This echoes: "Those who exalt themselves will be humbled" (Luke 14:11; cf. II Samuel 22:28; Job 40:11; Proverbs 3:34, 29:23; Isaiah 2:12, 17; I Peter 5:6). Throughout the book, this punishment becomes the outcome of those who oppose God. "Torment" tells us that the judicial response will bring pain over a period of time. This draws on another parallel in the third angel's message: "tormented with fire and brimstone" (14:10) on those who have the "mark of the beast" (enforcement of a false sabbath – addressed in chapters 10 and 13).

Grief – sorrow – is her end. Again, the "eye for an eye" and "tooth for a tooth" retribution rule is expressed (Matthew 7:2, Galatians 6:7-8). This unveils a distinct ethic or standard within Christianity.[2]

- A follower of Christ never repays evil for evil (Romans 12:14, 17; I Thessalonians 5:15; II Timothy 4:14; I Peter 3:9).
- The response is God's judicial right to rule against (*sentence*) apostasy and execute judgment (*punishment*) on wrong (Romans 12:19).

The wicked must be viewed as crossing over a line, never to return. Probation is closed. Repentance is no longer an option. The suffering in the end gives an incredible contrast to her luxury.

To illustrate the arrogance of Babylon – a symbol of the false trinity – God permits John to record one of her quotations. This is inserted to teach us exactly what God means when talking of sin, iniquity and pride of heart.

"I sit a queen, and am no widow, and shall see no sorrow." (vs 7)

This expression is in John's oft-used trilogy pattern or three phrases to reinforce the imagery. It introduces a fascinating contrast – a prostitute as a queen, representing a church that claims control of the world who is about to face torment! Her focus on self is portrayed as self-deification.[3]

"Son of man, say unto the prince of Tyrus, Thus saith the Lord GOD; Because thine heart *is* lifted up, and thou hast said, I *am* a God, I sit *in* the seat of God, in the midst of the seas; yet thou *art* a man, and not God, though thou set thine heart as the heart of God" (Ezekiel 28:2). This spirit is as the soliloquy of Nebuchadnezzar before his fall.

In the ancient world widowhood was often a fearful state. Some cultures didn't permit remarriage. Others forced the widow to live with the parents of the deceased. This harlot – truly ruling the world for a time – is noting that she has no want for intimate friends. She has lovers so close she functions as if she were married – "no widow." Fascinating is this spirit of Babylon which echoes the Laodicean church. "I am rich and increased in goods and have need of nothing" (Revelation 3:17).

Christianity tried to change these selfish bonds. "Pure religion and undefiled before God and the Father is this, To visit the fatherless and widows in their affliction, and to keep himself unspotted from the world" (James 1:27; cf. I Timothy 5:3-16). This was rejected.

Stunning is this arrogant queen of Babylon. It echoes again: "And thou saidst, I shall be a lady for ever: so that thou didst not lay these things to thy heart, neither

---

2   Thomas, Robert L.; *Revelation 8–22 – An Exegetical Commentary* (Moody Press, Chicago – 1992), p. 322.

3   *Ibid.*, p. 325.

didst remember the latter end of it.... Therefore shall evil come upon thee; thou shalt not know from whence it riseth: and mischief shall fall upon thee; thou shalt not be able to put it off: and desolation shall come upon thee suddenly, which thou shalt not know" (Isaiah 47:7, 11)!

As with Babylon of old, latter-day Babylon sees herself as mother to all her inhabitants. She has confidence that she will never be without the support of her children. As with the arrogant, God-defying ancient city/empire, the final metaphor will come to its end suddenly. Her proud security will be seen as a delusion (Jeremiah 50:31-32)[4] (see Appendix IV.)

Most provocative are the many first through third century writings that allude to either Isaiah 47 or Revelation 18, associating Babylon directly with a woman and Rome![5]

A provocative question has been raised: "Who executes God's administrative justice? The wrath of God is a defined theme in many places (i.e., Daniel 8:19, Revelation 14:10). A peek into the final cause/effect was given to us in 17:16: "And the ten horns which thou sawest upon the beast, these shall hate the whore, and shall make her desolate and naked, and shall eat her flesh, and burn her with fire."

Here, God permits the molding of circumstances where the wicked finally execute His vengeance. "Even though vengeance is the prerogative of God alone (Deuteronomy 32:35, Romans 12:19, Hebrews 10:30) (Card), God may choose His enemies to implement it."[6] He had used Cyrus (Isaiah 44:28, 45:1) and Nebuchadnezzar to execute His will. They serve as a model of what is ahead.

Who Is Mother Babylon with Power Over All?

"Holy **Mother Church,** like the loving mother she is, has provided us with the necessary guidelines on how to think and behave.... These are provided for us in what is called her teaching Magisterium.... The Church, which is the 'Body of Christ,' is as it were the presence of Christ in the World."
http://holyromancatholicchurch.org/rama/church.html

"In regard to the Bible – Old and New Testaments – scholarly study of the texts is not sufficient, it must be interpreted within the tradition of the Church, since both are equally inspired by the Holy Spirit." Divine Holy Teachings of **Mother Church** from Vatican II.
http://www.catholic.org/international/international_story.php?id=33332

"Here and elsewhere the conciliar documents affirm the language of the **Church as Mother** – even to those estranged from her visible communion. It is because they are true members of Christ's Body that **Mother Church** constantly prays for their entrance into the fullness of the Catholic Church."
http://covenant-communion.net/index.php/features/mother_church_and_christian_unity

---

[4]   Beale, G. K.; *The New International Greek Testament Commentary; The Book of Revelation* (William B. Eerdmans Publishing Company, Grand Rapids, Michigan – 1999), p. 903.

[5]   *Sib. Or.* 5.168-77; 143, 159; 4 Ezra 15:46-63; as quoted by Bauckham, *Climax of Prophecy*, p. 344.

[6]   Thomas, *op. cit.,* p. 323.

CHAPTER 40

THE CIRCLE IS COMPLETE

"Therefore shall her plagues come in one day, death, and mourning, and famine; and she shall be utterly burned with fire: for strong *is* the Lord God who judgeth her" (Revelation 18:8).

We've come full circle. The story began with Babylon coming to its end (16:19). Then one of the Vial angels told John that he was going to show what led to its demise (17:1). The story wove through chapter 17, then 13 and finally into this chapter. Here we return to the plagues.

"And the great city was divided into three parts, and the cities of the nations fell: and great Babylon came in remembrance before God, to give unto her the cup of the wine of the fierceness of his wrath" (Revelation 16:19).

The warning of these plagues was one reason believers were called to get out of Babylon (18:4).

"Therefore shall her plagues come in one day." (vs 8)

"One day" is similar to "one hour" (18:10, 17, 19). It does not express duration of time but figuratively reveals abruptness.[1] What does she experience? The immediate implication is that she becomes a widow and then loses her children. Exactly what she had said would not happen – came true.

Literal Babylon came to its end with Cyrus killing Belshazzer. The timing of "one day" suggests that "suddenly, in an instant"[2] apostate Babylon ceases.

John is inspired to begin this verse with "therefore." "On account of" (*dia touto*) is a common prophetic expression that addresses cause.

"death, and mourning, and famine;" (vs 8)

Note the marked contrast given in this trilogy.

Vs 8	Vs 7
Death	Lived deliciously
Mourning	See no sorrow
Famine	Sit a queen

Babylon's end is also Rome's end.[3] This is the end of the papacy – the Roman Catholic Church.

"and she shall be utterly burned with fire: for strong *is* the Lord God who judgeth her." (vs 8)

This echoes 17:16 where the ten horns (ten kingdoms of this world) "shall … burn her with fire." In 16:19 Babylon was the object of God's "cup of the wine of

1   Thomas, Robert L.; *Revelation 8–22 – An Exegetical Commentary* (Moody Press, Chicago – 1992), p. 326.

2   Mounce, Robert H.; *The Book of Revelation* (Wm. B. Eerdmans Publishing Co., Grand Rapids, Michigan – 1977), p. 329.

3   Aune, David E.; *World Biblical Commentary; Revelation 17–22*, vol. 52c (World Books; Publisher, Dallas, Texas – 1997), p. 996.

the fierceness of his wrath." We see this fascinating flow of judgment:

- Wine of God's wrath (*internal* divine judgment) (16:19)
- Burning with fire (*external* judgment) (18:8)

This imagery is one of total loss – ceasing to exist! (Isaiah 34:8).

Burning with fire, whether God's "final act" post-millennial or literal after capture of a city in the ancient world, *represents* His last step to rid all traces of the enemy's memory.

Noah was promised that the earth would never be destroyed again by water (Genesis 9:15), the "rainbow promise." But – it is in His blueprint to burn, totally annihilate, the earth with its unrepentant people (II Peter 3:10, 12). This imagery of Babylon ("she") being "utterly" burned – represents God's final act in ridding the universe of sin. There will be nothing left of Satan and his rebellion except for the scars of Christ. The universe will be "clean."

"One reminder alone remains: our Redeemer will ever bear the marks of his crucifixion. Upon his wounded head, upon his side, his hands and feet, are the only traces of the cruel work that sin has wrought. Says the prophet, beholding Christ in his glory, 'He had bright beams coming out of his side; and there was the hiding of his power.' [Hab. 3:4 ...] That pierced side whence flowed the crimson stream that reconciled man to God, –there is the Saviour's glory, there 'the hiding of his power.' 'Mighty to save,' through the sacrifice of redemption, he was therefore strong to execute justice upon them that despised God's mercy. And the tokens of his humiliation are his highest honor; through the eternal ages the wounds of

Calvary will show forth his praise, and declare his power."[4]

A wonderful contrast to those scars will be the vast throngs of the redeemed. They will be the judicial witnesses throughout eternity of Christ's greatness.

The queen of Babylon, who loses all, now stands in another contrast to the King of the universe, who has gained all – His kingdom. A stunning, wonderful, elevating and never-ending theme to immerse the mind in and engross the imagination is the final outcome.

"Who judges her is a reminder that God is the ultimate judge. He may use agents to inflict that punishment as in 17:16-17, but the divine side of it is the ultimate reality."[5]

"Flee out of the midst of Babylon, and deliver every man his soul: be not cut off in her iniquity; for this is the time of the LORD'S vengeance; he will render unto her a recompense.... Babylon is suddenly fallen and destroyed: howl for her; take balm for her pain, if so be she may be healed. We would have healed Babylon, but she is not healed: forsake her, and let us go every one into his own country: for her judgment reacheth unto heaven, and is lifted up even to the skies.... And the land shall tremble and sorrow: for every purpose of the LORD shall be performed against Babylon, to make the land of Babylon a desolation without an inhabitant" (Jeremiah 51:6, 8-9, 29).

Rome comes to its end by God's mighty power.[6] The circle of prophetic information is now complete.

---

4 White, Ellen G.; *The Great Controversy,* p. 674.
5 Thomas, *op. cit.,* p. 327.
6 Mounce, *op. cit.,* p. 329.

Appendixes

Appendix I

WHEN IN ROME **EXHIBITION**

1929-2009: EIGHTY YEARS OF VATICAN CITY STATE

■ BY MICAELA BIFERALI

WHERE
Charlemagne Wing,
St. Peter's Square
WHEN
Until May 10th, 2009
HOURS
Every day 10.00 am to 6.00 pm
Wednesdays 1 pm to 6.00 pm
TICKETS
Free admission
INFORMATION
Tel. +39 06 69882060
Fax +39 06 69885720
www.vaticanstate.va
eventi@scv.va

Here, St. Anne's Gate, one of the main entrances into the Vatican.
Top, Cardinal Gasparri and Benito Mussolini during the signing of the Lateran Treaty (February 11, 1929).
Right, construction of the Vatican train station

A new exhibition, *1929-2009: Eighty Years of Vatican City State*, promoted by the governorate of the city state, is on display in the Charlemagne Wing off St. Peter's Square.

This show, celebrating the 80th anniversary of the foundation of Vatican City State, opens with an extraordinary 3-D scale model reproducing the entire present Vatican City.

The exhibition is divided into five sections:

Section I
Vatican City State Before 1929
The items on display show the changes the city underwent over time. This section also points out the connection between Vatican City State and Rome, and covers the period of the "Roman question" (1870-1929).

SECTION II
Pope Pius XI
The second section is dedicated to the figure of Pope Achille Ratti, Pius XI (1922-1939), during whose reign the Italian government agreed to a legal framework for Vatican City State.

On display are the Pope's precious cope manufactured in Como, his beautiful miter, a little-known portrait, and many papers and antiques concerning him and his papacy.

SECTION III
The Lateran Treaty
The third section is dedicated to the Lateran Treaty (February 11, 1929). A treaty and a concordat were signed by the Vatican secretary of state, Cardinal Pietro Gasparri, and Benito Mussolini, head of the Italian government. Unpublished papers documenting the long negotiations preceding 1929 are on display. A rich set of photographic documentation coming from the collections of the Vatican Apostolic Library provides further documentary evidence for these historic events.

SECTION IV
The Construction of the State
The construction of the state is the core of the exhibition. Immediately after February 11, 1929,

the buildings and infrastructures of the new state began to be developed.

The projects and plans of the Head Office of Technical Services of the Governorate offer exhaustive documentation on the different buildings.

SECTION V
The Other Pontificates
Since Pius XI, there have been six papacies (Pius XII, John XXIII, Paul VI, John Paul I, John Paul II, Benedict XVI).

Each Pope is represented by his own portrait from the collections of the Vatican Museums.

At the end of the exhibition, visitors can see an artistic masterpiece created on purpose for the celebrations: the *Civitas Vaticana*, a new relief map of Vatican City State as it actually is,

engraved on copper and printed in a limited edition of 330 copies. The work, done by Pierluigi Isola for the Vatican Apostolic Library, aims to be the symbolic image of the Vatican City State of the 21st century, as the official map of Lorenzo Tealdy was in 1929. For this reason the two maps have been chosen as symbols of this exhibition.

For the occasion, the Vatican Apostolic Library has published a very comprehensive catalog of the whole exhibition. ●

Appendix II

Pope Sylvester I (314-335 A.D.) Decrees the Transfer of Sabbath Rest to Sunday

Rabanus Maurus (776-856), abbot [clergyman/priest] of Fulda and later archbishop of Mainz, Germany, was seen as one of the greatest theologians of his age and exceptionally learned in patristics [writings and lives of the "church fathers"]. He was a zealous defender of the papacy and its teachings. In one of his works, he notes:

"Pope Sylvester instructed the clergy to keep the feriae [Roman festival day].... From an old [honoring the god Mithra] custom he [now] called the first day [of the week] the 'Lord's [day],' on which the light was made in the beginning and also the resurrection of Christ is celebrated."[1]

Rabanus Maurus didn't mean that Sylvester was the first man who referred to the this feriae or who first started the observance of Sunday among Christians. He meant that, according to the testimony of Roman Catholic writers, Sylvester affirmed those practices and made them official dogma. Hence Maurus says elsewhere in his writings:

"Pope Sylvester first among the Romans ordered that the names of the days [of the week], which they previously called after the name of their gods, that is, [the day] of the Sun, [the day] of the Moon,

[the day] of Mars, [the day] of Mercury, [the day] of Jupiter, [the day] of Venus, [the day] of Saturn, they should call feriae thereafter, that is the first feria, the second feria, the third feria, the fourth feria, the fifth feria, the sixth feria, because that in the beginning of Genesis it is written that God said concerning each day: on the first, 'Let there be light:'; on the second, 'Let there be a firmament'; on the third, 'Let the earth bring forth verdure'; etc. But he [Sylvester] ordered [the bishops] to call the Sabbath by the ancient term of the law, [to call] the first feria the 'Lord's day,' because on it the Lord rose [from the dead], Moreover, the same pope decreed that the rest of the Sabbath should be transferred rather to the Lord's day [Sunday], in order that on that day we should rest from worldly works for the praise of God."[2]

Note particularly, he says that "the same pope [Sylvester I] decreed that the rest of the Sabbath should be transferred rather to the Lord's day [Sunday]."[3]

According to this statement, he was the first bishop to introduce the idea that the divinely appointed rest of the Sabbath day

---

[1] Rabanus Maurus, Liber de Computo (A book Concerning Computation), Chap. XXVII ("Concerning Festivals"), as translated by the writer from the Latin text in Migne's Patrologia Latina, Vol. CVII, col. 682.

[2] De Clericorum Institutione (Concerning the Instruction of the Clergymen), Book II, Chap. XLVI, as translated by the writer from the Latin text in Migne's Patrologia Latina, Vol. CVII, col. 361.

[3] The wording in the Latin text reads: "Statuit autem idem papa ut otium Sabbati magis in diem Dominicam transferretur, ut ea die a terrenis operibus ad laudandum Deum vacaremus."

should be transferred to the first day of the week. This was an *ecclesiastical decree* or law. This is significant, especially in view of the fact that it was during Sylvester's pontificate that the emperor of Rome [Constantine] issued the first *civil laws* compelling men to rest from secular labor on Sunday, and that Eusebius (265–340 A.D.), bishop of Caesarea, was the first theologian on record to present arguments, allegedly from the Scriptures, that Christ did transfer the rest of the Sabbath day to Sunday.

Decrees of Sylvester I

- The "rest" of the seventh-day Sabbath should be *transferred* to "the Lord's Day."

- "Every Sabbath [seventh day] on account of the burial [of Jesus] is to be regarded in execration [denunciation] of the Jews ... In fact it is not proper to observe, because of Jewish customs, the consumption of food and the ceremonies of the Jews."[4]

In his bitter anti-Semitism, he also wrote:

"Sunday is to be observed joyfully by the Christians on account of the resurrection, then every Sabbath on account of the burial is to be regarded in execration [loathing or cursing] of the Jews."[5]

Source: Sabbath and Sunday in Early Christianity, by Robert L. Odom, © 1977 by the Review and Herald Publishing Association (An 55 W Oak Ridge Dr. Hagerstown, MD 21740), pages 247–248.

4 "Pope" Sylvester, 314-335 C.E., *"Adversus Graecorum,"* S.R.E. Humbert, PL 143, p. 936.
5 Quoted by Cardinal S.R.E. Humbert, *Adversus Graecorum calumnias 6, PL* 143, 937 1054 AD.

Appendix III

Abomination Associated with Desolation
Only at the eth qets!

Introduction

It may be one of the Bible's most frightening words! It describes how God *feels* about a behavior or a worship practice that He despises. When He calls something an "abomination," you know He has raised His voice. He uses such language against cross-dressers (Deuteronomy 22:5). Solomon lists seven things that the Lord hates: "Yea, seven are abomination[s] to him" (Proverbs 6:16-19). "Lying lips" are an abomination to the Lord (Proverbs 12:22). He also hates heathen idols – they are an abomination (Deuteronomy 12:29-32). That is an especially sensitive issue with our sovereign God!

There are many deep religious issues that God addresses with this word. Even "new moons," Sabbaths and church gatherings are abominations if the worship experience is filled with vain oblations or liturgical mysteries (Isaiah 1:13). Jeremiah noted that building edifices to worship Baal in "high places" and causing children to walk through fire to the god Molech (Jeremiah 32:35) was an abomination. Molech was a heathen deity of the Ammonites. Babies were placed into the red hot hands of Molech's statute and sacrificed. Baal had been adopted from the Phonecians. It morphed into many forms in different cultures. But everywhere its place of honor was on a hill or an elevated eminence so the *heavens* could be seen and worshiped, *especially the sun.* Many ancient records even equate Baal worship with sun worship.

An abomination always represents something God *detests*. Frequently the issue relates to a *substitute* of Himself or something that tarnishes His character. The matters He abhors also include ***changing what He has irrevocably instituted***. That is why homosexuality is an abomination to Him (Leviticus 20:13). It is a *substitute* for God's plan of sexuality. It changes the nature and meaning of procreation instituted in Eden.

Jesus Points Out "the" Abomination

The pivotal time Jesus addressed a detestable matter was in His expose regarding the "end of time." The disciples had inquired what signs would tell them that the end of the world was about to arrive and what clue would reveal that His second advent was imminent. They also asked the "when" question. He unfolded crucial information in Matthew 24:15 (cf. Mark 13:14) that should rivet every Christian's attention. Those verses come right in the middle of other timing clues that tell "when" the end of time will occur. "*When ye therefore shall see the **abomination of desolation,** spoken of by Daniel the prophet, stand in the holy place, (whoso readeth, let him understand:)*" Matthew 24:15.

Jesus revealed in literal and typological language that there would be two ends of time.

1. When *physical* Jerusalem would fall
2. When *spiritual* Babylon would fall

Each of those, He said, would be preceded by an "abomination" (*bdelugma*); the latter *had already been detailed* by Daniel. That tie is found in chapters 8–12 of his book. Then Jesus personified this abomination by saying, "It stands where it shouldn't be" (Mark 13:14 – paraphrased). Matthew also said that the abomination is a sign of the end when it "stands in the holy place" (Matthew 24:15). Something God hates comes into the very precincts of the church. It will be specific and definable, and becomes a warning to God's true people – the remnant.

An additional clue to its meaning is: "Ye shall see Jerusalem compassed with armies" (Luke 21:20). That was a literal event in 68-70 A.D. A literal event often becomes a great spiritual metaphor for the very end of time! Often words or phrases illustrate deep truths which act like mini-prophecies. They become God's coded way of conveying, to a serious Bible student, wonderful messages about the future. The word "Jerusalem" is also in that category. It was literal. But Jesus personified it in Matthew 23:37: *"O Jerusalem, Jerusalem, thou that killest the prophets, and stonest them which are sent unto thee, how often would I have gathered thy children together, even as a hen gathereth her chickens under her wings, and ye would not!"* There, Jerusalem is a symbol of *God's people.* When enemies surround Jerusalem (God's peple), they will soon stand where they shouldn't be and finally come right into the church.

The key introductory statement that begins Jesus' "abomination" message is that timing word "when." "When you see" – it will be apparent. It will be so obvious, it shouldn't be missed. "When" you are aware that something detestable to God:

1. Takes its place among God's people where it shouldn't
2. Armies ready to impose their will or presence on them
   - You will know that a time of supreme danger has arrived.
   - It is time for you to act.

We can historically see that when Jerusalem, now seen as an apostate city, was surrounded by armies (beginning in 68 A.D.), it was about to fall (three-and-a-half-year period). To His faithful, that was the "when" sign that gave them a chance to escape, to "come out." In Revelation there is a message to another apostate "city:" "Babylon is fallen, *come out* of her my people" – escape.

The "Holy Place" (Matthew 24:15), when apostasy comes in, refers to the sanctuary, temple or church – at the very center of religious activity. That "abomination" is what His people are to urgently distance themselves from – "come out of her." What detestable *element* comes into God's church that destroys its purity? In Matthew, Mark and Luke, Jesus doesn't say. He only urges, "Go to Daniel."

Originally, the Jewish phrase "abomination of desolation" was an expression of contempt towards the heathen deity Zeus or Baal.

Zeus

The pagans referred to Zeus as "Lord of Heaven." The Jews referred to him as *siqqus somem* – the "abomination which desolates." The sky, celestial bodies, especially the sun were part of that worship.[1]

We will find that worship in a way God didn't command, tied to sun worship, is the abomination He is referencing.

Daniel Picks Up the Story

The word "desolation" (*somen* or *shamen*) is found in seven places in Daniel. It simply means **nothing is left.** Except for one (9:27), all the references *relate to* the consequences of an *abomination* or *sin*. This word is a helpful key in our quest to understand this "abomination." It all begins when Gabriel asks Jesus about the little horn vision that Daniel just saw (8:13) (that relates to the end-time antichrist). His key question relates to the little horn and its behavior. Daniel was told *in this vision setting:*

The Little Horn of Daniel 8:

1. Came from the north (vs 9)
2. Had power against the host of heaven (vs 10) – mighty power not of himself (vs 24) (it came from Satan) – "Host" is God's people
3. Persecuted them (vs 10) – even destroyed the holy people (vs 24)
4. Magnified himself to the prince of that host (vs 11) – Shall magnify (arrogant over another) himself (vs 25)
5. Then he stood up against the Prince of princes (Jesus) (vs 25)

1. Brown, Colin; *Dictionary of New Testament Theology* (Zondervan, Grand Rapids, MI) vol. 1, pp. 74-75.

6. This all caused the "place" of the sanctuary to be cast down (vs 11) – The place God's church held in the world was tarnished. Gabriel now describes how!
7. Because of a "transgression," truth was cast to the ground (vs 12). Now comes the **clue:** That "transgression" is what led to "desolation" (vs 13)!
8. All this occurs by a fierce-looking king (vs 23; cf. 11:40) (vicious in heart – another way to describe that "little horn") at a time when "transgressors" (those promoting **this** abomination) are come in full (vs 23).

This description relates to the antichrist, who sets himself against God and sits "in the temple of God (the Christian church), showing himself that he is God" (II Thessalonians 2:4). There it is again. He "stands" or occupies a place where he shouldn't be. He lords over the church in some remarkable way.

An antichrist, the "little horn," not only tries to displace God, but Daniel alludes to how this is done! There is a "transgression" that casts truth to the ground. The church is filled with transgressors. More than that, in Gabriel's follow-up timing question (8:13), he asked Jesus "when" this (the "transgression of **desolation**") would happen. Gabriel uses a very specific word to render its meaning more precise: transgression or *pesha* (H) results in desolation. As we will see, *pesha* **is** the abomination.

Pesha is one of several Hebrew words for sin. It has a special connotation, describing man committing a willful deed to spite God. It symbolizes rebellion, defiance by resisting God's authority. It represents an act that goes "beyond the limits" of

183

God's law.[2] It also describes sin against His covenant. All this was acknowledged as one of Israel's great failures in Daniel's prayer. In Daniel 9:24a it is the first "sin" that God's people must address.

We have the misdeeds of the little horn of Daniel 8 defying Jesus, His people and truth, taking over and destroying what the sanctuary or church really represents. Now Gabriel tells us how, in arrogance, that is done *through* his questions (8:13). The "sin" or "transgression" (*pesha*) challenges:

1. God's authority
2. God's covenant
3. God's law

Where is the center of those three things? Right in the center of the Decalogue. Study especially Deuteronomy 5:12-15. This foundational apocalyptic prophecy shows that the Sabbath will be a pivotal issue at the end. Gabriel notes that that is the transgression that leads to "desolation."

The next important use of "desolation" is in Daniel's prayer: "O my God, incline thine ear and hear; open thine eyes, and behold our *desolations*." Isn't that interesting? Daniel, in great humility, acknowledges their sin and now appeals to God to rescue his people from its desolating consequences. "Look God, how **desolate** our people and land are. Respond to this plea!"

How does God respond? Through Gabriel – while Daniel was yet praying. He outlined several steps that would bring *restoration*. Amazing, amazing, the very first issue that God's people must address is *pesha* or transgression against the Sabbath! We must discover even more what that refers to!

2   http://www.hebrew4christians.com/Meditations/ Chata_ah/chata_ah.html

This is so vital! It ties directly to Jesus' counsel regarding the end of time! Let's look at more verses in this chapter where *"desolation"* is used.

Daniel 9:26: Gabriel states that the end of resistance against Jesus and the "church" or "holiness" is *desolation.*

Daniel 9:27: The covenant will be confirmed by the Prince and God's people. The last week of the seventy weeks is split into two. One half is set aside for God to complete His part of that covenant. The other is set aside for His people to finish the covenant obligation (a separate timing study). Then a distinct thought is introduced (really like a separate paragraph).

Paraphrased: "Because abominations have spread everywhere, God is going to make everything desolate (*shamen*) at the time Jesus comes again." (The Second Coming is distinctly alluded to.)

That information is astounding. The Hebrew word there for "abomination" (*shiqquwts*) is the Greek equivalent of *bdelugma*, which Jesus talked about in the gospels when He said, "Go to Daniel!" It represents something detestable or abhorrent in God's sight. Now that we have brought together many clues from the gospels to the words "transgression" and "desolation," we know that some abominable sin will become universal, associated with the antichrist and against God's authority, law and covenant. In Gabriel's question of 8:13, he noted that it "cast truth to the ground." We will discover that it relates to a worship issue that *substitutes* a false Sabbath, something in place of God's directive to keep the seventh day.

"Desolation" will be a focus later in 11:31 related again to the antichrist and in a stunning timing prophecy that describes the very end of all things (12:11).

Background to the "Abomination"

The word *shiqquwts* is a very strong Hebrew word. It is meant to illustrate the *extreme* seriousness and wickedness of a particular sin. God is appealing to all to see it from His perspective and not man's (Deuteronomy 7:26).[3]

There's more in Daniel that we will visit, but we have come to a point where we must discover what God specifically means by transgression/abomination. What exactly makes it so detestable? The story begins with the Creation week. Those seven days represent a divine clock. It was set into man's flow of life by decree. Unrelated to any celestial body, God said right from the beginning that "days" would **be grouped into "sevens."** That may seem simplistic, and perhaps it is. But God associated that week with three important issues:

1. The sixth day was related to man.
2. The seventh day was related to God.
3. The days were declared to be an *evening and morning*. That signals not only its sequence but, in sacred *redemptive thought*, they were *set apart*.

The week motif became a metaphor for many sequential prophecies of "seven." There was a week of days (Creation week), week of months (Feast "year"), week of years (the key to understand end-time prophecy), seven weeks of years (related to man's final probation) and a week of seven millenniums (a timeframe in which to finish the great controversy issues).

---

[3]   Harris, R. Laird; *Theological Wordbook of the Old Testament* (Moody Press: Chicago, IL), 1980, p. 955.

Our focus here will be on the "week of years." God used language and phrases in that special seven-year cycle, which are like keys to unlock similar language concepts elsewhere, including the *abomination* and *desolation*. Jesus already told us that we must know those issues as it relates to the end of time.

The Sabbath was made as a grand finale to the Creation week. It was a day called "holy." Uniquely set as a block of time within a group of seven, God designed it for the Creator and the created to communicate and enjoy each other's company. When sin arrived, its meaning grew:

1. The Sabbath remained holy; therefore, it became a "sign" that man could become holy once again (Exodus 31:13).
2. It also became a *forever* promise of the covenant agreement God made *with* man that he could become holy (Exodus 31: 16-17).
3. It embodied a promise that within the Sabbath rest there would eventually come "deliverance" from sin into an eternal rest (Deuteronomy 5:12-15).

In that context we visit the "week of years."

"And the LORD spake unto Moses in mount Sinai, saying, Speak unto the children of Israel, and say unto them, When ye come into the land which I give you, then shall the land keep a sabbath unto the LORD. Six years thou shalt sow thy field, and six years thou shalt prune thy vineyard, and gather in the fruit thereof; But in the seventh year shall be a sabbath of rest unto the land, a sabbath for the LORD: thou shalt neither sow thy field, nor prune thy vineyard. That which groweth of

its own accord of thy harvest thou shalt not reap, neither gather the grapes of thy vine undressed: for it is a year of rest unto the land. And the sabbath of the land shall be meat for you; for thee, and for thy servant, and for thy maid, and for thy hired servant, and for thy stranger that sojourneth with thee, And for thy cattle, and for the beast that are in thy land, shall all the increase thereof be meat" (Leviticus 25:1-7).

Every seventh year, called a *shemita*, the land was to rest. It was far more than an agricultural order. That year was a Sabbath. It brought also *deliverance* to all Hebrews who had been bought as slaves (Exodus 21:2). The "week of years" established several principles:

1. The seventh represented deliverance.
2. The seventh symbolized restoration.
3. The seventh characterized man becoming holy, like God is holy.
4. The seventh became a great symbol of finishing the everlasting covenant.

What did God do to assure that there was adequate food for the year the land was at rest and for the following year when new crops were started? God said He would give double crop production on the *sixth*. The land would produce enough food that it would last through the seventh, into the eight, when the new crop would be planted to harvest the ninth! God made *supernaturally clear* on the sixth that the Sabbath rest could be observed. He provided evidence that preparations on the sixth could be so complete that the Sabbath *could* be kept holy (Leviticus 25:20): "And if ye shall say, What shall we eat the seventh year? behold, we shall not sow, nor gather in our increase: Then I will command my blessing upon you in the sixth year, and it shall bring forth fruit for three years. And ye shall sow the eighth

year, and eat *yet* of old fruit until the ninth year; until her fruits come in ye shall eat *of* the old *store."*

In this great illustration God revealed how all timing sequences of seven are to be viewed and applied. The *week of years* became typological and serves as a beautiful metaphor of redemption's story over seven millenniums – the "week of millenniums."

There is another amazing part to this story. Not only does the typology of the week of seven years define a success story related to the redeemed, it also includes elements which reveal the outcome of those who rebel and resist the "Sabbath" year provisions.

In Leviticus 26:14-39 God outlines what will happen to those who reject His decrees, abhor His commandments and, thus, violate the covenant. The:

1. Highways will become **desolate** (*shamen*) (vs 22)
2. Cities will lie in waste and churches will become **desolate** (vs 31)
3. The land will become **desolate** (vs 32)

Interesting! Resistance to God's "seventh" would result in "nothing left" – desolation.

God then said: As long as it (the land) lieth desolate, it will *rest* and *keep the Sabbath* because *they* did not keep the Sabbath! The desolation curse is tied directly to the Sabbath – *the sacred seventh!* Over and over the Jewish dispersion and desolation warnings relate to the great Sabbath theme.

"The land also shall be left of them, and shall enjoy her sabbaths, while she lieth desolate without them: and they shall accept of the punishment of their iniquity: because, even because they despised my judgments, and because their soul abhorred my statutes" (Leviticus 26:43).

When desolation (**shamen – Hebrew;** or *eremosis – Greek*) is used, it is the outcome of some sin or iniquity related to despising God's laws and statutes, especially the Sabbath!

- Break my sabbaths, statutes and laws (abomination)
- Mock my messengers – despise their words
- Scattered – bondage
- Desolation
- Land enjoys her Sabbaths

The shemita was so sacred it was the leading reason for the Babylonian captivity and desolation of Jerusalem! (II Chronicles 35:21). (When Jesus introduced us to the two ends of time, the Jews already had a lesson book from history regarding the pivotal abomination. But they weren't very attentive students.)

*"But they mocked the messengers of God, and despised his words, and misused his prophets, until the wrath of the LORD arose against his people, till there was no remedy. Therefore he brought upon them the king of the Chaldees, who slew their young men with the sword in the house of their sanctuary, and had no compassion upon young man or maiden, old man, or him that stooped for age: he gave them all into his hand.... And them that had escaped from the sword carried he away to Babylon; where they were servants to him and his sons until the reign of the kingdom of Persia: To fulfil the word of the LORD by the mouth of Jeremiah, until the land had enjoyed her sabbaths: for as long as she lay **desolate** she kept sabbath, to fulfil threescore and ten years"* (II Chronicles 36:16-17, 20-21).

Desolation is the final outcome of rebellion against the Sabbath! The above sequence not only applied to the Jews, it became a symbol for how God will deal with apostasy against His Sabbath at the very end of time! This is a key prophetic concept.

Defining Look at Abomination

God's throne relates to the "north" in direction: *"Beautiful for situation, the joy of the whole earth, is mount Zion, on the sides of the **north,** the city of the great King"* (Psalm 48:2). Satan, once Lucifer, said in his heart (when he began to act on his passions) that he would ascend into heaven, exalt his throne above the stars, to be like the Most High and sit on the "mount of the congregation" (representing Zion), which is on the sides of the ***"north"*** (Isaiah 14:12-14).

Apostasy leads to displacement of God from His rightful place. It *stands where it ought not be.* A false leader or standard is set up symbolically in the "north," trying to either represent God or be God. This is referred to as an abomination [*towebah* (Ezekiel) – or *shiqquwts* (Daniel)].

Ezekiel was given additional insight into the meaning of abomination. It began by his going into vision, associated with a dramatic encounter with God (Ezekiel 8:1-4). He was about to **see** and **hear** examples of things that God despises. Actions of individuals that violated the fundamental principles of a covenant relationship: "You shall have no other gods before me" and "You shall not make any idolatrous images for yourselves to worship and serve" (Exodus 20:3-6; Deuteronomy 4:1-20, 5:7-12).

Ezekiel is brought in vision to Jerusalem, symbolic of the center of God's people. He was initially brought to the north gate of the inner temple court. The glory of God was supposed to be in that area. But in that gate was a seated statue, "an image of jealousy." That begins the story of things God detests. God's glory is contrasted with this pathetic statue. Yet, the statue guarded the gate that led to the inner court and temple! The Hebrew message seems to describe the statue from God's viewpoint: "The outrageous statue of jealousy." Its appearance provoked His jealousy, thus, the "statue of jealousy." Amazing! In the northern gate – trying to be like God is a detestable idol!

God takes Ezekiel on a temple tour, introducing him to what "drives Him out of the sanctuary." These are things that *stand where they ought not be*. Verse 6 begins by God asking him to "look up." This is an eschatological phrase. Whatever historic application it might provide, there is a greater end-time typological meaning. He was to look up to the north at the statue and *then contemplate the abomination* of the people in the temple he was about to see. God then said, "You're going to see even greater abominations."

The flow of thought at the onset of this vision creates an anticipation of reprehensible activity. It envisions a remarkable picture of what God is extremely emotional about! Maybe we should say, "things He hates!" Ezekiel is then shown seventy elders or leaders of God's people, each with an incense censer, worshiping crawling creatures, beasts and idols. Scene one was an idol at the north entrance to the inner court and temple. Scene two is where church leaders are worshiping idols and creatures in the temple. They were doing it in the "dark" and claimed that "God won't see us." But

He does. He calls this another abomination (*towebah*).

The number seventy recalls the number of leaders who assisted Moses in guiding the affairs of His people (Exodus 24:1, 4; Numbers 11; 16, 24-25). Symbolically, it represents all of the key leaders of God's church here in apostasy. In the center of this group was another individual whose name was Jaazaniah, meaning "Yahweh listens." He apparently was a civic leader, suggesting a bond in apostasy between church and state. That is fascinating and has thematic ties to Revelation 13 and 17. God said, once again, that worse abominations were to come.

In the next scene, number three, Ezekiel comes toward the entrance of the north gate. He apparently had been inside the temple and now moves outside. The inner court is in full view. There are women sitting facing the temple (God's house), crying over the heathen god Tammuz. This god was raised to life annually. Their cry is for her virility and life to return once again.

The nature of the Hebrew expression, "*the* Tammuz," suggests that it is a chant for Tammuz, who is now dead. This means that these women are lamenting or even praying for or to the dead.

God again told Ezekiel that he would see even greater abominations. Though all are hideous and detestable to God, the last is worse than the previous!

He now is ushered into the east temple court and observes a ritual, a religious drama between the porch and altar of sacrifice. There are twenty-five men (not characterized) with their backs towards the temple. These individuals were prostrating themselves towards the sun. This represented physical homage to a celestial object. The imagery is specific – rejecting Yahweh, they gave obeisance to the sun (god). Solar or astral cults were strictly forbidden in Deuteronomy 4:19 and 17:2-5. Yet, these are God's people worshiping the sun.

Suddenly God says, "Does this all seem trivial to my people? This, along with violence occurring in the land, has now provoked me to anger. Mercy is ended, probation closed" (Ezekiel 8:17-18 – paraphrased).

What does this collectively state regarding God's hatred of all this specific behavior – abominations?

1. Man-made forms of worship are detestable – though it may be a tradition or even cultural.
2. Worship of nature, relics, and idols causes God to flee.
3. Prayer for and to the dead is abhorrent.
4. Worshiping the sun or any sun symbol disconnects man from God.

Worship on Sunday, the first day of the week, is a tradition that is idolatrous. It is a rebellious break from the sacred seventh. It is like turning one's back to God's Sabbath commands. Instead of honoring the resurrection of Jesus – something Christ never commanded – it's like honoring the resurrection of Tammuz, which mythologically occurred annually. Sunday was also the day when the sun was honored by worship. Even in Christ's day the Romans honored Mythrianism, where the first day was seen as sacred.

Abomination in the Cup

The harlot named "Mystery," "Babylon the Great" of Revelation 17 had a golden cup in her hand. Gold suggests purity, perfection or flawlessness. That was its veneer. It was in her hand so that it could be offered to others. The Word says that it

was "full" (*geno* – unable to fit in anymore) of abominations. What abomination (*bdelygmatien*)? Jesus used the same word to relate, once again, to significant end-time issues. He referred us to Daniel (which we will once more visit). But, it has led us now to the end-time harlot, the apostate church, with abominations she spreads around the earth.

This time another clue is added to the meaning of "abominations." It is described as the *"filthiness of her fornication."* The Greek word for "filthiness" or "unclean thing" is *akatharta*. This is cultic and implies an illicit relationship and/or religious blasphemy. In Revelation 16:13 John saw three *unclean* spirits going out to deceive the nations. Some deceptive or illicit religious teaching enamors the world. The saints clearly reject it because the harlot is there depicted as drunk with the blood of the saints.

The abomination refers to a religious "rite" she idolizes. *Akatharta*, with fornication (*porneras*), reveals that she is intimately relating with others over this "rite," belief or action.

What deceptive religious teaching or philosophy does the harlot bring to the world? The clues we have reviewed regarding the abomination, desolation and uncleanliness all point to a false worship related to the "sun!" God's sacred seventh is rebelled against. As ancient Israel broke that "sacred seven," the *shemita*, and brought desolation, so at the end, apostate Christianity breaks a Sabbath, which will lead to desolation.

The beast is a political power. The woman/harlot represents a blasphemous religious system. Slandering the name of God permeates Revelation 17. The Sabbath commandment was designed for people to "remember" God as Creator; it was designed to be a sign of His sovereign power, to be a reminder of the covenant promises and, finally, to be a symbol of deliverance from this world and restoration to God's original purpose. We are reminded that the harlot is the mother of the *abominations* on the earth resisting this truth. It is the *pesha* found in Daniel 8.

The collective evidence suggests that the harlot, epitomizing the antichrist, is a church that leads all other churches (her daughters) into rebellion against the Sabbath. This is end-time imagery. It becomes a mark of her power and authority since the world submits to her seductive influence. The world eventually seeks to kill the saints who resist this mark. This, then, fulfills a subsequent description of what is also in the cup – the blood of God's people.

The King of the North Connection

We were introduced to the antichrist – the papal little horn power (its second rise), back in Daniel 8. There is a sequel to that story. God uses varied symbols to describe prophetic powers and events. In chapter 11 the little horn is first referred to as a "vile person." Then in another section, it is "king of the north." The latter represents the *rest of the story* in Jesus' command to look at Daniel.

This king hates God's covenant (11:30). His practices pollute God's sanctuary (because he *stands where it ought not be*). **Then it says that he places** or decrees the abomination that leads to desolation (11:31). This is amazing! The King of the North not only seductively pollutes the church, but is associated with a decree or law that enforces it!

The "mother church" is the Roman Catholic Church. She admits it, and the Bible supports it. But – in the latter, only in a setting of apostasy! The question is

raised: Is the Roman Catholic Church interested in civil decrees to enforce Sunday keeping? If it is, the issues of that church related to the abomination would raise an alarm of fearful magnitude. It would be a fulfillment of end-time prophecy that threads its way from the very words of Jesus back to Daniel and forward to Revelation!

On July 5, 1998, the late Pope John Paul II wrote an *apostolic letter, Dies Domini,* of 50 plus pages. These are a few quotations:

66. *"In this matter, my predecessor Pope Leo XIII in his Encyclical Rerum Novarum spoke of Sunday rest as a worker's right which the State must guarantee." (110)*

67. "Therefore, also in the particular circumstances of our own time, **Christians <u>will naturally strive</u> to ensure that <u>civil legislation respects</u> their duty to keep Sunday holy.**"

47. "Even if in the earliest times it was not judged necessary to be prescriptive, the Church has not ceased to confirm this obligation of conscience, which rises from the inner need felt so strongly by the Christians of the first centuries. It was only later, faced with the half-heartedness of negligence of some, that *the Church had to make explicit the duty to attend Sunday Mass: more often than not, this was done in the form of exhortation, but at times the Church had to resort to specific canonical precepts.*"

"The present Code reiterates this, saying that 'on Sundays and other holy days of obligation the faithful are bound to attend Mass.' (82) *This legislation has normally* *been understood as entailing a <u>grave obligation</u>: this is the teaching of the Catechism of the Catholic Church, (83) and it is easy to understand why if we keep in mind how <u>vital Sunday is for the Christian life</u>.*"

48. Bishops must ensure that Christians appreciate Sunday. [Hmmm, how does that happen? By using the power of civil law – decrees!]

This document was a communiqué to Catholic Church leaders around the world and directly reflects the ties that Daniel predicted would come at the end of time! Rebellion against the Sabbath is a detestable issue with God. He ties it to the words *pesha* and *shiqquwts*, which prophetically leads to utter *desolation*.

This all happens when the "daily" or true Sabbath is taken away. Daniel's message is nearly finished. There is one more factoid that is vital to the understanding of the abomination. God tells us how long that decree to observe a false sabbath will last.

From the onset of the decree or command to take away the "daily" and set up the abomination which makes the desolation of the earth will be 1290 days (12:11). That represents the last segment of time before Jesus returns (another study).

What an amazing amount of information tucked into the crevasses of so many prophecies. They all have a *consistent* message. They all define how God addresses the Sabbath. It is clear – its holiness never changes. Equally important, it is the pivotal issue at the end of time.

Coming now full circle, we return to Matthew 24. In verse 20 Jesus invited His people to "pray that your flight (escape) be not … on the Sabbath day." Why? It would make observing that sacred day difficult. Jesus is consistent. This end-time issue is not Sabbaths (plural). The grand finale of history relates to a single holy day that began at Creation week a little over 6000 years ago.

Appendix IV

Catholic References Regarding Motherhood and the Church

Please refer to this website:

endtimeissues.com

Under "Books" menu at top

Scroll down to this book's icon – Appendix IV

Prophecy Research Initiative

P.O. Box 829

Lucerne Valley, CA 92356-0829 USA

prophecy-research@earthlink.net

Web: www.endtimeissues.com

For other materials available, see website above.

Printed in the United States
By Bookmasters